International College
Information Resource Center
2655 Northbrooke Drive
Naples, Florida USA 34119
www.internationalcollege.edu

AMERICA
UNBOUND

AMERICA UNBOUND

THE BUSH REVOLUTION IN FOREIGN POLICY

IVO H. DAALDER

JAMES M. LINDSAY

BROOKINGS INSTITUTION PRESS

Washington, D.C.

Copyright © 2003
THE BROOKINGS INSTITUTION
1775 Massachusetts Avenue, N.W., Washington, D.C. 20036
www.brookings.edu

Library of Congress Cataloging-in-Publication data

Daalder, Ivo H.
  America unbound : the Bush revolution in foreign policy /
Ivo H. Daalder, James M. Lindsay.
    p.   cm.
Includes bibliographical references (p.   ) and index.
  ISBN 0-8157-1688-5 (cloth : alk. paper)
    1. United States—Foreign relations—2001– 2. United States—Foreign relations—Philosophy. 3. Bush, George W. (George Walker), 1946—Views on international relations. 4. Balance of power. 5. Unilateral acts (International law) 6. War on Terrorism, 2001—Diplomatic history. 7. September 11 Terrorist Attacks, 2001—Influence. I. Lindsay, James M., 1959– II. Title.
  E902.D23 2003
  327.73—dc22   2003016767

9 8 7 6 5 4 3

The paper used in this publication meets minimum requirements of the American National Standard for Information Sciences—Permanence of Paper for Printed Library Materials: ANSI Z39.48-1992.

Typeset in Adobe Caslon

Composition by Cynthia Stock
Silver Spring, Maryland

Printed by Phoenix Color
Hagerstown, Maryland

To

MARC *and* MICHAEL

and

IAN, CAMERON, FLORA, *and* MALCOLM

The highest proof of virtue is to
possess boundless power without abusing it.

—Lord Macaulay

Contents

THE BUSH REVOLUTION

G EORGE W. BUSH had reason to be pleased as he peered
down at Baghdad from the window of Air Force One in
early June 2003. He had just completed a successful visit to Europe and
the Middle East. The trip began in Warsaw, where he had the opportunity to personally thank Poland for being one of just two European
countries to contribute troops to the Iraq War effort. He then traveled
to Russia to celebrate the three hundredth birthday of St. Petersburg
and to sign the papers formally ratifying a treaty committing Moscow
and Washington to slash their nuclear arsenals. He flew on to Évian, a
city in the French Alps, to attend a summit meeting of the heads of the
world's major economies. He next stopped in Sharm el-Sheik, Egypt,
for a meeting with moderate Arab leaders, before heading to Aqaba,
Jordan, on the shore of the Red Sea to discuss the road map for peace
with the Israeli and Palestinian prime ministers. He made his final stop
in Doha, Qatar, where troops at U.S. Central Command greeted him
with thunderous applause. Now Bush looked down on the city that
American troops had seized only weeks before. As he pointed out land-
marks below to his advisers, the pilot dipped Air Force One's wings in
a gesture of triumph.

Bush's seven-day, six-nation trip was in many ways a victory lap to
celebrate America's win in the Iraq War—a war that many of the leaders Bush met on his trip had opposed. But in a larger sense he and his
advisers saw it as a vindication of his leadership. The man from Midland

had been mocked throughout the 2000 presidential campaign as a know-nothing. He had been denounced early in his presidency for turning his back on time-tested diplomatic practices and ignoring the advice of America's friends and allies. Yet here he was traveling through Europe and the Middle East, not as a penitent making amends but as a leader commanding respect.

As Air Force One flew over Iraq, Bush could say that he had become an extraordinarily effective foreign policy president. He had dominated the American political scene like few others. He had been the unquestioned master of his own administration. He had gained the confidence of the American people and persuaded them to follow his lead. He had demonstrated the courage of his convictions on a host of issues—abandoning cold-war treaties, fighting terrorism, overthrowing Saddam Hussein. He had spent rather than hoarded his considerable political capital, consistently confounding his critics with the audacity of his policy initiatives. He had been motivated by a determination to succeed, not paralyzed by a fear to fail. And while he had steadfastly pursued his goals in the face of sharp criticism, he had acted pragmatically when circumstances warranted.

In the process, Bush had set in motion a revolution in American foreign policy. It was not a revolution in America's goals abroad, but rather in how to achieve them. In his first thirty months in office, he discarded or redefined many of the key principles governing the way the United States should act overseas. He relied on the unilateral exercise of American power rather than on international law and institutions to get his way. He championed a proactive doctrine of preemption and deemphasized the reactive strategies of deterrence and containment. He promoted forceful interdiction, preemptive strikes, and missile defenses as means to counter the proliferation of weapons of mass destruction, and he downplayed America's traditional support for treaty-based nonproliferation regimes. He preferred regime change to direct negotiations with countries and leaders that he loathed. He depended on ad hoc coalitions of the willing to gain support abroad and ignored permanent alliances. He retreated from America's decades-long policy of backing European integration and instead exploited Europe's internal divisions. And he tried to unite the great powers in the common cause of fighting terrorism and rejected a policy that sought to balance one power against another. By rewriting the rules of America's engagement in the world, the man who had been dismissed throughout his political career as a lightweight left an indelible mark on politics at home and abroad.

Nevertheless, good beginnings do not always come to good endings. Even as Bush peered out the window of Air Force One to look at Baghdad, there were troubling signs of things to come. American troops in Iraq found themselves embroiled in what had all the makings of guerrilla war. Anger had swelled overseas at what was seen as an arrogant and hypocritical America. Several close allies spoke openly about how to constrain America rather than how best to work with it. As the president's plane flew home, Washington was beginning to confront a new question: Were the costs of the Bush revolution about to swamp the benefits?

THE QUESTION OF how the United States should engage the world is an old one in American history. The framers confronted the question only four years after ratifying the Constitution when England went to war with France. President George Washington ultimately opted for neutrality, disappointing partisans on both sides. The hero of Valley Forge calculated that the small and fragile experiment in republican government would likely be crushed if it joined a battle between the world's two greatest powers.

America's relationship with Europe remained an issue throughout Washington's presidency. He discussed the topic at length in his magisterial address announcing his decision to retire to his beloved Mount Vernon. He encouraged his countrymen to pursue peace and commercial relations. "Harmony, liberal intercourse with all nations are recommended by policy, humanity, and interest." But he discouraged them from tying their political fate to the decisions of others. "It is our true policy," Washington counseled, "to steer clear of permanent alliances with any portion of the foreign world." His argument for keeping political ties to a minimum was simple: "Europe has a set of primary interests which to us have none or a very remote relation. Hence she must be engaged in frequent controversies, the causes of which are essentially foreign to our concerns."[1]

Washington concluded his Farewell Address by noting, "I dare not hope [that my advice] will make the strong and lasting impression I could wish."[2] He should not have feared. His vision of an America that traded happily with Europe but otherwise stood apart from it became the cornerstone of the new nation's foreign policy. John Quincy Adams eloquently summarized this sentiment and gave it an idealistic twist in an address he made before the House of Representatives on July 4, 1821. America applauds those who fight for liberty and independence, he argued, "but she goes not abroad, in search of monsters to destroy. She is the well-wisher to the freedom and independence of all. She is the champion and vindicator only of her own." America stuck to its own business not merely for pragmatic reasons, but because to do otherwise would repudiate its special moral claim. "The fundamental maxims of her policy would insensibly change from *liberty* to *force*," Adams warned. "She might become the dictatress of the world. She would be no longer the ruler of her own spirit."[3]

However, even liberal, democratic spirits can be tempted by changed circumstances. When Adams spoke, the United States was an inconsequential agrarian country of twenty-three states, only one of which—Louisiana—was west of the Mississippi. By the end of the nineteenth century, it was an industrial colossus that spanned a continent. Its new status as a leading economic power brought with it growing demands from within to pursue imperial ambitions. Intellectuals used the reigning theory of the day, Social Darwinism, to advocate territorial expansion as a demonstration of American superiority and the key to national survival. Church groups saw American imperialism as a means to spread Christianity to "primitive" areas of the world. Commercial interests hoped to reap financial gain by winning access to new markets for American goods. Anti-imperialists such as Andrew Carnegie and Mark Twain challenged these arguments for expansion with great passion, but they were fighting a losing battle. As William McKinley's secretary of state John Hay put it, "No man, no party, can fight with any chance of success against a cosmic tendency; no cleverness, no popularity avails against the spirit of the age."[4]

The opportunity that imperialists had waited for came with the Spanish-American War. The windfall from that "splendid little war," as its supporters took to calling it, was an empire that stretched from Puerto Rico in the Caribbean to the Philippines in the Pacific. With victory safely in hand, concerns that America would lose its soul if it went abroad quickly faded. Under Teddy Roosevelt's corollary to the Monroe Doctrine, which had been largely forgotten for seven decades after it was first issued, Washington assumed the role of policeman of the Western Hemisphere. The former Rough Rider denied that "the United States feels any land hunger or entertains any projects as regards the other nations of the Western Hemisphere." Nonetheless, he insisted that the United States could not stand idly by while Latin American nations mismanaged their economies and political affairs. Latin American nations needed to "realize that the right of such independence can not be separated from the responsibility of making good use of it."[5] In the view of Roosevelt and his successors, they failed to do that. Between 1904 and 1934, the United States sent eight expeditionary forces to Latin America, took over customs collections twice, and conducted five military occupations. The Caribbean was soon nicknamed Lake Monroe.

With the Spanish-American War and the Roosevelt corollary to the Monroe Doctrine, internationalists for the first time triumphed over isolationists in the struggle to define the national interest. However, the imperialist cause would soon begin to struggle. Part of the problem was the cost of empire. America's new subjects did not always take easily to Washington's rule. In the Philippines, the United States found itself bloodily suppressing a rebellion. American occupations of several Caribbean countries failed to produce the stability that Roosevelt had promised. By then, the imperialists were confronted by another, more serious challenge. This one came not from isolationists, but from within the internationalist camp itself.

WOODROW WILSON TOOK office in 1913 determined to concentrate on domestic concerns. Shortly before taking the oath of office, he told an old colleague: "It would be the irony of fate if my administration had to deal chiefly with foreign affairs."[6] Yet fate had precisely that destiny for Wilson. His domestic policies are long forgotten; his foreign policy legacy is historic. Wilson's importance rests not on his achievements—

he ultimately failed to see his proposal for a new world order enacted—but on his vision of America's role in the world. It was a vision that would dominate American politics after World War II.

Wilson shared with all his predecessors an unwavering belief in American exceptionalism. "It was as if in the Providence of God a continent had been kept unused and waiting for a peaceful people who loved liberty and the rights of men more than they loved anything else, to come and set up an unselfish commonwealth."[7] But whereas that claim had always been used to argue that America would lose its soul if it went abroad in search of monsters to destroy, Wilson turned it on its head. America would lose its soul if it did not go abroad. His liberal internationalism set forth a moral argument for broad American engagement in world affairs.

"We insist," Wilson told Congress in 1916, "upon security in prosecuting our self-chosen lines of national development. We do more than that. We demand it also for others. We do not confine our enthusiasm for individual liberty and free national development to the incidents and movements of affairs which affect only ourselves. We feel it wherever there is a people that tries to walk in these difficult paths of independence and right."[8] Not surprisingly, when Wilson requested a declaration of war against Germany—thereby doing the unthinkable, plunging the United States into a European war—he did not argue that war was necessary because Germany endangered American interests. Rather, the United States must fight because "the world must be made safe for democracy."[9]

Wilson's commitment to a world in which democracy could flourish was by itself revolutionary. Equally revolutionary was the second component of his vision—the belief that the key to creating that world lay in extending the reach of international law and building international institutions. The former college president—who ironically during his first term had enthusiastically used American military power to enforce the Roosevelt corollary to the Monroe Doctrine—called on the victorious powers to craft an international agreement that would provide "mutual guarantees of political independence and territorial integrity to great and small states alike."[10] He went to the Paris Peace Conference in December 1918 to push his idea on deeply skeptical European leaders.

He was ultimately forced to compromise on many of the particulars of his plan. Nevertheless, in the end he prevailed on the core point. The Treaty of Versailles, signed in July 1919, established a League of Nations that would "respect and preserve as against external aggression the territorial integrity and existing political independence of all."[11] Wilson returned to the United States convinced that the idea of collective security—"one for all and all for one"—would prevent war and remake world politics.

The idea of the League of Nations was also revolutionary for American politics. Wilson was asking Americans to do more than just cast away their aversion to entangling alliances. The United States, after all, had fought World War I as an "associated" power and not an "allied" one in deference to the traditional reluctance to become tied militarily to other countries. He was asking them to spearhead an international organization that would seek to protect the security of its members, however far they might be from American shores. That would prove the rub.

The Senate's rejection of the Treaty of Versailles is usually recounted as a triumph of traditional isolationism. Isolationists certainly were the treaty's most vociferous critics. The "irreconcilables" and "bitter-enders," as they were called, were led by Republican Senator William E. Borah of Idaho, a man who had a reputation as an expert on world affairs despite never having left American soil. The irreconcilables were traditional isolationists who vehemently opposed entangling the country in foreign alliances. Borah insisted that if he had his way the League of Nations would be "20,000 leagues under the sea" and he wanted "this treacherous and treasonable scheme" to be "buried in hell." Even "if the Savior of men would revisit the earth and declare for a League of Nations," he declared, "I would be opposed to it."[12]

Although Borah and his fellow irreconcilables lacked the votes to carry the day, many of the Senate's most ardent internationalists and imperialists also opposed the treaty. What bothered them was not that Wilson wanted to involve the United States in affairs beyond its borders. They were all for that. They simply opposed the way Wilson intended to engage the world. These anti-League internationalists, who included most Republicans and a few Democrats, believed that the United States had to preserve a free hand to act abroad, not tie its fate to the whims and interests of others. They charged that the League would trump the Constitution and usurp Congress's power to declare war. The leader of the anti-League internationalists, Republican Senator Henry Cabot Lodge of Massachusetts, went to the heart of the matter when he asked his colleagues: "Are you willing to put your soldiers and your sailors at the disposition of other nations?"[13]

The victory of the anti-treaty forces heralded for a time the continuation of the policy of the free hand that Lodge and others so loved. By the beginning of the 1930s, however, this unilateral internationalism began giving way to rising isolationist sentiment. As the country entered the Great Depression and war clouds gathered on the European horizon, Americans increasingly retreated to Fortress America. Some isolationists argued that war would not occur. In July 1939 Senator Borah confidently predicted, "We are not going to have a war. Germany isn't ready for it. . . . I have my own sources of information."[14] Others admitted war might occur and that it would be best for the United States to remain apart. Regardless of the reason, the German invasion of Poland, the Battle of Britain, and Germany's invasion of the Soviet Union came and went without convincing most Americans of the need to act. It took Pearl Harbor to do that.

THE FOREIGN POLICY questions Americans faced at the end of World War II had little to do with what the United States *could* do abroad. By every measure, America dominated the world as no nation had ever done before. All the other major powers, whether victor or vanquished, were devastated. The United States, in contrast, emerged from the war not only unscathed, but far stronger than it was when it entered the hostilities. Its economy was by far the world's largest. It possessed the world's strongest navy and most powerful air force. And it alone held the secret to the world's most terrifying weapon: the atomic bomb.

The foreign policy questions facing Americans dealt much more with what the United States *should* do abroad. Some Americans wanted to "bring the boys back home" from Europe and the Pacific and to return to a "normal" life. Others warned against a return to isolationism. But internationalists themselves disagreed on important questions. Should the United States define its interests regionally or globally?

What were the threats to U.S. security? How should the United States respond to these threats?

The task of answering these questions fell to President Harry Truman, a man who in many ways was ill prepared for it. By his own admission he was "not a deep thinker."[15] A product of the Democratic political machine in Kansas City, he had cut his political teeth on domestic issues. He had served in the Senate for ten years with modest distinction before becoming Franklin Roosevelt's surprise choice in 1944 to be his running mate. When FDR died in April 1945, Truman had been vice president for less than three months and had not been included in the administration's foreign policy deliberations. Indeed, he did not learn that the United States was building an atomic bomb until *after* he was sworn in as president.

Whatever Truman lacked in experience he more than made up for with a commitment to pursuing Woodrow Wilson's aims without making his mistakes. During his seven years as president, Truman remade American foreign policy. In March 1947 the former Kansas City haberdasher went before a joint session of Congress and declared what became known as the Truman Doctrine: "It must be the policy of the United States to support free peoples who are resisting attempted subjugation by armed minorities or by outside pressures."[16] Three months later his secretary of state, George C. Marshall, unveiled the Marshall Plan in a commencement address at Harvard, claiming a major role for the United States in rebuilding a war-torn Europe. Two years later, Truman signed the treaty creating the North Atlantic Treaty Organization (NATO). With the stroke of his pen, he cast off America's traditional aversion to entangling alliances and formally declared that Washington saw its security interests as inextricably linked with those of Western Europe.

The hallmark of Truman's foreign policy revolution was its blend of power and cooperation. Truman was willing to exercise America's great power to remake world affairs, both to serve American interests and to advance American values. However, he and his advisers calculated that U.S. power could more easily be sustained, with less chance of engendering resentment, if it were embedded in multilateral institutions. During his presidency, Truman oversaw the creation of much of the infrastructure of the international order: the United Nations, the International Monetary Fund, the World Bank, the General Agreement on Tariffs and Trade, and the Organization of American States among other multilateral organizations. In creating these institutions, he set a precedent: Even though the United States had the power to act as it saw fit, it accepted, at least notionally, that its right to act should be constrained by international law. In marked contrast to the epic League of Nations debate, the Senate overwhelmingly endorsed this multilateral approach.

Nonetheless, Truman's foreign policy choices were not unanimously applauded. The challenge, however, did not come from isolationists. The smoke pouring from the USS *Arizona* had shown the vulnerability of Fortress America. The complaints instead came from hard-line conservatives who thought Truman's policy of containing the Soviet Union was too timid. These critics believed that the United States had a moral and strategic interest in working to liberate nations that had fallen under Soviet control. Truman rejected these calls for "rollback" because he judged the costs of the wars that would inevitably follow as too high.

Proponents of rollback thought they had found their leader in Truman's successor, Dwight Eisenhower. Ike campaigned in 1952 criticizing Truman's foreign policy and particularly his handling of Korea. The official Republican Party platform denounced containment as a "negative, futile, and immoral" policy that abandoned "countless human beings to a despotism and Godless terrorism."[17]

However, it is one thing to campaign, another to govern. Once Eisenhower was in office, his actions made clear, in the words of one historian, that Republican rhetoric about "'liberation' had been aimed more at freeing the government in Washington from Democrats than at contesting Soviet influence in Eastern Europe."[18] In June 1953 the former Supreme Allied Commander stood by as Soviet troops crushed a revolt in East Germany. The following month he brought the Korean War to an end not by invading North Korea but by signing an armistice with Pyongyang. The next year he rebuffed a French appeal for U.S. military help to relieve the French forces trapped at Dien Bien Phu. Two years after that, Washington again did nothing when Soviet tanks rolled into Hungary, crushing yet another revolt against communist rule. Eisenhower's reason for inaction was not timidity but prudence. Any effort to liberate Eastern Europe by force of arms could have led to a nuclear war that turned American cities into smoking, radiating ruins. With the cost of being wrong so high, the appeal of rollback policies dimmed.

EISENHOWER'S EMBRACE OF Truman's foreign policy blueprint solidified America's basic approach to world affairs for the next half century. Even with the debacle in Vietnam, a basic foreign policy consensus held. The United States had extensive interests overseas that it must be prepared to defend. Washington actively cultivated friends and allies because in a world with a superpower adversary it was dangerous to be without them. International organizations, and especially military alliances, were a key instrument of foreign policy.

At the same time, however, the ever-present Soviet threat muffled the continuing disagreement between the intellectual descendants of Woodrow Wilson and those of Henry Cabot Lodge. Those in the Wilson school cherished the contribution of international law to world stability and prosperity. They took pride in the fact that Washington had championed the creation of international organizations such as NATO and the United Nations and that by doing so the United States was laying the groundwork for the gradual expansion of the rule of law in international affairs. Those in the Lodge school longed for the policy of the free hand but were comforted by the fact that America's great wealth and military might enabled it to dominate international organizations. In NATO, for example, the United States was not simply Italy with more people. It was the superpower that provided the alliance's ultimate security guarantee, and as a result it had a disproportionate say over alliance policy. When multilateral organizations refused to heed American wishes, the United States could—and frequently did—act alone.

As the cold war ground on and America's allies became less willing to follow Washington's lead, it became harder to paper over the differences between those who emphasized cooperation and those who stressed the free exercise of power. While the former saw new possibilities for building multilateral organizations, the latter decried the ineffectiveness of many international organizations and despaired at the constraints they placed on America's freedom to act. These differences flared into the open in the 1990s with the demise of the Soviet Union. Suddenly those who emphasized international institutions and law lost the trump card they had long held over those who favored the unilateral exercise of American power—the prospect that going it alone might produce costs that were unbearably high.

The foreign-policy debates of the 1990s were at first mistakenly seen as a replay of the debates between isolationists and internationalists of the 1930s. True, some voices called for America to return home, but this was a distinctly minority view. Most Americans had little interest in disengaging from the world. They quite liked American predominance and saw it as costing them little. As a result, politicians such as Patrick Buchanan, who thought they could ride an isolationist tide to power, instead sank without leaving a ripple.

The real debate in the 1990s was not over *whether*, but *how* the United States should engage the world. Bill Clinton's presidency in most ways represented a continuation of the traditional Wilsonian approach of building a world order based on the rule of law. Clinton and his advisers argued that globalization was increasing economic, political, and social ties among nations and that this growing interconnectedness made fulfillment of Wilson's vision all the more important. In keeping with this thinking, the Clinton administration pursued traditional arms control agreements such as the Comprehensive Test Ban Treaty and a strengthening of the Biological Weapons Convention. It also sought to create new international arrangements such as the Kyoto Protocol and the International Criminal Court to deal with a new set of policy challenges.

Clinton's opponents criticized his decisions on numerous grounds, but one in particular stood out: He had failed to recognize that, with the demise of the Soviet Union, the United States now had the freedom to act as it saw fit. In their view, Clinton not only failed to assert American primacy; he also ensnared the country in multilateral frameworks that did not even serve broader international interests. As the columnist Charles Krauthammer put it, "An unprecedentedly dominant United States . . . is in the unique position of being able to fashion its own foreign policy. After a decade of Prometheus playing pygmy, the first task of the new [Bush] administration is precisely to reassert American freedom of action."[19] America, in short, could and should be unbound.

GEORGE W. BUSH delivered the revolution that Krauthammer urged. It was not a revolution that started, as many later have suggested, on September 11, 2001. The worldview that drove it existed long before jet planes plowed into the Twin Towers and the Pentagon. Bush outlined its main ideas while he was on the campaign trail, and he began implementing parts of it as soon as he took the oath of office. What September 11 provided was the rationale and the opportunity to carry out his revolution.

But what precisely was the Bush revolution in foreign policy? At its broadest level, it rested on two beliefs. The first was that in a dangerous world the best—if not the only—way to ensure America's security was to shed the constraints imposed by friends, allies, and international institutions. Maximizing America's freedom to act was essential because the unique position of the United States made it the most likely target for any country or group hostile to the West. Americans could not count on others to protect them; countries inevitably ignored threats that did not involve them. Moreover, formal arrangements would inevitably constrain the ability of the United States to make the most of its primacy. Gulliver must shed the constraints that he helped the Lilliputians weave.

The second belief was that an America unbound should use its strength to change the status quo in the world. Bush's foreign policy did not propose that the United States keep its powder dry while it waited for dangers to gather. The Bush philosophy instead turned John Quincy Adams on his head and argued that the United States should aggressively go abroad searching for monsters to destroy. That was the logic behind the Iraq War, and it animated the administration's efforts to deal with other rogue states.

These fundamental beliefs had important consequences for the practice of American foreign policy. One was a decided preference for unilateral action. Unilateralism was appealing because it was often easier and more efficient, at least in the short term, than multilateralism. Contrast the Kosovo war, where Bush and his advisers believed that the task of coordinating the views of all NATO members greatly complicated the war effort, with the Afghanistan war, where Pentagon planners did not have to subject any of their decisions to foreign approval. This is not to say that Bush flatly ruled out working with others. Rather, his preferred form of multilateralism—to be indulged when unilateral action was impossible or unwise—involved building ad hoc coalitions of the willing, or what Richard Haass, an adviser to Colin Powell, called "a la carte multilateralism."[20]

Second, preemption was no longer a last resort of American foreign policy. In a world in which weapons of mass destruction were spreading and terrorists and rogue states were readying to attack in unconventional ways, Bush argued that "the United States can no longer solely rely on a reactive posture as we have in the past. . . . We cannot let our enemies strike first."[21] Indeed, the United States should be prepared to act not just preemptively against imminent threats, but also preventively against potential threats. Vice President Dick Cheney was emphatic on this point in justifying the overthrow of Saddam Hussein on the eve of the Iraq War. "There's no question about who is going to prevail if there is military action. And there's no question but what it is going to be cheaper and less costly to do now than it will be to wait a year or two years or three years until he's developed even more deadly weapons, perhaps nuclear weapons."[22]

Third, the United States should use its unprecedented power to produce regime change in rogue states. The idea of regime change was not new to American foreign policy. The Eisenhower administration engineered the overthrow of Iranian Prime Minister Mohammed Mossadegh; the CIA trained Cuban exiles in a botched bid to oust Fidel Castro; Ronald Reagan channeled aid to the Nicaraguan contras to overthrow the Sandinistas; and Bill Clinton helped Serb opposition forces get rid of Slobodan Milosevic. What was different in the Bush presidency was the willingness, even in the absence of a direct attack on the United States, to use U.S. military forces for the express purpose of toppling other governments. This was the gist of both the Afghanistan and the Iraq wars. Unlike proponents of rollback, who never succeeded in overcoming the argument that their policies would produce World War III, Bush based his policy on the belief that nobody could push back.

GEORGE W. BUSH presided over a revolution in foreign policy, but was he responsible for it? Commentators across the political spectrum said no. They gave the credit (or blame) to neoconservatives within the administration, led by Deputy Secretary of Defense Paul Wolfowitz, who they said were determined to use America's great power to transform despotic regimes into liberal democracies. One critic alleged that Bush was "the callow instrument of neoconservative ideologues."[23] Another saw a "neoconservative coup" in Washington and wondered if "George W fully understands the grand strategy that Wolfowitz and other aides are unfolding."[24] Pundits weren't the only ones to argue that the Bush revolution represented a neoconservative triumph. "Right now, the neoconservatives in this administration are winning," Democratic Senator Joseph Biden, the ranking member of the Senate Foreign Relations Committee, said in July 2003. "They seem to have captured the heart and mind of the President, and they're controlling the foreign policy agenda."[25]

This conventional wisdom was wrong on at least two counts. First, it fundamentally misunderstood the intellectual currents within the Bush administration and the Republican Party more generally. Neoconservatives—who might be better called democratic imperialists— were more prominent outside the administration, particularly on the pages of *Commentary* and the *Weekly Standard* and in the television studios of Fox News, than they were inside it. The bulk of Bush's advisers, including most notably Dick Cheney and Defense Secretary Donald Rumsfeld, were not neocons. Nor for that matter was Bush. They were instead assertive nationalists—traditional hard-line conservatives willing to use American military power to defeat threats to U.S. security but reluctant as a general rule to use American primacy to remake the world in its image.

Although neoconservatives and assertive nationalists differed on whether the United States should actively spread its values abroad, they shared a deep skepticism of traditional Wilsonianism's commitment to the rule of law and its belief in the relevance of international institutions.

They placed their faith not in diplomacy and treaties, but in power and resolve. Agreement on this key point allowed neoconservatives and assertive nationalists to form a marriage of convenience in overthrowing the cold-war approach to foreign policy even as they disagreed about what kind of commitment the United States should make to rebuilding Iraq and remaking the rest of the world.

The second and more important flaw of the neoconservative coup theory was that it grossly underestimated George W. Bush. The man from Midland was not a figurehead in someone else's revolution. He may have entered the Oval Office not knowing which general ran Pakistan, but during his first thirty months in office he was the puppeteer, not the puppet. He governed as he said he would on the campaign trail. He actively solicited the counsel of his seasoned advisers, and he tolerated if not encouraged vigorous disagreement among them. When necessary, he overruled them. George W. Bush led his own revolution.

GEORGE BUSH AND
THE VULCANS

G EORGE W. BUSH sat down for the interview with WHDH-TV in Boston in early November 1999 expecting it to be like the dozens of other local television interviews he had done around the country since declaring himself a presidential candidate months earlier. He would chat with the reporter for a dozen or so minutes, use key passages from his stump speech to answer questions, and then move on to his next interview. Reporter Andy Hiller had something different in mind, however. Bush had been knocked for knowing little about foreign affairs. So Hiller intended to find out what the Texas governor knew about the world beyond America's shores.

"Can you name the president of Chechnya?" Hiller asked.

"No, can you?" Bush replied.

Hiller ignored the gibe and went to his next question: "Can you name the president of Taiwan?" Bush answered, "Yeah, Lee," getting right at least the family name of Taiwanese president Lee Teng-hui.

"Can you name the general who is in charge of Pakistan?" asked Hiller, referring to General Pervez Musharraf, who three weeks earlier had led a military coup that overthrew Pakistan's corrupt, though democratically elected, government.

"Wait, wait, is this fifty questions?" retorted a clearly uncomfortable Bush.

Hiller pressed on. "No, it's four questions of four leaders in four hot spots."

Bush fumbled, looking for an answer. "The new Pakistani general, he's just been elected—not elected, this guy took over office. It appears this guy is going to bring stability to the country and I think that's good news for the subcontinent."

Hiller again refused to relent. "Can you name him?"

Bush replied: "General. I can name the general. General."

"And the prime minister of India," asked Hiller.

Bush responded: "The prime minister of India is—no." But having been put on the spot, the Texas governor wanted to return the favor. Drawing on his knowledge of Mexican political leaders, he challenged Hiller: "Can you name the foreign minister of Mexico?"

"No sir," replied the reporter, "but I would say to that, I'm not running for president."[1]

Bush's three-minute exchange with Hiller quickly became a national—even international—news story. Bush's critics argued that his performance showed him unprepared to move into the Oval Office. Al Gore's spokesperson predictably insisted that the vice president would have named all four leaders if asked. Meanwhile, Bush's supporters rushed to his defense, insisting that the pop quiz was both demeaning and misleading. "The person who is running for president is seeking to be the leader of the free world, not a 'Jeopardy!' contestant," said Karen Hughes, one of Bush's closest confidantes and communications director for his campaign.[2] And truth be told, Hiller's foreign policy pop quiz was unfair. When the story first broke, staffers at Washington think tanks delighted in administering the quiz to their colleagues. Few went four for four.

Yet as brief and unfair as Hiller's pop quiz was, it dogged Bush for the remainder of the campaign. His foreign policy gaffes earlier in the year, such as confusing Slovakia and Slovenia and referring to Greeks as "Grecians," had already made him the butt of jokes by Jay Leno and David Letterman. Now he had seemed to confirm what those jokes had implied all along: he didn't know enough about the world to be president. Making matters worse, polls showed that although few Americans could say what Bush proposed to do as president, most knew that he had flunked a foreign policy pop quiz. The not-too-surprising result was that many Americans came away from the campaign believing that the Texas governor was an amiable dunce who was, as one journalist put it, "ambling into history."[3]

Bush tried to turn weakness into strength. He freely admitted that he had much to learn about world affairs. "This is a big world," he said, "and I've got a lot to learn."[4] He repeatedly reassured voters that he would compensate for the gaps in his own knowledge by surrounding himself with seasoned advisers. Bush's critics saw this as his greatest vulnerability—he risked being a puppet whose decisions would be guided by others. Bush, however, touted his willingness to rely on experts as his greatest asset. He was a man who knew what he didn't know and was secure enough to turn to others to find out what he needed to know. That fit perfectly with his vision of the president as the chief executive officer of the United States. He would set the broad goals and strategies for his administration, make the tough calls, and then leave it to his Cabinet to turn his decisions into reality.

IMPECCABLE FOREIGN POLICY credentials have never been a requirement to win the White House—or to stay there. During the cold war voters elected Jimmy Carter and Ronald Reagan. Both were governors who had never been tested by foreign policy crises before they entered the Oval Office. After the Soviet Union collapsed, voters cashiered the elder George Bush despite his mastery of foreign affairs. In his place, they elected Bill Clinton, the governor of one of the nation's smallest states and a man whose informal campaign slogan—"It's the economy, stupid"—made clear that foreign policy would not be his top priority.

However, candidates Carter, Reagan, and Clinton generated far fewer doubts about their ability to handle foreign policy than the younger Bush did. No one doubted Carter's smarts—he finished in the top third of his class at the Naval Academy and had been a nuclear submariner. Critics often ridiculed Reagan for being too dumb to be commander in chief. But he had had a long political career, first as a union president, then as a two-time governor of the nation's most populous state and a three-time presidential candidate. Clinton, like Carter, oozed smarts. He had finished near the top of his classes at Georgetown and Yale Law School and had gone to Oxford as a Rhodes Scholar. He was also a gifted speaker who could seemingly hold his own with experts on any topic.

Bush lacked these credentials. He attended three of America's most prestigious schools without distinguishing himself in the classroom. He never made the honor roll at Andover, he was a C student at Yale, and he scarcely left a footprint at Harvard Business School. At Yale, by his own admission, he was more interested in partying than in studying. His main achievement during his time in New Haven was being elected president of Delta Kappa Epsilon, known on campus as the "jock" fraternity. He also seemed oddly indifferent to the great issue of the day—Vietnam. While many of his generation marched off to fight in the war and others protested it, he remained largely outside that great debate. He volunteered for the Texas Air National Guard, knowing that this would minimize his chances of being sent to Indochina.

There was no evidence that Bush's interest in world affairs deepened as he aged. Aside from frequent visits to Mexico during his governorship, he seldom traveled abroad. His insistence on bringing his favorite pillow with him as he crisscrossed the country during the campaign, along with his frequent complaints to the press about having to spend time away from home, contributed to his image as a provincial unconcerned with the broader world.

Bush's factual misstatements, mediocre grades, and infrequent international travel might have attracted less notice if he hadn't also inherited his father's gift for malapropisms and mangled syntax. It is a singular conceit among academics and journalists that people who don't speak well can't think well—that is, if they think at all. Bush provided the doubters with plenty of grist for their mills. He called for free-trade policies that knocked down "bariffs and terriers," turned a "vital" hemisphere into a "vile" one, and warned about terrorists holding Americans "hostile" rather than "hostage." Kosovars became "Kosovians" and the East Timorese "East Timorians." His gaffes provided red meat for every critic with a pen or a microphone. Garry Trudeau depicted Bush in his *Doonesbury* comic strip as a giant cowboy hat sitting atop an asterisk. David Letterman joked, "The guy may have 'bonehead' stamped all over him."[5] Maureen Dowd of the *New York Times* wrote that Dick Cheney would be Bush's "baby sitter."[6]

These cracks were in many ways unfair. By any objective measure Bush was no dunce. He scored 566 out of 800 on the verbal section of the SAT and 640 out of 800 on the math section. His combined score of 1206—which would have been 75 points higher under the adjusted scoring system that the SATs adopted in 1994—was one that most high school students would be delighted to have and one that some of his presidential rivals could not match. Bill Bradley, for instance, who was often praised for his intellect, scored only 485 on the verbal part of the SAT. By the same token, Bush's unimpressive grades at Yale turned out to be not much different from those that Al Gore earned during much of his time at Harvard, and they came before grade inflation turned a gentleman's C into a B. They were also much higher than those of John McCain, who finished near the bottom of his class at the Naval Academy.

The cracks about Bush's intelligence also missed how he grew more comfortable in discussing foreign policy as the campaign progressed. He performed far better in his three debates with Al Gore, for instance, than he had in debates with his rivals for the Republican nomination months earlier. Then his answers often bore only a faint relationship to the question asked, and they often ended long before his allotted time was up. Against Gore, whose reputation as a fierce debater willing to draw blood prompted the *Atlantic Monthly* to run a cover depicting him as a vampire, Bush held his own. His oratorical skills may not have made listeners forget Churchill or Lincoln, but largely gone were the halting answers and the painful pauses of a man unsure of what to say.

Bush's greater ease in discussing foreign policy no doubt reflected the fact that he knew more about world affairs at the end of the campaign than he did at the start. But his early discomfort—and the impressions it helped create—probably owed as much to a well-justified fear that the news media were playing "gotcha" with him on foreign policy. That, after all, had been the point of the foreign policy pop quiz. Over time Bush learned, as do all successful presidential candidates, how to handle the media. The problem for Bush was that a presidential candidate seldom gets a second chance to make a first impression. And the first impression many Americans had of him was that he was lost when it came to foreign affairs.

BUSH KNEW HE could not credibly claim to be a foreign policy expert like his father, and he wisely never tried. "Nobody needs to tell me what to believe," he said on the campaign trail. "But I *do* need somebody to tell me where Kosovo is."[7] To help him locate Kosovo, Bush assembled a group of eight Republican experts, nicknamed the Vulcans, to tutor him on world affairs. The group was drawn mostly from people who had served in the third and fourth tiers of his father's administration. It was led by Condoleezza Rice, the former provost at Stanford University and his father's White House adviser on the Soviet Union, and Paul Wolfowitz, the dean of the Johns Hopkins School of Advanced International Studies (SAIS) and undersecretary for defense policy in the first Bush administration. The other Vulcans were Richard Armitage, assistant secretary of defense for international security affairs in the Reagan administration; Robert Blackwill, White House adviser on European and Soviet affairs in the first Bush administration; Stephen Hadley, assistant secretary of defense for international security policy in the first Bush administration; Richard Perle, assistant secretary of defense for international security policy during the Reagan administration; Dov Zakheim, deputy undersecretary of defense for planning and resources in the Reagan administration; and Robert Zoellick, undersecretary of state for economic affairs and White House deputy chief of staff during the first Bush administration.

Rice had the most interesting personal history of any of the Vulcans. She named the group to honor her hometown of Birmingham, Alabama, a steel city whose symbol is a statue of the Roman god of fire and metalworking. Rice grew up in a segregated, middle-class neighborhood in the final, dangerous days of Jim Crow. One of the four young girls killed in the 1963 Birmingham church bombing was a friend and classmate. Her father joined with other men in the neighborhood to patrol the streets at night armed with shotguns to protect their families against white racists. In this atmosphere of hate and bigotry, Rice's parents pushed her to achieve. She began taking piano lessons at the age of three, was tutored in French and Spanish while in elementary school, and entered the eighth grade at the age of eleven. She and her family moved to Denver for high school, driving across the country and not being able to stay at motels or eat in restaurants. At the age of fifteen, she enrolled at the University of Denver. There she became a protégé of Josef Korbel, the father of Secretary of State Madeleine Albright. Rice fell in love with Russian history. After graduating from Denver at the age of nineteen, she took a master's degree at Notre Dame. She returned to Denver to earn a Ph.D. under Korbel's tutelage, writing her dissertation on the relationship between the Soviet and Czechoslovak militaries. She eventually joined the political science faculty at Stanford University.

Although Rice's parents were Republicans—her father wanted nothing to do with the South's Dixiecrats—she initially registered as a Democrat. She switched parties in 1982, she later said, because she had been appalled by the naïveté inherent in Jimmy Carter's remark two years earlier that he had been shocked by the Soviet invasion of Afghanistan.[8] Despite her change of political heart, she informally advised Gary Hart in his 1984 bid for the Democratic presidential nomination. That same year, however, the direction of Rice's life changed. At a dinner at Stanford, she challenged the substance of a talk given by General Brent Scowcroft, then chair of President Reagan's Commission on Strategic Forces. Impressed by "this little slip of a girl," Scowcroft decided, "that's someone I've got to get to know."[9] He arranged for her to be invited to high-level conferences in the mid-1980s. She also won a prestigious fellowship from the Council on Foreign Relations that enabled her to spend a year in Washington working for the Joint Chiefs of Staff, handling among other issues, nuclear strategy. When the elder George Bush made Scowcroft his national security adviser, Scowcroft asked Rice to join his staff as an adviser on the Soviet Union.

The National Security Council (NSC) appointment came at an auspicious time for a Soviet expert—the once rising Soviet Union was coming apart at the seams. Rice, like her boss, Scowcroft, and his boss, the president, favored working with Soviet leader Mikhail Gorbachev as long as possible. In 1989 she gained notoriety by physically preventing Boris Yeltsin, then the leader of Russia's reform movement, who was demanding a meeting with President Bush rather than General Scowcroft, from leaving the NSC's offices in the White House to go in search of the Oval Office.

Despite the magnitude of the events taking place in the Soviet Union, or perhaps because of them, Rice left the first Bush administration after only two years to return to Stanford. Backed by powerful supporters like former secretary of state George Shultz, she was named Stanford's provost, the university's number-two officer and the one primarily responsible for overseeing the faculty, in 1993. She was not only the first woman and first African American to hold the post, but at age thirty-nine she was also by far the youngest. Indeed, it was an almost unheard-of feat for someone only a dozen years removed from receiving her Ph.D. and without any experience in university administration to be named provost. Her supporters also succeeded in placing her on the boards of several major corporations, including the Chevron Corporation, which named one of its supertankers after her.

Rice and George W. Bush first met in the mid-1990s. They bonded almost immediately over their mutual love of sports and exercise. Rice, a die-hard fan of football's Cleveland Browns—their games were broadcast in Birmingham when she was growing up—often said her dream job was to be commissioner of the National Football League. While at Stanford she had a rigorous workout regimen overseen by the university's football coach, prompting *George* magazine to run a story about her entitled "Bush's Kissinger: She Can Kick Your Butt Too." (The story came with photos of her in the gym.) Bush and Rice also shared a deep religious devotion—Rice was a devout Presbyterian— and an equally deep desire for order, punctuality, and predictability. (She kept two mirrors at her desk so she could always check the back as well as the front of her hair. "I do try to make sure everything is in place.")[10] As Bush mulled over whether to run for the presidency, she became his personal foreign policy tutor. As he told an interviewer during the campaign, she is the one person who "can explain foreign policy matters in a way that I can understand." Perhaps just as important, he regarded her as "a close confidante and a good soul."[11]

Wolfowitz, the cochair of the Vulcans, could not match Rice's close relationship with Bush or point to a ship bearing his name. He could match her, however, in intellect and accomplishment. He grew up in Ithaca, New York, the son of a Cornell University statistics professor who had immigrated to the United States from Poland in the 1920s. He attended Cornell, where he was a student of the philosopher Allan Bloom, who later wrote the national bestseller *The Closing of the American Mind*. He initially aimed to enroll in MIT's graduate program in biophysical chemistry, partly to please his father, who wanted him to study a real science. He eventually opted to study political science at the University of Chicago, where a series of student deferments spared him from having to serve in Vietnam.

When Wolfowitz showed up in Chicago in 1965, Albert Wohlstetter, who had just joined the faculty after a distinguished career at RAND, a Pentagon-financed think tank in Santa Monica, California, took him under his wing. Wohlstetter was one of the seminal strategists of the nuclear age. His work in the 1950s warning that U.S. bombers might be vulnerable to a Soviet attack helped persuade the Pentagon to develop long-range ballistic missiles and supposedly made him one of the models for the character Dr. Strangelove. Wohlstetter introduced Wolfowitz to Paul Nitze, another pivotal postwar thinker and policy practitioner who had written the famed NSC-68 policy memo, which, on the eve of the Korean War, essentially laid out the blueprint for the policy of containment that Washington would pursue for the next four decades. In 1969 Nitze persuaded Wolfowitz to come to Washington to work on a campaign seeking to counter criticisms of President Nixon's plan to build an antiballistic missile (ABM) system. While in the nation's capital, Wolfowitz worked with another Wohlstetter protégé, Richard Perle. Wolfowitz eventually returned to Chicago, earned his Ph.D., and joined the faculty at Yale.

In 1973 Wolfowitz abandoned the classrooms of New Haven to work in Washington at the U.S. Arms Control and Disarmament Agency. He was soon drawn into the bitter debate within the Nixon and Ford administrations over the wisdom of the policy of détente. Hard-liners argued that the U.S. intelligence community was downplaying the Soviet Union's aggressive efforts to gain military supremacy because of the White House's love affair with arms control. With the controversy threatening to sap conservative support for Gerald Ford's 1976 presidential bid, George H. W. Bush, then director of Central

Intelligence, set up "Team B" to review the top-secret data that the intelligence agencies used. Its ten members, all hard-liners, included Wolfowitz. Not surprisingly, given the intellectual makeup of its members, Team B depicted the Soviet Union as bent on world domination and willing to fight a nuclear war if necessary. These conclusions, which were adroitly leaked to the press, gave conservatives critical ammunition with which to attack the Strategic Arms Limitation Talks (SALT) treaties and to push for a reversal in the Vietnam-inspired free fall in defense spending. (In retrospect, Team B proved to be a classic example of worst-case analysis; none of its reports recognized the significance of the political, demographic, and economic rot already eating away at the Soviet system.) Wolfowitz, however, was not a central player on Team B or a major contributor to its headline-grabbing conclusions. His contribution analyzed the role that medium-range missiles played in Soviet military strategy.

After the Ford administration ended, Wolfowitz spent the next fifteen years shuttling back and forth between jobs at the Defense and State Departments. He was deputy assistant secretary of defense under Jimmy Carter; director of the State Department's policy planning staff, assistant secretary for East Asian and Pacific affairs, and U.S. ambassador to Indonesia (the country with the world's largest Muslim population) under Ronald Reagan; and undersecretary of defense for policy under the first George Bush. Wolfowitz's status as a quintessential Washington insider earned him a literary distinction of a sort. He was the model for a minor character in Saul Bellow's 2001 book *Ravelstein*, a novel whose main character is a thinly disguised Allan Bloom. (The Wolfowitz character, a Pentagon official named Philip Gorman, calls Ravelstein occasionally to share Washington gossip.)

Wolfowitz spent the Clinton years outside of government, primarily as the dean at SAIS. Whereas Rice wrote and spoke publicly about current events only intermittently during the 1990s, Wolfowitz actively participated in Washington debates. He frequently criticized what he saw as Bill Clinton's missteps, particularly his administration's handling of Iraq. Wolfowitz had been heavily involved in planning the Gulf War in his post as undersecretary of defense for policy, and he had quickly concluded that the elder Bush had erred by not ordering U.S. troops to

march on Baghdad in March 1991. He also served on the congressionally mandated Commission to Assess the Ballistic Missile Threat, informally known as the Rumsfeld Commission after its chair, Donald Rumsfeld. The commission, which essentially was another Team B exercise,
concluded in 1998 that the U.S. intelligence community had underestimated the growing ballistic missile threat to the United States from
countries such as North Korea, Iran, and Iraq. Just six weeks after the
commission released its report, Pyongyang fired a rudimentary inter-
continental missile, seemingly confirming the commission's conclusion.

Richard Armitage, a lifelong weight lifting aficionado who in his
mid-fifties could still bench-press nearly four hundred pounds, was in
many ways Wolfowitz's opposite, more a doer than a thinker. Born in
Boston in 1945 and the son of a cop, he graduated from the Naval
Academy. He did three tours of duty in Vietnam, witnessed the fall of
Saigon in 1975, and then served two years as a military attaché in Iran.
In the late 1970s he worked as an administrative assistant to Senator
Bob Dole of Kansas. During the Reagan administration, he worked as
deputy assistant secretary of defense for East Asian and Pacific Affairs
before becoming assistant secretary of defense. Under the elder President Bush, he served in a variety of special envoy jobs. Among other
things, he negotiated the transfer of U.S. military bases in the Philippines back to the Filipino government. Armitage made no pretense to
having a grand foreign policy vision. He saw himself, and was seen by
others, as an experienced diplomatic troubleshooter with a deep knowledge of Asia.

Robert Blackwill was a classic example of what the John F. Kennedy
School of Government at Harvard University likes to call its "scholar
practitioners." A Peace Corps volunteer in Malawi, he joined the foreign service in 1967 and was thus the only Vulcan with experience as a
State Department foreign service officer. After serving in Kenya,
Britain, and Israel, as well as on the NSC staff and in the State Department, he left the foreign service in 1983 to become associate dean at the
Kennedy School. Over the next seven years, he alternated teaching
stints at Harvard with tours of duty back in government, first as the
chief U.S. negotiator at the Vienna talks on mutual and balanced force
reductions under Reagan and then as the NSC's top European expert

under the elder Bush. In the latter job, he was Rice's immediate boss during her first year at the White House and heavily involved in the diplomacy surrounding German reunification. The Federal Republic of Germany recognized his contributions by awarding him one of its highest honors, the Commander's Cross of the Order of Merit.

If Blackwill was the only former foreign service officer among the Vulcans, Stephen Hadley was the only practicing lawyer. He had attended Cornell University and then Yale Law School. Over his career he moved back and forth between his law practice, which focused on international business and regulatory issues, and a variety of government posts. He worked for Brent Scowcroft on the NSC staff during Gerald Ford's presidency. In 1987 he served as an unpaid counsel to the Tower Commission, which President Reagan set up to investigate the origins of the Iran-contra affair. He eventually became one of the two principal authors of the commission's highly praised final report. While serving as assistant secretary of defense during the first Bush administration, he was responsible for defense policy concerning NATO and nuclear weapons. He then returned to his law practice and also signed on as a principal in Scowcroft's international consulting firm. He was viewed by many of his colleagues as a negotiator and mediator more than as a strategist. Unlike most of the Vulcans, he wrote little and was never seen arguing policy positions on the television talk show circuit.

Richard Perle, by contrast, was widely known in Washington and in many European capitals. He first came to Washington because of his connections to Albert Wohlstetter. Unlike Wolfowitz, Perle first got to know the strategist around the Wohlstetter family pool rather than in a classroom. He attended Hollywood High School with Wohlstetter's daughter and went over to the Wohlstetters to swim. In this undistinguished student—Perle was flunking high-school Spanish at the time—Wohlstetter found an attentive pupil for his theories of military strategy and the inexorable impact of technological change on warfare. Perle graduated from the University of Southern California and then attended Princeton. (Chicago rejected him.) Like Wolfowitz, he received a phone call from Nitze in 1969 asking him to come to Washington to work for approval of the planned ABM system. Unlike Wolfowitz, he did not return to academia once the campaign ended. He instead landed a job on the staff of Democratic Senator Henry "Scoop" Jackson of Washington, a post he held for the next eleven years. As Jackson's senior aide, Perle led his attack on the Nixon-Ford policy of détente with the Soviet Union. After Perle helped engineer passage of the 1974 Jackson-Vanik Amendment, which restricted trade benefits for the Soviet Union because of Soviet restrictions on Jewish emigration, then–Secretary of State Henry Kissinger angrily predicted: "You just wait and see! If that son of a bitch Richard Perle ever gets into an administration, after six months he'll be pursuing the same policies I've been attempting and that he's been sabotaging."[12] Kissinger was wrong. During his six years in the Reagan administration, Perle earned the nickname "Prince of Darkness" for fiercely resisting any U.S. movement on arms control. He left the Reagan administration in 1987 to pursue business interests and to serve as a senior fellow at the American Enterprise Institute, a conservative think tank in Washington. During the 1990s he distinguished himself as a relentless critic of the Clinton administration's policy toward Iraq and a staunch supporter of Iraqi exile groups looking for U.S. aid in their bid to topple Saddam Hussein. Despite his membership in the Vulcans, Perle remained a registered Democrat.

Like Perle, Dov Zakheim was a veteran of the Defense Department. A Brooklyn native, he graduated from Columbia and earned his doctoral degree in politics and economics from Oxford. In the 1970s he worked as a national security analyst at the Congressional Budget Office. After Ronald Reagan's landslide victory in 1980, Zakheim moved over to the Defense Department, eventually rising to the post of deputy undersecretary of defense for planning and resources. While at the Reagan Pentagon he played a lead role in the campaign to kill Israel's Lavi jet fighter program, which was being funded primarily by U.S. military aid. After leaving the Defense Department, he worked first for McDonnell Douglas and then for System Planning Corporation, a defense contractor that analyzed defense issues for the Pentagon and manufactured components for weapons systems. He eventually became SPC's chief executive officer. In addition to his corporate work,

Zakheim pursued a career as a defense intellectual. He wrote extensively for both experts and the broader public on a wide range of defense topics, including a book on the Lavi dispute. However, his main focus was criticizing the missteps of the Clinton administration, especially what he saw as its misguided penchant for engaging U.S. troops in peacekeeping operations.[13]

Robert Zoellick was the Vulcans' economics and trade expert. Born and raised in a Chicago suburb, he earned an undergraduate degree from Swarthmore and then public policy and law degrees at Harvard. A former professor persuaded him to take a post at the Reagan Treasury Department, where he became a top aide to the secretary, James Baker. When Baker moved from Treasury to the State Department in 1989, Zoellick went with him. He first served as counselor of the department, a job that led some to dub him Baker's "second brain" because he reviewed every piece of paper before it went to the secretary.[14] Zoellick later served as undersecretary for economic and agricultural affairs. Among his many accomplishments at State was helping to negotiate the reunification of Germany. When Baker left Foggy Bottom to become White House chief of staff in the waning days of the elder Bush's presidency, Zoellick once again followed, this time serving as deputy chief of staff. He held several positions in the 1990s, including executive vice president of Fannie Mae, the giant mortgage investment firm, and lecturer at the Naval Academy.

The Vulcans were not the only ones offering advice to the younger Bush. He stayed in close touch with his father, though both resolutely refused to discuss what they talked about. Numerous other Republican foreign policy luminaries, including former secretaries of state Henry Kissinger and George Shultz, traveled to Austin to discuss world affairs. Bush also called on the expertise of his father's chief advisers, most notably Dick Cheney and Colin Powell. The importance of Cheney, then the head of the Dallas-based oil services firm Halliburton, became clear when Bush tapped him to be his running mate. Bush's relationship with Powell, the former national security adviser under Reagan and chairman of the joint chiefs during the Gulf War, was more distant. Powell seldom appeared publicly with Bush during the campaign, often refusing requests to attend campaign events, and he did not form a deep bond with the candidate. However, Powell's popularity and his unquestioned national security credentials helped burnish Bush's image. The Texas governor may not have been a foreign policy expert, but he certainly knew plenty of people who were.

Although other experts got to share their views with Bush, the Vulcans ran the foreign policy aspects of the campaign on a day-by-day basis. For that reason Bush's choice of these eight advisers was significant—it provided the first clue to his own foreign policy beliefs. In the 1990s the loudest Republican voices on foreign policy in Congress, and especially in the House, were "sovereigntists." They were deeply suspicious of engagement abroad and saw most international institutions, whether political or economic in nature, as eroding American sovereignty. Although they were a minority in the Republican caucus, the sovereigntists often succeeded in setting the party's foreign policy agenda on Capitol Hill. They pushed legislation to bar presidents from putting U.S. combat troops under the command of a foreign officer, voted against sending peacekeeping troops to the Balkans, sought to prevent the World Trade Organization from being able to compel changes in American consumer and environmental laws, opposed efforts to pay U.S. back dues to the United Nations, and denounced the war in Kosovo. In contrast to this mixture of isolationist and protectionist policies, the Vulcans supported international engagement and free trade.

By the same token, however, the Vulcans hardly represented the views of all internationalist Republicans. Largely missing from Bush's core foreign policy team were moderate Republicans from his father's administration, most notably Brent Scowcroft, James Baker, and Lawrence Eagleburger—the elder Bush's national security adviser and his two secretaries of state. The Vulcans were instead for the most part intelligent hard-liners. When asked to characterize her views, Rice would tell reporters that she was "very conservative" in foreign policy.[15] Wolfowitz, Perle, and Zakheim also prided themselves on being hawks. They had demonstrated over the years that they were willing to criticize anyone, Republican or Democrat, who they believed failed to measure up to their hard-line standards.

BUSH'S MISCUES ON foreign policy did not mean he had no idea how to be president. On the contrary, he had well-developed views on leadership. They drew in part from his Harvard Business School education and from running a company. They also drew from watching his father's triumphs and failures. During the 1988 presidential campaign he assumed the role, as one journalist put it, of "official kibitzer."[16] He kept a watchful eye on the staff and rebuked them when he thought they were putting their own interests before his father's. After the election, he occasionally returned to Washington to play the heavy in intra-White House politics, most notably in firing John Sununu as chief of staff. Unlike most presidential candidates, he had firsthand experience in the White House. And his perspective was unique: never before had someone watched a president both as a staff member and as a son.

During the 2000 campaign, Bush described how he viewed the president's role—it was as the country's chief executive officer. As he wrote in his campaign autobiography, that meant he had "to outline a clear vision and agenda."[17] A belief in the need for clear objectives is hardly surprising for a man whose father's reelection campaign had foundered over "the vision thing." The younger Bush pushed the point further in his first major foreign policy address as a candidate: "Unless a president sets his own priorities, his priorities will be set by others—by adversaries, or the crisis of the moment, live on CNN."[18] Moreover, Bush believed that a president should act boldly. Leaders did not merely tinker at the margins. As he said about becoming governor: "I wanted to spend my capital on something profound. I didn't come to Austin just to put my name in a placecard holder at the table of Texas governors."[19] His presidential campaign platform—a $1.6 trillion dollar tax cut, Social Security privatization, and deployment of an ambitious missile defense—attested to his desire not to spend his political capital on small things.

"The next challenge" of leadership, according to Bush, is "to build a strong team of effective people to implement my agenda."[20] He saw his reliance on others as a sign of strength. He repeatedly reminded voters, "I've assembled a team of very strong, smart people. And I look forward to hearing their advice."[21] He used his advisers' foreign policy qualifications to deflect questions about his own. "I may not be able to tell you exactly the nuance of the East Timorian situation but I'll ask Condi Rice or I'll ask Paul Wolfowitz or I'll ask Dick Cheney. I'll ask the people who've had experience."[22] His job, then, was to be decisive—to pick among the options his advisers presented. "There's going to be disagreements. I hope there is disagreement, because I know that disagreement will be based upon solid thought. And what you need to know is that if there is disagreement, I'll be prepared to make the decision necessary for the good of the country."[23]

Bush also insisted that as a CEO president he would stick to his positions even if public opinion moved the other way. His campaign mantra was: "We have too much polling and focus groups going on in Washington today. We need decisions made on sound principles."[24] This insistence on standing firm no doubt made for good politics. However, it probably also reflected Bush's true feelings, particularly if it is understood as skepticism of conventional wisdom. His personal history showed that experts were often wrong and opinions could change. Few took him seriously when he decided to run for governor. Most political pros were convinced that his younger brother Jeb was the upcoming star in the family. Pundits dismissed him as a daddy's boy running on his father's name and ridiculed his refusal to go "off message" in endlessly repeating his main campaign themes. He proved the skeptics wrong and defeated the popular Ann Richards. Once in office, he succeeded in enacting some of his priorities and failed in others. Still, his governing style was in keeping with his philosophy: "I believe you have to spend political capital or it withers and dies."[25]

Underlying this approach to presidential leadership was tremendous self-confidence. It was a quality of Bush's that impressed his advisers. "The first time I met Bush 43 I knew he was different," Perle said, using the White House lingo for distinguishing the younger Bush from his father, the forty-first president. "Two things became clear. One, he didn't know very much. The other was that he had the confidence to ask questions that revealed he didn't know very much. Most people are reluctant to say when they don't know something, a word or term they haven't heard before. Not him. You'd raise a point, and he'd say, 'I didn't realize that. Can you explain that?' He was eager to learn."[26]

Outsiders might question whether this self-confidence was justified.

After all, how would someone who was still learning about the world choose the right foreign policy priorities, decide whom to listen to when his seasoned advisers disagreed on what to do, know when his advisers reached a flawed consensus, or recognize when the conventional wisdom was actually right? Then again, Bush had reason to be self-confident. As Cheney explained it: "Well, but think of what he's done. He's the guy who went out and put his name on the ballot, got into the arena, captured the Republican nomination, devised a strategy to beat an incumbent vice president at a time of considerable prosperity in the country. None of the rest of us did that. And that's the test."[27]

For Bush, the campaign was the culmination of a remarkable journey that began not at Andover and Yale, but when he was forty years old and living in Lubbock, Texas. He was running a failing business, drinking too much, and ambling through life, not into history. How many Americans have turned their lives around so completely that within a dozen years they became a two-time governor of the nation's second most populous state and a serious contender for the highest office in the land?

THREE

BUSH'S WORLDVIEW

W HEN FOREIGN POLICY came up during the 2000 Bush campaign, the discussions typically focused on what the Texas governor knew about world politics and whether it was enough to be commander in chief. Often overlooked was a different, and more important question: What did he believe? The fixation on how much George W. Bush knew is in many ways understandable. Journalists and intellectuals often assume that beliefs are built on a foundation of facts. This assumption is usually wrong. Just listen to the visceral pronouncements on talk radio. As these show, people generally come to their beliefs about how the world works long before they encounter facts. And while Bush's store of foreign policy knowledge may have been low, he was emphatic that "I know what I believe in."[1]

At the start of the campaign it was difficult to pin down exactly what Bush believed about America's role in the world. Unlike Al Gore, he had not cast hundreds of congressional votes or written books and articles outlining his vision for the United States abroad. Bush was a doer, not a thinker; his natural element was action, not analysis. During his two terms as Texas governor he had worked on some foreign policy issues. However, these typically involved matters such as managing water resources in the Rio Grande basin—concerns that would be at the fringes of any president's policy agenda. Bush's lack of eloquence, bordering at times on incoherence, made it harder to discern his core beliefs. Bill Clinton probably had even less firsthand experience with foreign policy when he first ran for the presidency in 1992, but his capacity to think conceptually, coupled with his ability to talk lucidly and at great length, gave voters clear insight into how he saw America's role in the world.

Nonetheless, anyone who followed Bush closely during the campaign could see that he was outlining, albeit at times faintly, a coherent foreign policy philosophy. It could be seen more clearly in the writings and statements of the people he chose to advise him on foreign policy. This philosophy was unremarkable in what it posited as the goals of America's engagement abroad: security, prosperity, and freedom. What made it distinctive was what it said about how the United States should seek to achieve these goals. It should look primarily to the unilateral exercise of American power and not to international or multilateral organizations.

LIKE VIRTUALLY EVERY major presidential candidate since World War II, and unlike third-party candidates Patrick Buchanan and Ralph Nader, Bush argued that the United States must play an active role in world affairs. In an implicit rebuke to the sovereigntist wing of the Republican Party, he criticized those who argued that the wisest course for the United States at the start of the twenty-first century was to withdraw behind its own borders. In his first major speech on foreign affairs, he warned that giving in to the temptation "to build a proud tower of protectionism and isolation" would be a "shortcut to chaos, . . . invite challenges to our power," and result in "a stagnant America and a savage world." He insisted that "American foreign policy cannot be founded on fear. Fear that American workers can't compete. Fear that America will corrupt the world—or be corrupted by it." A Bush administration, he pledged, would "not shrink from leadership."[2]

Bush's foreign policy aspirations mirrored those of virtually every other major presidential candidate since World War II in another way—he accepted Woodrow Wilson's view that the United States's foreign policy should seek to promote its values abroad as well as its interests. "Some have tried to pose a choice between American ideals and American interests—between who we are and how we act," Bush declared in a speech at the Ronald Reagan presidential library in November 1999. "But the choice is false. America, by decision and destiny, promotes political freedom—and gains the most when democracy advances."[3] The United States, he argued, had a "great and guiding goal: to turn this time of American influence into generations of democratic peace."[4]

Although on one level Bush's foreign policy could be described as consistent with his predecessors', on another level it could be summarized as ABC—Anything But Clinton. Bush's public pronouncements and those of the Vulcans dripped with disdain for the forty-second president. Lurking in the background of these criticisms was always the reality that Clinton had been the one who had denied his father a second term in office. But in Bush's judgment, Clinton had also committed the cardinal sin of leadership—he had failed to set priorities. Bush clearly had Clinton in mind when he declared that presidents should not let the nation "move from crisis to crisis like a cork in a current."[5] The result was "action without vision, activity without priority, and missions without end—an approach that squanders American will and drains American energy."[6]

Clinton's failure to set priorities, Bush argued, was most visible in the way his administration had promiscuously deployed U.S. military forces around the globe. "Rarely has our military been so freely used—an average of one deployment every nine weeks in the last few years."[7] In places such as Somalia and Haiti, both of which were tangential to core U.S. interests, Clinton had compounded the problem by committing American forces to nation-building when their true mission was "to fight and win war."[8] Bush stuck to this position even when he was asked what he would do if another Rwanda occurred. "We should not send our troops to stop ethnic cleansing and genocide in nations outside our strategic interest," he said on ABC's *This Week*. "I don't like genocide and I don't like ethnic cleansing, but the president must set clear parameters as to where troops ought to be used and when they ought to be used."[9]

Despite these statements, Bush was not flatly opposed to U.S. intervention abroad. During his second debate with Al Gore he volunteered that he agreed with every one of Clinton's decisions to intervene militarily except for Haiti. He supported Clinton on Kosovo, though he (and many others inside and outside the administration) criticized

Clinton for appearing to rule out the possibility of sending in U.S. ground forces when he announced the war's start. Bush also publicly urged congressional Republicans not to cut off funding for the war or mandate an early withdrawal of U.S. peacekeeping troops from the Balkans. Clinton's mistake, in Bush's view, was not that he had actively exercised American military might; it was that he had expended it on matters of secondary importance, leaving U.S. troops dispirited, frustrated, and overstretched. The solution was to replace "diffuse commitments with focused ones" and "uncertain missions with well-defined objectives."[10]

Bush and the Vulcans also criticized Clinton for appeasing a rising China and indulging a corrupt Russia. Bush mocked Clinton for his inconsistency and wishful thinking in dealing with China. First Clinton said China was "run by 'the butchers of Beijing,'" and then a few years later he aspired to make the Chinese government America's "strategic partner." In Bush's view, Washington "must deal with China without ill-will—but without illusions." In the case of Russia, Bush criticized the Clinton White House for "focusing our aid and attention on a corrupt and favored elite" and for excusing "Russian brutality" in Chechnya and elsewhere. What was needed was "nothing short of a new strategic relationship to protect the peace of the world."[11]

Bush's disdain for Clinton's stewardship carried over to relations with allies. He and the Vulcans repeatedly attacked Clinton for undermining U.S. alliances by alienating America's friends. The source of this criticism lay partly in Clinton's decision to return directly to Washington from his one trip to China. "Never again," Bush declared, "should an American president spend nine days in China, and not even bother to stop in Tokyo or Seoul or Manila. Never again should an American president fall silent when China criticizes our security ties to Japan." The criticism of Clinton also reflected a belief that he had been too willing to follow his European counterparts and not bold enough to lead them. "For NATO to be strong, cohesive and active, the President must give it consistent direction: on the alliance's purpose; on Europe's need to invest more in defense capabilities; and, when necessary, in military conflict."[12]

Bush promised voters he would deliver abroad what he said Clinton had not—a clear set of priorities based on a hard-nosed assessment of America's national interests. "These are my priorities," he said in his first major foreign policy address. "An American president should work with our strong democratic allies in Europe and Asia to extend the peace. He should promote a fully democratic Western Hemisphere, bound together by free trade. He should defend America's interests in the Persian Gulf and advance peace in the Middle East, based upon a secure Israel. He must check the contagious spread of weapons of mass destruction, and the means to deliver them. He must lead toward a world that trades in freedom."[13]

This pledge shows that Bush's foreign policy goals were thoroughly conventional. Indeed, his proposals for dealing with Beijing and Moscow looked considerably like Clinton's. Bush did relabel Beijing a strategic "competitor," but he defended Clinton's policy of improving trade relations with China because "economic freedom creates habits of liberty. And habits of liberty create expectations of democracy." Bush called for working with Russia to develop missile defense systems, but he also pledged to ask Congress "to increase substantially our assistance to dismantle as many of Russia's weapons as possible, as quickly as possible."[14]

Bush's stances on the two foreign policy issues that would come to define his presidency—terrorism and Iraq—were equally conventional. He vowed in his first campaign speech to "put a high priority on detecting and responding to terrorism on our soil."[15] For the most part, however, Bush (and Al Gore) seldom mentioned terrorism during the campaign. He did not raise the subject in any of the three presidential debates, nor was he asked about it. This is surprising in retrospect. The third debate came just days after al Qaeda operatives bombed the USS *Cole* in the Yemeni port of Aden, killing seventeen American sailors. When Bush did mention terrorism, he almost always did so in the context of discussing the ballistic missile threat to the United States and the need for national missile defense, even though terrorists had killed thousands with car, truck, and human bombs, but had never used a ballistic missile in an attack—and had never shown any inclination or capability to do so. While Bush insisted that "the protection of America itself will assume a high priority in a new century" and that "homeland defense has become an urgent duty," his remarks made clear that he saw missile defense and homeland defense as one and the same.[16] Like most people in American political life before September 11, he offered no plan for improving what we now call homeland security.

Bush's views on Iraq were closely followed throughout the campaign, given speculation that he itched to avenge Saddam Hussein's attempt to assassinate his father in 1993. Asked during a December 1999 debate with Republican rivals how he would respond, if he became president, to the discovery that Iraq had resumed manufacturing weapons of mass destruction, he appeared to say he would "take him out." When the moderator immediately followed up this answer, Bush said he would "take out his weapons of mass destruction." The next day he said his original answer was "take 'em out," which people had mis-interpreted because of his Texas drawl. "My intent was the weapons—them, not him."[17] His standard line subsequently became that there would be "consequences" if Iraq developed weapons of mass destruc-tion, though he studiously avoided saying what those consequences might be. He never said that he intended to use the U.S. military to unseat Saddam Hussein. Instead, like Gore, he supported the 1998 Iraq Liberation Act, which gave the State Department $97 million to par-cel out among Iraqi exile groups dedicated to toppling Saddam's gov-ernment. He also agreed with Gore that the policy of containing Iraq with sanctions should continue, insisting, "I want them to be tougher."[18]

ANYONE WHO FOCUSED on what George Bush said he wanted to achieve abroad could be forgiven for concluding that he intended to stick with the status quo. What made Bush's proposed foreign policy different—and potentially even radical—were not its goals but its logic about how America should act in the world. It rejected many of the assumptions that had guided Washington's approach to foreign affairs for more than half a century.

The logic that underlay Bush's foreign policy has its roots in a strain of realist political thinking best labeled hegemonist. At its most basic, the hegemonist argument contends that America's immense power and the willingness to wield it, even over the objections of others, is the key to securing America's interests in the world. This idea is not new. Echoes of hegemonist thought can be found in Senator Henry Cabot Lodge's denunciation of the League of Nations and in the arguments of those who urged Presidents Truman and Eisenhower to roll back Soviet domination of Eastern Europe. Hegemonist arguments were updated in the early 1990s, when the Soviet Union's collapse meant that the United States was no longer checked by a rival superpower. An initial contribution was a 1992 Pentagon study prepared for Dick Cheney and Paul Wolfowitz. The study, according to a draft leaked to the *New York Times*, maintained that U.S. national security policy after the cold war should seek to transform the unipolar moment into a unipolar era by precluding "the emergence of any potential future global competitor."[19]

If Bush's remarks on foreign policy reflected hegemonist thinking, it is fair to ask whether he would have recognized the term or been able to articulate its logic. Probably not in the closely argued style of Cheney and Wolfowitz. The man from Midland was, by his own admission, a "gut player" rather than an intellectual, someone more interested in action than introspection.[20] However, to repeat an earlier point, it is a mistake to assume that someone cannot have a foreign policy philosophy until he has written a book on the subject or at least read a range of books written by others. Bush may not have spent any time consciously trying to develop a philosophy about foreign affairs. However, a lifetime of experience had left deeply formed beliefs—instincts might be more precise—about how the world works and, just as important, how it does not. In that respect, Bush was a bit like Molière's M. Jourdain, who was surprised to discover he had been speaking prose his whole life. The fact that Bush could not translate his gut instincts into a form that would please political science Ph.D.s really did not matter.

What, then, do hegemonists believe? Their philosophy rests on five propositions—four of which are familiar to anyone steeped in the realist tradition of world politics championed until recently by generations of European leaders. The first is that the United States lives in a dangerous world, one closer to Thomas Hobbes's state of nature, in which life is "war of all against all," than to Immanuel Kant's perpetual peace, "in which the idea of a law of world citizenship is no high-flown or exaggerated notion." For Bush and his advisers, the Soviet Union's demise had prompted too many people to ignore the dangers beyond America's borders and see only the opportunities. "This is," Bush maintained, "still a world of terror and missiles and madmen."[21] He routinely criticized Clinton for confusing the world as it is with the world as it ought to be. This was the gist of his complaint about Clinton's seeing China as a potential strategic partner rather than as an actual "competitor."[22] Cheney shared this dark vision of the world. The perils that the United States faced abroad—from China, Russia, Iraq, North Korea, terrorists—were a staple of his conversations.[23] Condoleezza Rice criticized the Clinton administration for being soft in its Russia policy, saying, "if we have learned anything in the last several years it is that a romantic view of Russia—rather than a realistic one—did nothing to help the cause of stability in Russia."[24] The one-time superpower, the Stanford professor argued, in fact "is a threat to the West and to our European allies in particular."[25]

The second element of the hegemonist view is that self-interested nation-states are the key actors in world politics. Political and academic thinkers became enamored in the 1990s of the idea of globalization—the growing economic, political, and social interconnectedness of nations that had resulted from increased trade and financial ties and the rapid advance in communications technology. They believed that globalization was undercutting the authority of individual states, with power flowing to nonstate actors such as private corporations and transnational activist groups; the result was nothing less than a fundamental reordering of the structure of world politics. Bush and his advisers would have none of it. Aside from trade, they seldom mentioned globalization when discussing foreign policy. Whenever they mentioned terrorism, they almost always linked it to rogue regimes and hostile powers. The assumption was that terrorists were the creatures of states, and they would wither without state support. For Bush and his advisers, then, world politics at the beginning of the twenty-first century looked no different than it had to Cardinal Richelieu or Prince von Metternich. States sought to advance their own narrow interests, not to create what Rice called "an illusory international community."[26]

Hegemonists also see power, and especially military power, as the coin of the realm even in a globalized world. "Power matters," Rice wrote, "both the exercise of power by the United States and the ability of others to exercise it."[27] And if power matters, great powers matter most of all. "I believe the big issues are going to be China and Russia," Bush argued. "There will be moments when situations, incidents will flare up. It's important for the President to think globally. But in the long run, security in the world is going to be how do we deal with China and how do we deal with Russia."[28] In dealing with Beijing and Moscow, however, the United States had the advantage of "unrivaled military power, economic promise, and cultural influence." The challenge he faced, then, was "to turn these years of influence into decades of peace."[29] In short, American primacy in world affairs was both real and usable.

But power is about more than just capability. It is also about will. Here Bush and his advisers scorned what they saw as Clinton's hesitancy to flex America's military muscle in defense of core national interests. "There are limits to the smiles and scowls of diplomacy," Bush argued. "Armies and missiles are not stopped by stiff notes of condemnation. They are held in check by strength and purpose and the promise of swift punishment."[30]

The Bush team's thinking about how to apply power was decidedly unsentimental. They talked about exercising American power solely in terms of American interests. Rice explicitly criticized those who believed "that the United States is exercising power legitimately only when it is doing so on behalf of someone or something else."[31] Moreover, Washington should not be afraid of throwing its weight around. The lesson of America's "remarkable record" of building coalitions during the cold war, Wolfowitz wrote, was that leadership consists of "demonstrating that your friends will be protected and taken care of, that your enemies will be punished, and that those who refuse to support you will live to regret having done so."[32] The demonstration of resolve was as crucial for friends as for foes. They both needed to be convinced that the United States intended to back up its words with deeds; otherwise, their suspicion that Washington might change its mind and leave them in the lurch could lead them to ignore American policy or even resist it. Wolfowitz told the story of how Saudi Arabia rejected the elder president Bush's offer to send a fighter squadron to help defend the desert kingdom immediately after the Iraqi invasion of Kuwait. Only after Secretary of Defense Cheney traveled to Riyadh and assured King Fahd that the administration would send hundreds of thousands of U.S. troops did the Saudis conclude that Washington was committed to "finish the job."[33] The lesson was clear: if America leads, others will follow.

The fourth basic proposition of the hegemonist worldview is that multilateral agreements and institutions are neither essential nor necessarily conducive to American interests. Bush did not flatly rule out working through international institutions. On the contrary, he at times spoke of working to strengthen organizations such as NATO, the United Nations, and the International Monetary Fund. However, he and his advisers articulated a distinctively instrumental view of formal multilateral efforts—they were fine if they served immediate, concrete American interests. As a practical matter, international institutions would usually be found wanting. That would force Washington to form "coalitions of the willing." The 1992 draft Pentagon planning document argued that coalitions "hold considerable promise for promoting collective action" and that "we should expect future coalitions to be ad hoc assemblies, often not lasting beyond the crisis being confronted, and in many cases carrying only general agreement over the objectives to be accomplished." But since America might often find itself alone, the planning document argued, "the United States should be postured to act independently."[34] To borrow a metaphor popularized by one Republican thinker, the United States would be the "sheriff" who organized the townspeople into a posse.[35] If the townspeople did not want to ride out to meet the bad guys, Washington would happily take on the role of Gary Cooper in *High Noon* and face the bad guys alone.

The skepticism that the Bush campaign had for international institutions carried over to many international agreements. Part of Bush's critique was that many cold-war agreements had outlived their usefulness. The 1972 Antiballistic Missile (ABM) Treaty, which severely limited any national missile defense system, topped the list. The broader argument, however, was that the Clinton administration had stopped viewing international agreements as a means to achieving

American interests. It had instead transformed them into ends in and of themselves by pursuing what Rice called "symbolic agreements of questionable value."[36] Bush and his advisers rejected the notion, popular with many in the Clinton administration and in Europe, that committing good words to paper would create international norms capable of shaping state behavior. In Bush's view, such agreements constrained only the United States and other law-abiding countries, not rogue states bent on harming American interests. That was his reason for opposing the Comprehensive Test Ban Treaty, which he argued "offers only words and false hopes and high intentions—with no guarantees whatever."[37] With treaties unable to deliver real security to the United States, Washington would be better able to advance its interests by jettisoning constraints on its freedom of action. This policy of the free hand rested on an important assumption: the benefits of flexibility far outweigh the diplomatic costs of declining to participate in international agreements that are popular with friends and allies.

Washington could get away with disappointing its allies because of the fifth tenet of the hegemonist faith: the United States is a unique great power and others see it as such. This is the one proposition alien to the realist worldview, which treats the internal make-up and character of states as irrelevant. But it is a proposition virtually all Americans take as self-evident. "America has never been an empire," Bush argued in 1999. "We may be the only great power in history that had the chance, and refused—preferring greatness to power and justice to glory."[38] America's "national interest has been defined instead," argued Rice, "by a desire to foster the spread of freedom, prosperity, and peace."[39] The purity of American motives is crucial because it meant that the exercise of American power would jeopardize only those threatened by the spread of liberty and free markets. A Washington that confidently exercised power would not alienate its friends or disappoint people ruled by tyrants. What Washington wanted was what everyone wanted.

Most of Bush's advisers accepted this billiard-ball view of the world, where the United States was the biggest (and most virtuous) ball on the table and could move every other ball when and where it wanted. The one exception was Colin Powell, a pragmatic internationalist who understood the importance of power, but also worried about the costs of alienating other countries. His time in Vietnam had left him acutely sensitive to the limits of American power and the whims of public support. While chairman of the Joint Chiefs of Staff, he had promulgated the so-called Powell Doctrine, which argued that the United States should use force only as a last resort against clear threats, and even then only if the American public were prepared to support the use of overwhelming force. During the buildup to the Gulf War he had been the most enthusiastic of the elder Bush's advisers about the usefulness of economic sanctions and the least persuaded about the wisdom of using U.S. troops to liberate Kuwait. Powell also saw more virtue in multilateral efforts and agreements; he was the only member of the Bush team to endorse the Comprehensive Test Ban Treaty. And as a career Army man, he was skeptical about the merits of technological panaceas such as missile defense. He was convinced that America's ability to win wars depended ultimately on the willingness of its young men to fight and die on the ground in far-off places.

Powell's views had over the years put him at odds with the rest of Bush's foreign policy team. (The exception was Armitage. The two had been close friends ever since meeting in the early years of the Reagan administration.) Most of the Vulcans dismissed Powell's cautious approach to American power as timidity. They savaged him privately to their allies in the press, complaining that he had no strongly held views on foreign affairs. He was instead a foreign policy manager who preferred to repair rips in the status quo rather than chart a bold course for the United States. He and Wolfowitz had staked out opposite positions during the Gulf War. The memory of that dispute apparently lasted with Wolfowitz. When he was asked why he agreed to become deputy secretary of defense for the younger Bush, he reportedly gave a one-word answer: "Powell."[40]

While the hegemonists in the Bush campaign were united in dismissing Powell's views, they disagreed among themselves over a key question: To what extent should the United States use its power to promote America's ideals? A minority, led by Wolfowitz and Richard Perle, was what the press often referred to as neoconservatives, but they might be more accurately called democratic imperialists. This group argued that the United States should actively deploy its overwhelming military, economic, and political might to remake the world in its image—and that doing so would serve the interests of other countries as well as the United States. They were less worried about the dangers of nation-building and more willing to commit the nation's resources not just to toppling tyrants, but also to creating democracies in their wake. After September 11, and especially after the Iraq War, many commentators explored the intellectual links between the democratic imperialists and Leo Strauss, a European émigré and longtime political philosopher at the University of Chicago who died in 1973. These efforts, which frequently resembled the parlor game "Six Degrees of Kevin Bacon," gave too much credit to the author of obscure books like *Xenophon's Socratic Discourse*. Strauss's belief that western democracies would be safe from the forces of tyranny and his rejection of moral relativism, while powerfully argued, were hardly novel.

The efforts to uncover signs of Strauss's influence on Bush's advisers also missed a more important point: most of Bush's foreign policy advisers—and to judge by his comments on the campaign trail, the president himself—were not democratic imperialists. They were instead assertive nationalists deeply skeptical of nation-building, especially when it involved the U.S. military, and scornful that American power could create what others were unable to build for themselves. The U.S. military "is not a civilian police force," Rice argued. "It is not a political referee. And it is most certainly not designed to build a civilian society."[41] She wrote at another point, "There is nothing wrong with doing something that benefits all humanity, but that is, in a sense, a second-order effect."[42] Rice and Cheney saw the purpose of flexing America's military might as more limited—to deter and defeat potential threats to the nation's security. Because these threats also imperiled others, America's willingness to stare them down enhances not only U.S. security, but international security as well. As the controversial 1992 Pentagon study put it, "the world order is ultimately backed by the U.S."[43] Or, as Rice explained, "America's pursuit of the national interest will create conditions that promote freedom, markets, and peace. Its pursuit of national interests after World War II led to a more prosperous and democratic world. This can happen again."[44]

BUSH RETURNED REPEATEDLY throughout the election campaign to his argument that the United States needed clear foreign policy priorities. He did not, however, make foreign policy his top priority in the race. Unlike Ronald Reagan, who spoke incessantly and unapologetically about the need to confront Soviet power, Bush did not put any foreign policy initiative at center stage. His top two priorities were instead both domestic initiatives—a $1.6 trillion tax cut and education reform. While Bush provided detailed plans on how he intended to achieve these two objectives, his discussion of foreign policy initiatives— whether military readiness, missile defense, or better relations with Mexico—never went beyond listing aspirations.

Bush's decision to make foreign policy a secondary theme reflected his own background and political vulnerabilities. Candidates taking remedial courses in world affairs are poorly positioned to tell the country to look overseas. Another political calculation also played a role— foreign policy was not a topic on the minds of most voters. Polls throughout the 1990s found that fewer than 10 percent of Americans—and often less than 5 percent—named any defense or national security issue as the most important problem facing the United States. Even when people were pressed to name a foreign policy problem, they often could not. If there is one rule of American politics it is this: politicians seeking election avoid issues that do not interest voters and gravitate toward those issues that do.

Indeed, a suspicion that Americans were at heart isolationists suffused Bush's campaign remarks. In his first foreign policy address he warned, "America's first temptation is withdrawal."[45] At many junctures, Bush seemed to play to these sentiments, despite his avowed commitment to providing strong American leadership in world affairs. He repeatedly complained that the Clinton administration had been promiscuous in sending troops overseas and thereby had stretched the U.S. military to its breaking point. This appeared to be part of a deliberate effort to reassure voters that he, unlike his opponent, would not plunge the United States into protracted foreign engagements. He refused to acknowledge that virtually every major U.S. overseas military deployment predated Clinton's presidency and that, except for the Balkans, those begun under Clinton involved very few U.S. troops and were invariably carried out in concert with others. And he failed to mention that ending any of America's major troop deployments overseas would strain alliance relations and potentially upset international stability. Bush insisted that, when deciding whether to use American power, the first question he would ask would be, "What's in the best interests of the United States?"[46] This managed to say both nothing and everything. No one would recommend that a president not act in the country's interests, and it seemed to reassure a country lacking enthusiasm for foreign adventures. That was probably the point.

What the campaign suggested was that for Bush, as for Bill Clinton in 1992, foreign policy was not a matter of passion. He had to speak about world affairs to demonstrate his political credibility. He attempted to do so in ways that maximized his appeal to voters, or at least limited the chances that he would offend. On a few issues, most notably better relations with Mexico, he showed genuine enthusiasm and comfort, though obviously domestic political considerations played a part, given America's rapidly growing Latino population. But the main message he sent to the American electorate was that his would not be a foreign policy presidency.

FOUR

BUILDING A TEAM

G EORGE W. BUSH won the 2000 presidential election, but hardly in the way he expected. In the final weeks of the campaign his advisers confidently predicted victory. Karl Rove, Bush's chief political strategist, told Bush that he would beat Al Gore by 4 to 7 percentage points in the popular vote and pick up 320 votes in the Electoral College.[1] Election Day, however, produced arguably the closest presidential race in American history. Bush drew 540,000 fewer votes than Gore. The dispute over the vote count in Florida threw the outcome into doubt for five weeks. It took a ruling by the Supreme Court, voting along ideological lines, to settle the matter. When Bush took the oath of office in January 2001, he became only the fourth man to lose the popular vote and win the Electoral College. Oddly enough, one of those men was John Quincy Adams, the only other son of a president to become president himself.

The election left many Americans openly doubting the legitimacy of Bush's presidency. Several members of the House of Representatives walked out in protest when the Electoral College votes were officially counted. Equally troubling for Bush was that large numbers of voters, including many who voted for him, doubted his qualifications for the job. Exit polls found that 44 percent of voters believed he did not know enough to be president, and 42 percent believed that he could not handle a foreign policy crisis. Half of those who voted for Bush said they had doubts about their vote.[2]

IT WAS AGAINST this backdrop of skepticism and in some quarters downright hostility that Bush launched his presidency. Only days after the disputed Florida vote recount was halted, Bush moved to name his cabinet. In his 1999 autobiography he had written that one of the challenges of leadership "was to build a strong team of effective people to implement my agenda." In Texas, his philosophy had been to "recruit the very best."[3] The pressure to do so again was great, not only because of his inexperience and gaps in his knowledge, but also because he had likened the presidency to the position of a chief executive officer. As CEO, he would head a corporation with a $2 trillion budget and 2.7 million employees, including 1,000 senior-management positions requiring Senate confirmation and another 6,000 middle-management positions.

The task of filling several of the top foreign policy jobs was easy. In mid-December, Washington's worst-kept secret was revealed when Bush named Colin Powell secretary of state, the first African American to hold the post. The choice of Powell was a no-brainer. Polls showed that he was the most popular political figure in the United States. He even had his own limited-edition G.I. Joe action figure, complete with a uniform, ribbons, and stars. Many Democrats and Republicans had hoped Powell would follow Dwight Eisenhower's lead and run for president. Bush reportedly had tried hard to persuade Powell to be his running mate. (The retired general apparently said no to the presidency and the vice presidency because his wife, Alma, said she would leave him if he did: "If you run, I'm gone.")[4] In introducing Powell as his nominee, Bush gushed that he was an "American hero."[5] Powell's selection gave Bush instant credibility and reassured those voters who worried that he was too green to handle a major foreign policy crisis.

The day after nominating Powell, Bush named Condoleezza Rice to be his national security adviser. She was not the first African American to hold the post—Powell held that distinction—or, at forty-six, the youngest—McGeorge Bundy became John F. Kennedy's national security adviser at the age of forty-one. She was, however, the first woman ever named to the job. The new post would test her ability to master foreign policy subjects well outside her scholarly expertise on the Soviet Union and the Czechoslovak Army, neither of which existed anymore.

"I've been pressed to understand parts of the world that have not been part of my scope," she admitted during the campaign. "I'm really a Europeanist."[6] To help her run a foreign policy decisionmaking process that involved far more of the world than Europe, Rice tapped her fellow Vulcan, Stephen Hadley, as the deputy national security adviser.

In naming Rice as national security adviser, Bush did not give her cabinet rank, as Bill Clinton had done with his two national security advisers. The decision reflected Bush's desire to streamline the size of the cabinet. It had grown substantially under Clinton, encompassing not just the heads of the cabinet departments but also a variety of other senior government and White House officials. The decision most certainly was not a comment on Bush's estimation of Rice's abilities— neither General Scowcroft nor any of his predecessors had cabinet status. Bush drove the point home in announcing her appointment. "I want Condi to come to every Cabinet meeting," he said, thereby informally bestowing on her the main perk that accompanies cabinet rank. "But I think it's best that she be an equal partner of the senior team in the White House." The president then went on to point out the great advantage she would hold over almost every government official with cabinet rank. "I will be seeing her on a daily basis."[7]

FAR HARDER WAS deciding whom to appoint as defense secretary. Paul Wolfowitz wanted the job and had the experience and intellectual credentials for it. However, Bush and his closest advisers worried that the notoriously disorganized Wolfowitz lacked the managerial skills to run what was essentially a conglomerate with an annual budget of more than $300 billion. They feared he would be another Les Aspin, the congressman-cum-defense-intellectual Bill Clinton chose as his first secretary of defense and who lasted less than a year on the job.

Senate Majority Leader Trent Lott lobbied Bush to appoint Dan Coats. The former Indiana senator had served on the Senate Armed Services Committee for ten years. He enjoyed good relations on both sides of the aisle in Congress, a plus for a post that required spending considerable time stroking egos on Capitol Hill. A private meeting between Bush and Coats in mid-December went poorly, however. Bush aides subsequently let it be known that the president-elect was unimpressed with Coats's commitment to defense transformation—the idea of using advances in communications, computers, and other new technologies to make American combat forces faster, stealthier, and deadlier. Bush had hit on the defense transformation theme repeatedly during the campaign, in part because it offered the prospect of a more effective bang for the buck. However, he never spelled out what it would mean in practice, particularly which existing weapons systems, and the factories that made them, would be mothballed.

Perhaps a more important question about Coats was whether the retired senator had the necessary political heft to make a mark on the Bush team. The president-elect worried that the courtly Indianan, who began his political career as a staff assistant to Representative Dan Quayle, lacked the credibility and gravitas to stand up to the strong personalities in the Bush cabinet, particularly Dick Cheney and Powell. This was critical because Bush's approach to managing his national security team rested on having advisers who would be unafraid to push dissenting views.

As Christmas passed, media speculation about who would run the Pentagon mounted. In late December, three weeks before his term was to begin, Bush unveiled a surprise choice: Donald Rumsfeld. The former Navy fighter pilot, Illinois congressman, U.S. ambassador to NATO, and White House chief of staff had been secretary of defense once before. Gerald Ford named him to the post in 1975 at the age of forty-three, making him the youngest man ever to hold the job. Now he would be the oldest.

Rumsfeld had had a varied career after leaving the Pentagon when Ford's term ended in 1977. He served as CEO of several major corporations, none of them a defense contractor. Even as he moved about in the corporate world, he stayed involved in politics and policy. In the 1980s and 1990s, he served several stints as chairman of the board and a trustee of RAND. In 1996 he agreed to manage Bob Dole's faltering presidential campaign. In 1998 he won the admiration of hard-liners on Capitol Hill when the congressionally mandated commission he chaired concluded unanimously that the U.S. intelligence community had underestimated how much progress rogue states had made in developing long-range ballistic missiles, thereby strengthening the case for national missile defense. He chaired another, lesser known blue-ribbon panel in 2000 that urged the U.S. military to exploit space more aggressively.

What made Rumsfeld's appointment surprising was that for many years he had been a rival and critic of the elder Bush. In 1975, when Rumsfeld was Ford's chief of staff, he arranged for Bush to be moved from U.S. liaison to China to director of central intelligence, apparently because Rumsfeld hoped to neutralize politically someone he saw as a threat to his own presidential ambitions. (Bush agreed, cabling Henry Kissinger: "I do not have politics out of my system entirely, and I see this as the total end of any political future.")[8] During his tenure as defense secretary, he regularly criticized Bush's CIA for grossly underestimating the level of Soviet military spending. It was no accident that Rumsfeld spent the years of the elder Bush's administration outside of government.

The younger Bush, always fiercely protective of his father, overlooked these transgressions because of the credibility that Rumsfeld brought to the team. He had long championed the defense-transformation cause that Bush had made a centerpiece of his defense policy platform. He clearly had the stature to take on the heads of the uniformed military, most of whom could be expected to endorse transformation of the other services but resist transformation of their own. Just as important, Rumsfeld could hold his own with the rest of Bush's foreign-policy "dream team." As the president-elect put it in his press conference announcing Rumsfeld's nomination, "General Powell's a strong figure and Dick Cheney's no shrinking violet, but neither is Don Rumsfeld, nor Condi Rice. I view the four as being able to complement each other."[9]

THE LAST MAJOR position on the national security team to be filled was the director of central intelligence. Rumsfeld at one point had been the leading candidate for the job. Wolfowitz was another candidate, but he said flatly he was not interested. With inauguration day rapidly drawing near, Bush announced in mid-January that he had asked George Tenet, the incumbent CIA director, to stay on for a transition period. The decision was a surprise. It had been nearly three decades since a CIA director had survived a change in partisan control of the White

House. Bush's father had been the victim of just such a transition when Gerald Ford gave way to Jimmy Carter.

Tenet's ability to swim against the tide of political history owed something to his knack for making friends in high places. In the late 1980s the New York native and son of Greek immigrants impressed Senator David Boren of Oklahoma, the respected chair of the Senate Intelligence Committee, with his work for the panel. Boren rewarded Tenet by making him staff director and championing his rise up the intelligence ladder. When Bill Clinton was elected in 1992, Boren's recommendation led to Tenet's being named the senior director for intelligence on the NSC staff, a post that involved coordinating the efforts of the federal government's multiple intelligence agencies. In 1995 Clinton named him deputy CIA director. Two years later, Clinton promoted Tenet to director of central intelligence, a position that put him in charge of running the CIA and overseeing the U.S. intelligence community as a whole.

If Tenet's close friendship with David Boren was critical to helping him become CIA director, the good relations he cultivated with the elder George Bush were critical to keeping him there. In 1991, when Tenet was staff director of the Senate Intelligence Committee, Bush nominated Robert Gates, who had been deputy CIA director during the Iran-contra affair, to be director of central intelligence. Tenet earned the White House's gratitude by helping persuade skeptical Democratic senators to approve the controversial nomination. Once Tenet became CIA director himself, he worked to maintain good ties to the elder Bush. It was Tenet's idea to rename the CIA's headquarters in 1999 the George Bush Center for Intelligence to honor the only man to be both CIA director and president of the United States.

When the younger Bush was seeking to put together his national security team in early 2001, Boren and others recommended that he keep Tenet on as CIA director. They urged the president-elect to solicit his father's opinion. He did. The elder Bush offered what amounted to high praise in the family's vocabulary: "From what I hear, he's a good fellow."[10] The younger Bush soon came to the same conclusion. He wanted frequent, to-the-point briefings, not opaque, cover-your-ass assessments. Tenet obliged. "He wasn't puffed up or pompous," Cheney said of Tenet. "The President clearly likes that."[11] Talk of finding a new CIA director faded away. George Tenet was part of the Bush team.

IN FILLING THE top slots on his national security team, Bush passed over the Vulcans, with Rice being the notable exception. Although they all had extensive government experience—again with Rice as the exception—all of them had worked three or four rungs down the bureaucratic hierarchy. The decision not to give top jobs to those who had been the campaign's big thinkers led to grumbling among some conservatives that the watchword of the Bush administration was NINA—no intellectuals need apply.

Nonetheless, Bush did reward all the Vulcans with senior, if not necessarily cabinet, posts. Wolfowitz ended up as deputy secretary of defense. Armitage took himself out of the running for that post with a move that instantly became part of Washington lore. When Rumsfeld told him he had only a "50-50 chance" of being named his deputy, Armitage corrected him, saying he had a "zero chance" because he had no interest in working under Rumsfeld. Armitage's consolation prize was to be named deputy to his good friend Powell. Robert Blackwill, the expert on European affairs, was named U.S. ambassador to India, and moved to the White House two-and-a-half years later as Rice's deputy responsible for Iraq, Iran, Afghanistan, Pakistan, and India. Richard Perle was offered the number-three position at Defense but turned it down, partly for family reasons and partly because he was reluctant to have his financial dealings scrutinized by the Senate. He instead accepted an unpaid position to head up the Defense Policy Board, a previously obscure body of dignitaries that provided advice (often unheeded) to the secretary of defense. Dov Zakheim was named comptroller of the Pentagon, essentially making him the department's chief financial officer. Robert Zoellick ended up as the U.S. Special Trade Representative, where he beat back an effort by other Bush advisers to strip the job of cabinet status.

BY FILLING THE top defense and foreign policy posts with battle-tested veterans of previous administrations, Bush had assembled a national security team that resembled nothing so much as his father's team. However, there was an important twist. In the first Bush administration, Cheney had been the outlier. He was the assertive nationalist who frequently found himself butting heads with pragmatic internationalists such as Scowcroft, Powell, James Baker, and the president himself. In the second Bush administration, Powell was the outlier. Cheney, Rumsfeld, Rice, and Bush were all to his right—with Cheney and Rumsfeld considerably so. Bush respected the former four-star general, but was wary of him. And at least initially, Powell seemed strangely out of touch with Bush's own views. In the press conference announcing his nomination to be secretary of state, Powell all but ignored what Bush had said about foreign policy during the campaign, focusing his remarks on opportunities to make this a better world rather than on threats that make it a dangerous world. He also explicitly rejected the president-elect's insistence that the White House would set the policy agenda. "During your administration you will be faced with many challenges," the former national security adviser and chairman of the Joint Chiefs of Staff warned, "and crises that we don't know anything about right now will come along."[12]

Bush and Cheney sensed from the start that Powell could be too much his own man, and they worked to make sure he would not be. That they saw a threat is hardly surprising. Powell's popularity ratings were substantially higher than the president's, and the press was full of speculation that he would be "the star of the administration" and "the most powerful secretary of state since Kissinger"—someone Cheney had wrangled with during his stint as Ford's chief of staff.[13] The decision to select Rumsfeld was in part a move to keep Powell in check. Powell had virtually no input into the appointment of Rumsfeld. He learned in a phone call from a Bush aide that the president was strongly considering Rumsfeld for defense secretary, by which time Bush and Cheney had already interviewed him. Powell expressed reservations about nominating Rumsfeld—he argued instead for Pennsylvania governor Tom Ridge, a marine and decorated Vietnam veteran—but his concerns were ignored.

Powell was also isolated by the fact that he was not close to the other major figures on the foreign policy team. Similar interests and constant contact during the campaign had helped Bush and Rice form a virtual mind meld. Bush had increasingly looked to Rice to validate his foreign policy intuitions—which she did. Bush had also come to rely heavily on Cheney, as the decision to tap him for the vice presidency showed. Cheney and Rumsfeld had a relationship that dated back to 1969 when Rumsfeld picked Cheney to be his deputy at the Office of Economic Opportunity in the Nixon administration. They had reprised that boss-deputy role at the Cost of Living Council later in the Nixon administration and then again in the Ford White House, where Rumsfeld was the chief of staff. The two had remained friends over the years, with Rumsfeld and his wife attending the Cheneys' thirty-fifth wedding anniversary in Wyoming in 1999.

Powell and Cheney had a correct but distant relationship. Cheney felt that Powell, during his time as secretary of defense, had been too eager to stray beyond the confines of his military charge and to meddle in political matters. Cheney was outraged that Powell's speech accepting the nomination to be secretary of state treated Bush's own foreign policy pronouncements as an afterthought.[14] Powell and Rice shared the bond of race, and Powell's wife, Alma, hailed from the same Birmingham, Alabama, background as Rice. However, Powell and Rice had seldom worked together before Bush's inauguration, and she owed her position to the president, not the secretary of state. Powell's comment that he regarded Rice "like a daughter" suggested he thought of her as a subordinate rather than an equal, a perception that probably was not lost on the national security adviser.[15]

Powell's isolation within the administration was reinforced from the start by the fact that the people named to most of the number-two and -three spots in the national security bureaucracy dismissed his pragmatic approach to foreign policy and were close to Cheney, Rumsfeld, or both. Hadley and Wolfowitz had worked for Cheney when he was secretary of defense. Wolfowitz had worked with Rumsfeld as a member of the Rumsfeld Commission. Cheney would later tease the deputy secretary by giving him a signed photograph showing him flanked by the past and present secretary of defense. The inscription read: "Paul, Who is the best Secretary of Defense you ever worked for? Dick."[16]

In addition to installing Wolfowitz in the deputy secretary of defense slot, Cheney and Rumsfeld succeeded in stacking most other major Defense Department positions with hegemonists. In particular, Douglas Feith, a prolific polemicist who had been Richard Perle's special counsel at the Pentagon during the Reagan administration, was named to the number-three job in the Defense Department. The White House also insisted that Powell take on John Bolton, a fervent supporter of missile defense and a vocal skeptic of international treaties, as the undersecretary for arms control and international security, the top arms control post at State. (Bolton had gained a brief flicker of fame during the Florida vote recount as the man with the walrus mustache peering over the shoulders of Broward County officials as they tried to determine whether hanging chads counted as legal votes.) Powell compounded his isolation by deciding, in an understandable bid to rebuild morale at the perennially dispirited State Department, to rely heavily on career foreign service officers to fill out most of the other mid- and senior-level positions at Foggy Bottom. As a result, he had only two close allies in government—Armitage, his deputy, and Richard Haass, the former director of the foreign policy studies program at the Brookings Institution, whom he tapped to be director of the office of policy planning, State's in-house think tank.

While Powell was on the defensive at the start of the Bush administration, Cheney aggressively staked out a major role in national security policy. He created his own mini-NSC staff, hiring a dozen national security specialists of unusually high caliber. Al Gore's staff was half the size and made up almost entirely of mid-career military officers. This larger staff of professionals enabled OVP, as the Office of the Vice President is known inside the bureaucracy, to operate essentially as an independent agency. Through his staff Cheney had input at virtually every level of the interagency decisionmaking process and then again in private as the president's counselor. Cheney tapped I. Lewis "Scooter" Libby to run the OVP staff and serve as his personal national security adviser. Libby had been a student of Wolfowitz's at Yale and one of the authors of the controversial 1992 Defense Planning Guidance that the first Bush administration had been forced to disavow.

Cheney also attempted to place Rice under his direction. He pushed to be named chair of the so-called principals committee, where the cabinet members on the national security team gather in the president's absence to thrash out issues and decide on policy recommendations. The task of chairing the principals committee traditionally belonged to the national security adviser; indeed, it was a critical source of the position's power. The dispute over who would run the principals committee delayed by nearly a month completion of the basic document outlining the National Security Council's structure and operating procedures. Nearly every administration since Nixon's had produced this document on its first day in office. Bush eventually denied Cheney's request and affirmed the traditional responsibilities of Rice's job. Cheney, however, did not lose out completely. He would be a regular participant in meetings of the principals—a substantial break with the practice of previous administrations.

Bush's decision to have Rice chair the principals committee enhanced her standing within the administration and negated any fallout she might have experienced from not being awarded cabinet rank. Many inside and outside the White House openly doubted that the first female national security adviser, armed with only three years of Washington experience, could match bureaucratic wits with wily veterans such as Cheney, Powell, and Rumsfeld—all of whom had sat around the principals' table in previous administrations. Her victory on what was to most outsiders an obscure procedural issue attested to her own infighting skills. It also underscored what had always been true of the national security adviser's post: what mattered was not the length of the resume but closeness to the president. Rice clearly had Bush's ear.

Nonetheless, the dispute over assigning roles in the national security decisionmaking process was a sign of the dangers inherent in staffing a national security team with eight-hundred-pound bureaucratic gorillas. Cheney, Powell, and Rumsfeld were men used to getting their way, even if it meant trampling over colleagues. Rumsfeld had a particular reputation for having sharp elbows in bureaucratic competition. Henry Kissinger, in one of his many memoirs, approvingly quoted a veteran journalist who wrote that Rumsfeld's machinations during the Ford administration earned him a "welter of suspicion and hatred—the word hatred is justified"—of his colleagues.[17]

Bush understood and even hoped that his advisers would disagree, perhaps even strongly at times. He wanted to use their disagreements to sharpen his policy choices. However, private disagreements in Washington have a way of escalating into public food fights and dividing the foreign policy bureaucracy into warring camps. The bitter struggle between National Security Adviser Zbigniew Brzezinski and Secretary of State Cyrus Vance over the direction of Jimmy Carter's foreign policy played out in the nation's newspapers and helped reinforce the image of Carter as a man who couldn't control his own administration much less face down the Soviet threat. Secretary of Defense Caspar Weinberger and Secretary of State George Shultz bickered constantly over almost every aspect of national security during the Reagan years. The resulting bureaucratic infighting created havoc with Reagan's policies. Friends and foes often were unsure whether Reagan's decisions would stick or even what those decisions were.

So Bush faced two challenges. He had to make sure that the creative tension among his headstrong advisers was sufficient to give him the information he needed to make decisions, but not so intense that it grew into internal warfare. By the same token, he also had to make sure that all of his advisers understood that he was the commander in chief, however skimpy his foreign-policy resume. If he failed to meet either challenge, he risked seeing his presidency plunge into bitter wrangling and incoherence.

The First
Eight Months

WORLD AFFAIRS MIGHT not have been at the top of George
W. Bush's priority list during the presidential campaign,
but many of his supporters expected him to move quickly to revamp
U.S. national security policy. Hawks assumed he would turn the
defense budget tap wide open. Missile defense enthusiasts predicted a
rapid U.S. withdrawal from the ABM Treaty and a new Manhattan
Project to build a national missile defense. Beijing haters anticipated a
push to redirect the U.S. military to counter a rising China, a blunt declaration of the administration's intent to defend Taiwan, and massive
arms sales to Taipei. Sovereigntists on Capitol Hill looked forward to
the rapid withdrawal of U.S. troops from Bosnia and Kosovo. Latino
activists expected a major overhaul of U.S.-Mexico migration policy.
Free traders looked forward to a push to revive the talks on a free trade
agreement for the Americas and a new round of world trade talks.
Saddam-haters and armchair psychologists assumed that the administration would move aggressively on regime change in Iraq.

Bush mostly disappointed these expectations during his first eight
months in office. A case in point was defense spending. Throughout
the campaign, he had argued that American military capability had
eroded because the Clinton administration had failed to address growing problems of "poor pay, shortages of spare parts and equipment, and
rapidly declining readiness."[1] Dick Cheney used his speech accepting
the Republican vice presidential nomination to reassure the men and

women in the military that "help is on the way."[2] In early February, however, Bush told members of Congress that "there will be no new money for defense this year."[3] Instead, he decided to proceed with the Clinton administration's proposed 2002 defense budget request of $310 billion. He also declined to seek a supplemental appropriation to add more funds to the 2001 budget. The thrust of these decisions was that the Pentagon would have to close the gap between what it hoped to buy and what it got to spend by killing outdated weapons systems and rethinking how it did business. This philosophy of "starving the beast" to force internal reform was in keeping with Bush's campaign pledge to "skip a generation of technology" and create "a new architecture of American defense for decades to come."[4]

Bush took a similarly deliberate approach to the other major defense issue he emphasized during the campaign—national missile defense. Despite calls from many conservatives for immediate action, he did not use his first months in office to withdraw from the ABM Treaty or order rapid construction of a system capable of defending America from ballistic missiles. Bush finally gave a major address on missile defense in early May. The speech's main theme was that the ABM Treaty was destined for history's dustbin. "This treaty does not recognize the present, or point us to the future," Bush argued. "It enshrines the past. No treaty that prevents us from addressing today's threats, that prohibits us from pursuing promising technology to defend ourselves, our friends and our allies is in our interests or in the interests of world peace."

Nonetheless, Bush also made clear that he intended to prepare the diplomatic ground for a U.S. withdrawal from the ABM Treaty rather than present the world with a fait accompli. He pledged to "consult closely on the important subject with our friends and allies who are also threatened by missiles and weapons of mass destruction." To that end, he announced that he was sending Richard Armitage, Stephen Hadley, and Paul Wolfowitz to allied capitals to begin discussions on missile defense. Just as important, Bush spoke at length about his desire "to create a new framework for security and stability" with Russia. "This new cooperative relationship should look to the future, not to the past," the president argued. "It should be reassuring, rather than threatening. It should be premised on openness, mutual confidence and real opportunities for cooperation, including the area of missile defense. It should allow us to share information so that each nation can improve its early warning capability, and its capability to defend its people and territory. And perhaps one day, we can even cooperate in a joint defense."[5]

The cooperative tone in Bush's missile defense speech was in many ways surprising. In March he had ordered the expulsion of fifty Russian diplomats in the United States in the wake of FBI agent Robert Hanssen's arrest for espionage. It was the largest expulsion order in fifteen years. Meanwhile, both Donald Rumsfeld and Wolfowitz had publicly accused Russia of being "an active proliferator," an accusation that Russian officials heatedly denied.[6] Despite these flaps, Bush insisted, "I'm confident we can have a good relationship with the Russians."[7]

Bush got his chance to make his case for a new relationship directly with Russian President Vladimir Putin. In mid-June the two leaders met for the first time at a summit in Slovenia. Bush emerged from their meeting singing Putin's praises. "I was able to get a sense of his soul," Bush told reporters. He is a man "deeply committed to his country and the best interests of his country." To underscore just how successful the meeting had been, Bush announced that he had invited Putin to visit him in Crawford, Texas, a prized invitation that he had pointedly declined to extend to the leaders of several close U.S. allies. "I wouldn't have invited him to my ranch if I didn't trust him," Bush joked.[8] He later told people that he felt a close personal connection when the Russian leader showed him the crucifix his mother had given him when he was a boy. Whether Putin's story was genuine, and whether Bush truly believed it, can be debated. What was clear is that by mid-summer 2001, Bush's public approach to Russia was far more sympathetic than might have been expected based on his comments and those of his advisers during the campaign.

Bush's reluctance to undertake major new foreign policy initiatives during his first few months in office was evident on issues besides defense spending and missile defense. Secretary of State Powell announced in February that the United States would not remove its troops from Bosnia or Kosovo without the agreement of the NATO allies, saying: "The simple proposition is: We went in together, we will come out together."[9] Bush made a point of taking his first foreign trip to Mexico, and he declared (just days before September 11), "The United States has no more important relationship in the world than our relationship with Mexico."[10] Nonetheless, he offered no concrete plans for resolving the outstanding issues in U.S.-Mexican relations. The administration's trade policy remained stuck in the interagency process. Finally, Bush did not move ahead aggressively on a policy of regime change in Iraq, either through direct U.S. action or by empowering Iraqi exile groups to do so on America's behalf. Instead, the administration moved to replace the existing Iraqi sanctions with so-called smart sanctions that expedited trade in civilian goods but tightened controls on military goods.

RATHER THAN UNVEILING new initiatives, Bush's foreign policy during his first eight months in office focused on extracting the United States from existing ones. In March Bush abandoned his campaign pledge to curtail emissions of carbon dioxide from power plants. Condoleezza Rice subsequently told European Union ambassadors at a private lunch that the Kyoto Protocol, an international agreement on global warming signed by eighty-four countries, was "dead."[11] The announcement effectively torpedoed international hopes that Kyoto might provide the basis for an effective global response to the problem of climate change. The United States was far and away the world's largest emitter of the heat-trapping gases responsible for global warming. Bush's refusal to participate did not prevent other countries from agreeing to put the Kyoto accord into effect—which they did to great fanfare in July 2002. However, without U.S. participation most countries would likely balk at paying the potentially substantial economic costs they would incur in fulfilling their pledges to reduce their emissions of heat-trapping gases.

Bush followed up on his opposition to Kyoto by directing his administration to oppose a string of international agreements, among them: a pact to control trafficking in small arms, a new protocol to the Biological Weapons Convention, the Comprehensive Test Ban Treaty, and the International Criminal Court (ICC). Washington's opposition to these agreements was determined and often heavy handed. This was especially true with the ICC, which Clinton had signed in the waning days of his administration. Bush not only made clear he would not submit the ICC treaty to the Senate for approval; he also sought to persuade other signatories to agree that they would never hand over any Americans to the tribunal. This diplomatic effort led the Bush administration and its European allies to trade bitter recriminations that each was using the prospect of a no vote in the ongoing process of NATO expansion to bully eastern European countries into taking its side in the dispute.

Bush's "Just-Say-No" foreign policy was not limited to international agreements. In the first months of his administration, he also reined in a variety of U.S. efforts to broker peace around the world. At the top of the list was the Israeli-Palestinian conflict, which administration officials saw as the black hole of U.S. diplomacy. In a sharp break with Clinton, who had become personally enmeshed in negotiations between Israelis and Palestinians, Bush put U.S. engagement in the Middle East peace process on hold. He declined to send an envoy to the last-ditch Israeli-Palestinian peace talks at Taba, Egypt, in late January 2001. The White House eventually eliminated the post of special Middle East envoy that Dennis Ross had held for eight years, and three months into the administration the NSC staff still did not have a senior director for Middle East affairs. The reason for this inaction, as Powell repeatedly said, was, "in the end, we cannot want peace more than the parties themselves."[12] By June escalating violence prompted the White House to rethink its decision to de-emphasize the peace process. Bush dispatched George Tenet to the Middle East as his special envoy to negotiate a cease-fire, thereby having the CIA director reprise a role he had played for Bill Clinton. However, Bush declined to give Tenet the sort of political support he needed to make any significant progress in bringing the Israelis and Palestinians together.

Bush took a similar approach to North Korea. Clinton had undertaken a serious effort in the closing days of his administration to strike a deal freezing North Korea's missile program. In October 2000 Secretary of State Madeleine Albright made a historic visit to Pyongyang, where the North Koreans offered to end the production, testing, and deployment of mid- and long-range missiles in return for a presidential visit and help in launching three satellites a year. When the outcome of the U.S. presidential race dragged into December, thereby making it impossible for Clinton to discuss his plans with his successor, he decided that "there is not enough time while I am president to prepare the way for an agreement with North Korea."[13] When South Korean president Kim Dae Jung traveled to Washington in March 2001, Bush used the visit to publicly quash the idea that he would seek to close the deal that Clinton had begun negotiating and to close the door, at least for the time being, to any further discussions with Pyongyang. Bush also signaled that he did not support Kim's "sunshine policy" toward North Korea.

Bush took a similar hands-off approach to mediating the conflict in Northern Ireland. Whereas Clinton gladly played the role of peace broker, Bush announced he was "going to wait to be asked by the Prime Minister" of Britain. Tony Blair politely acknowledged the White House's withdrawal by saying, "It's difficult to perceive the exact circumstances in which I might pick up the phone and ask the President to help."[14] Bush also rejected suggestions that Washington do more to help end Colombia's civil war. He declined a request by Colombian president Andres Pastrana to have a U.S. envoy participate as an observer on peace talks between the government and its main guerrilla opponent. Twenty-five other countries accepted the request.

The lesson many observers drew from these decisions was, as one newspaper columnist put it, "In the Bush administration, engagement is a dirty word."[15] Foreign capitals may have put stock in such efforts, but Bush himself did not. And the president had no intention of letting anyone else set his agenda, if he could help it. He soon discovered, though, that sometimes he could not.

BUSH WAS ENJOYING his new ritual of spending the weekend relaxing at Camp David, the presidential retreat in Maryland, when the phone rang late on Saturday evening March 31. The call brought word of the first crisis of his presidency. A Chinese fighter jet had collided with a U.S. EP-3E reconnaissance aircraft seventy miles off China's southeast coast. The collision destroyed the Chinese plane and killed its pilot. The badly damaged American plane barely managed to make an emergency landing on Hainan Island. The American crew, along with the supersensitive equipment used to monitor Chinese military communications, was now in the hands of the People's Liberation Army.

Beijing immediately blamed the collision on the American pilot and detained the crew. Pentagon officials in turn blamed a hot-dogging Chinese pilot who had previously flown so close to an EP-3E that the American pilots could read the sign he held up advertising his e-mail address. These officials also noted that China had been formally warned that aggressive attempts by its pilots to intercept U.S. aircraft flying in internationally recognized airspace made a collision all too likely. "We went to the Chinese and said, 'Your aircraft are not intercepting in a professional manner. There is a safety issue here,'" recalled Admiral Dennis Blair, the head of the U.S. Pacific Command. "It's not normal practice to play bumper cars in the air."[16]

Bush at first took reports of the collision in stride. He and his advisers expected that the Chinese would treat the incident as an accident and send the crew on its way. When that did not happen, he took a hard line with Beijing. This was the approach he had used from the moment he entered the Oval Office. He had pointedly excluded Chinese president Jiang Zemin from the list of heads of state to whom he placed a courtesy call in the first days after his inauguration. Moreover, all of Bush's senior aides counseled taking a tough line with Beijing. This was in keeping with their general approach to diplomacy, and it also reflected the fact that none of them had much experience dealing with China.

Thus, three days after the unexpected phone call at Camp David, Bush strode into the Rose Garden to deliver a stern message: "We have allowed the Chinese government time to do the right thing," he said. "But now it is time for our servicemen and women to return home." He promised that there would be consequences if China ignored his advice. "This accident has the potential of undermining our hopes for a fruitful and productive relationship between our two countries."[17] Within the administration, discussions began about possible ways to punish China for detaining the American crew. The options ranged from opposing Beijing's bid to host the 2008 Olympics and canceling Bush's scheduled fall visit to China to imposing sanctions on Chinese exports to the United States.

Jiang's response later that day was not what Bush had hoped for. Rather than backing down, the seventy-five-year-old veteran of Communist party politics dug in his heels and insisted that the United States "bear full responsibility" for the collision.[18] These tough words sent Bush backpedaling. The next day he told his advisers he wanted to find "a way out."[19] He turned to Powell to find a negotiated solution. The White House also gave a green light to several Republican luminaries, including Brent Scowcroft and Henry Kissinger, to use their contacts in China to help free the American crew. The solution ultimately came in the form of a carefully crafted letter negotiated with the Chinese. The letter, which was written by the U.S. ambassador to China and addressed to the Chinese foreign minister, stated that the United States was "very sorry" for the loss of the Chinese pilot and "very sorry" that the American plane had entered Chinese airspace without receiving clearance to land at Hainan Island.[20] The "letter of the two sorry's" did not amount to the full-blown apology that Beijing had wanted. Nor did it come with an American pledge to stop reconnaissance flights off China's coast, as Beijing had demanded. Nonetheless, it was sufficient to free the detained American fliers.

The return of the EP-3E crew was a feather in Powell's cap and perhaps the high point of his first eight months as secretary of state. The crisis in many ways played to his strength. A military solution was unthinkable, thereby silencing hard-liners in the Pentagon and elsewhere who in other circumstances would have denigrated diplomacy. With the possibility of using force off the table, the challenge was to find a diplomatic solution that gave China a way to save face without requiring Washington to give up anything significant. At the same time, the EP-3E crisis attested to Bush's own flexibility and decisiveness. He quickly concluded that he had blundered in taking a tough public line with Beijing. Instead of compounding the problem, he moved to cut his losses.

The pragmatism that Bush showed in resolving the EP-3E crisis continued even after China released the American crew. In late April he broke with the practice of past administrations and authorized the sale of eight diesel submarines to Taiwan. In what administration officials acknowledged was a clear nod to Beijing's concerns, however, he decided against selling Taipei destroyers equipped with the advanced Aegis radar defense system. Two days after the arms sales were announced, Bush told ABC's *Good Morning, America* that the United States would do "whatever it took to help Taiwan defend herself."[21] Within hours the president backtracked, saying he had not changed long-standing U.S. policy toward Beijing. His advisers confirmed that statement publicly and privately. A little more than a month later, Bush extended normal trade relations status for China for another year, stating, "The United States is committed to helping China become part of the new international trading system."[22] If Bush felt any animus toward Jiang for holding American servicemen and women for eleven days, he did not let it overtly influence his policy toward China.

Bush's pragmatic approach in dealing with China may have staved off a confrontation with the Middle Kingdom. However, it angered many conservative commentators. The *Weekly Standard* editorialized that the apology to China amounted to a "national humiliation" that revealed Bush's "weakness" and "fear: fear of the political, strategic, and economic consequences of meeting a Chinese challenge."[23] Gary Bauer, one of the men Bush defeated in winning the Republican presidential nomination, argued that if Al Gore had said he was sorry to the Chinese, "there would be nothing less than dozens of Republicans at the microphone yelling, 'Sellout!'"[24]

The criticisms of Bush's handling of the EP-3E crisis tied in to a broader dissatisfaction among many conservative activists during his first eight months in office that Bush had failed to deliver the foreign policy he had promised during the campaign. The list of disappointments was long. In refusing to open the defense budget tap, the administration "had turned its back" on the pressing problems facing the U.S. military.[25] In pronouncing Putin a "fine Russian," he "sounded naive" and showed that he didn't understand that foreign policy "can't be run on a heartfelt embrace and a prayer."[26] In pursuing smart sanctions on Iraq, Bush looked "content to continue walking down dangerous paths in foreign and defense policy laid out over the past eight years by Bill Clinton."[27]

Nonetheless, in not rushing to make major departures in American foreign policy during his first months in office, Bush was delivering precisely the presidency he had promised. He had focused on a few key priorities and worked them hard. Those priorities just happened to involve domestic policy—notably tax cuts—not foreign policy.

THE STEPS THAT Bush did take in foreign policy, however, suggested a keen sensitivity to domestic politics, and especially the demands of core Republican constituencies, if not Republican intellectuals. On his third day in office, Bush reinstated the "Mexico City Policy," the executive order that Ronald Reagan had imposed and Bill Clinton repealed mandating that nongovernmental organizations receiving federal funds agree to neither perform nor promote abortion as a method of family planning in other nations. The practical importance of the decision was questionable, but the symbolic importance was not—pro-life groups had demanded reinstatement of the policy. With the stroke of a pen Bush shored up his support with the Republican base, many of whose members had previously doubted his conservative credentials. The decision to proceed deliberately on missile defense was calculated at least in part to deny his opponents a political issue. Democrats believed they had scored significant political points in the 1980s attacking Ronald Reagan's "Star Wars" missile defense. They hoped to repeat those successes by accusing Bush of endangering what they saw as the "cornerstone" of international stability. In contrast, by publicly reaching out to Russia, the White House hoped to minimize the chances that its policy on missile defense could be labeled reckless.

Domestic politics figured prominently in other Bush decisions. He based the decision to withdraw the United States from the Kyoto Protocol solely on domestic considerations, arguing that the "idea of placing caps on CO_2 does not make economic sense for America."[28] Powell later admitted that the decision had been handled badly. When the international "blowback came I think it was a sobering experience that everything the American president does has international repercussions."[29] The decision to delay action on a major trade initiative reflected a desire not to complicate the efforts to complete action on other, higher presidential priorities. Bush also showed he was not above reversing course to accommodate domestic political realities. His decision to stick with the Clinton administration's defense budget proposals angered defense hawks on Capitol Hill, who moved quickly to open the spending tap. Rather than risk being trumped by Congress, the White House changed its tune. By August 2001 Bush had submitted a 2001 defense appropriation supplemental request and raised the 2002 defense budget request $33 billion, to $343.3 billion.

The flip side to Bush's sensitivity to American domestic politics was his insensitivity to reactions in foreign capitals. During President Kim's visit to Washington in March, Bush angered the South Koreans when he used a joint public appearance to express his "skepticism" that the North Koreans could be trusted to keep their word.[30] The abrupt announcement of the decision to abandon Kyoto set the tone for a world already primed, as one analyst put it, to believe Bush would pursue a foreign policy marked by "more arrogance and more unilateralism."[31] As complaints abroad about American unilateralism grew in the spring of 2001, the White House did not back down. On the eve of his first trip to Europe in June 2001, Bush reiterated his opposition to Kyoto. While admitting that the surface temperature of the earth was warming and that human activity seemed to be a contributing factor, he offered only to fund programs to study the problem, not action to reduce the emission of heat-trapping gases, as his critics demanded.[32] As White House speechwriter David Frum later wrote, "Bush was extraordinarily responsive to international criticism—but his response was to tuck back his ears and repeat his offense."[33]

The Bush administration's willingness to step on diplomatic toes surprised many observers, who pointed to Bush's constant refrain during the campaign that he intended to strengthen America's alliances and that his foreign policy would show "purpose without arrogance."[34] Critics suggested that he instead pursued a foreign policy of arrogance without purpose. Nonetheless, Bush's unsentimental diplomacy flowed directly from his core beliefs. If all states pursue their self-interest, if power matters above all else, and if American virtue is unquestioned, then U.S. foreign policy should not be about searching for common policies. Rather it should be about pushing the world in the direction Washington wanted it to go, even if the initial reaction was resistance. As Powell told European journalists, Bush "makes sure people know what he believes in. And then he tries to persuade others that is the correct position. When it does not work, then we will take the position we believe is correct and I hope the Europeans are left with a better understanding of the way in which we want to do business."[35] Nor was it lost on the Bush team that the allies' harsh words were unmatched by equivalent deeds. With the allies unwilling or unable to make the United States pay a price for its actions, a change in policy hardly seemed necessary. The attitude Bush took to challenges to his domestic initiatives applied here as well: "We aren't going to negotiate with ourselves."[36]

Two other factors encouraged the administration's conclusion that it could ignore complaints from foreign capitals. One was the firm belief that Bush was paying the price for Clinton's eagerness to do what pleased the allies, especially the Europeans, rather than what was right. Most of Bush's advisers believed that Clinton had indulged the Europeans in their misguided view that international agreements were as much ends in themselves as they were means. Changing that mind-set required emphatic demonstrations that the old way of doing business was dead. Such "tough love" would produce vocal complaints, at least in the short run. Nonetheless, most officials in the Bush administration believed that if they stuck to their guns, the complaints would die away, and the allies would adjust to the new style of American leadership.

The other factor reinforcing the administration's willingness to ruffle diplomatic feathers was Bush's firm belief that chief executives do not change simply because their actions earn bad reviews. Shortly after returning from his first state visit to Europe, he told Peggy Noonan, once Ronald Reagan's speechwriter:

> I think Ronald Reagan would have been proud of how I conducted myself. I went to Europe a humble leader of a great country, and stood my ground. I wasn't going to yield. I listened, but I made my point.
>
> And I went to dinner . . . with 15 leaders of the EU, and patiently sat there as all 15 in one form or another told me how wrong I was [about the Kyoto Protocol]. And at the end I said, "I appreciate your point of view, but this is the American position because it's right for America."[37]

Bush's description sounded more fitting to a cold war summit with Soviet leaders than a peacetime meeting with America's closest allies. Nevertheless, he was supremely confident in the goals he had set for U.S. policy, and he was willing to exercise patience in his effort to achieve them.

Bush's vision of the president-as-CEO showed itself in another way—he made clear to everyone in his administration that he was in charge. Unlike Reagan, who often could not decide between his feuding friends even when it would have been in his interest to do so, or Clinton, who always saw every side to an argument, Bush quickly demonstrated his decisiveness. Once decisions were made, he delegated authority to his subordinates to carry them out. Contrary to suggestions that he would be a pawn of his more seasoned cabinet secretaries, he dominated them. At one point or another during his first eight months in office, he overturned their decisions or spurned their recommendations. Rumsfeld was the first victim. His public commitment in February to seek a supplemental defense appropriations bill was quickly countermanded by the White House. In March Powell had to retract his statement that the Bush administration would "pick up where the Clinton administration left off" in dealing with North Korea—"I got a little far forward on my skis," he later told reporters.[38] When Powell told Europeans in July that the administration would have a plan for combating climate change by fall, Rice followed by saying that there was no deadline and no plan. Environmental Protection Agency Director Christine Whitman and Treasury Secretary Paul O'Neill saw Bush reject their recommendation for action to combat global warming. In short, advisers advised; they did not decide. And no one emerged as Bush's regent.

IN PUTTING HIS mark on his administration, however, Bush failed to push his advisers to tackle the issue that would come to dominate his presidency—terrorism in general and al Qaeda in particular. He seldom mentioned terrorism publicly during his first months in office. In early May, he announced a new Office of National Preparedness for terrorism at the Federal Emergency Management Agency, but gave it no new resources. Except on the handful of occasions in which he justified abandoning the ABM Treaty because of the "terrorist threats that face us," he did not mention the subject of terrorism again publicly before September 11.[39] By all accounts, things were not much different in private. None of this is surprising. Bush and his advisers looked at the world in terms of states—whether great powers or rogue nations—not stateless actors.

The outgoing Clinton administration—whose own handling of the al Qaeda threat was not above reproach—tried to challenge that assumption. Before Bush took office, Rice met with the man she was replacing as national security adviser, Samuel Berger. He told her, "You're going to spend more time during your four years on terrorism generally and al Qaeda specifically than any other issue."[40] Other Clinton administration officials repeated the same message just as bluntly. About a week before the inauguration, Tenet met with Bush, Cheney, and Rice. He told them that al Qaeda was one of the three gravest threats facing the United States and that this "tremendous threat" was "immediate."[41] (The other two grave threats were the proliferation of weapons of mass destruction and China's rising power.) Brian Sheridan, the outgoing assistant secretary of defense for special operations and low-intensity conflict, said he told Rice that terrorism is "serious stuff, these guys are not going away. I just remember her listening and not asking much."[42] Lieutenant General Donald Kerrick, the outgoing deputy national security adviser, sent the NSC front office a memo on "things you need to pay attention to." About al Qaeda it said: "We are going to be struck again."[43] During Bush's first week in office, Richard Clarke, the top NSC staffer on terrorism during the Clinton years who held his post into the new administration, handed Rice an action plan that said a high-level meeting on al Qaeda was "urgently needed." A subsequent memo argued: "We would make a major error if we underestimated the challenge al-Qaeda poses."[44]

In fairness to the Bush administration, none of these warnings from the outgoing Clinton team suggested an attack of the magnitude of September 11. Nevertheless, the Clinton warnings did not persuade the Bush team to move terrorism up on its list of priorities or to act quickly on its own prescription for stopping al Qaeda. Rice did not schedule the meeting of the principals committee that Clarke had requested.

Instead she reorganized the NSC's handling of terrorism and effectively demoted Clarke. The new structure did nothing to elevate the prominence of the terrorism issue. Kerrick, who stayed through the first four months of the Bush administration, said, "candidly speaking, I didn't detect" a strong focus on terrorism. "That's not being derogatory. It's just a fact. I didn't detect any activity but what Dick Clarke and the CSG [the Counterterrorism Strategy Group he chaired] were doing."[45] General Hugh Shelton, whose term as chairman of the Joint Chiefs of Staff began under Clinton and ended under Bush, concurred. In his view, the Bush administration moved terrorism "farther to the back burner."[46]

Bush's advisers later argued that throughout the summer of 2001, and especially around July 4, they worked to prevent a possible al Qaeda attack. The intelligence community had picked up increasing "chatter" in late spring indicating greater terrorist activity. Officials worried that Bush himself might be a target. They changed the venue for his meeting with Pope John Paul II in July to limit his potential vulnerability. These concerns did not, however, spur the administration to take more aggressive action. Bush's senior foreign policy advisers did not meet formally to discuss the intelligence intercepts. Nor did they revive the Clinton administration's practice of keeping submarines armed with cruise missiles on alert near Afghanistan to strike if the intelligence community located Osama bin Laden. Treasury Secretary O'Neill actually suspended U.S. participation in multilateral efforts to track terrorist money flows. Clarke's proposal to go after al Qaeda wound its way slowly through the bureaucracy. Bush's senior advisers met for the first time to discuss the strategy—which was dedicated to "rolling back" al Qaeda—on September 4.

After September 11, administration officials insisted that President Bush had complained during the spring and summer of 2001 that they were not moving fast enough to confront al Qaeda. "I'm tired of swatting flies," he reportedly said. "I'm tired of playing defense. I want to play offense. I want to take the fight to the terrorists."[47] Bush's own assessment of how he handled the al Qaeda threat was far less flattering. "There was a significant difference in my attitude after September 11," he said. "I was not on point, but I knew he was a menace, and I knew he was a problem. I knew he was responsible, for the [previous] bombings that killed Americans. I was prepared to look at a plan that would be a thoughtful plan that would bring him to justice, and would have given an order to do that. I have no hesitancy about going after him. But I didn't feel that sense of urgency, and my blood was not nearly as boiling."[48]

Bush also refused to blame his advisers. When leading Republicans accused Tenet of negligence in failing to prevent what they called the worst intelligence disaster since Pearl Harbor, Bush came to his defense. "We cannot be second-guessing our team," Bush told members of Congress who had joined him aboard Air Force One in late September 2001, "and I'm not going to. The nation's at war. We need to encourage Congress to frankly leave the man alone. Tenet's doing a good job. And if he's not, blame me, not him."[49]

Bush had done what he promised during the campaign. He had stuck to his own agenda. Counterterrorism just was not high on his list. He would soon discover the truth of Secretary-designate Powell's warning and the lesson inherent in the EP-3E crisis: Events abroad do not always observe the priorities and plans of even the most disciplined of presidents.

SIX

September 11

B Y Labor Day 2001, the political winds were beginning to blow against George W. Bush. The slumping economy, the Enron scandal, growing anger in foreign capitals over the administration's unilateralism, and criticism of his month-long "working" vacation in Crawford had obscured his impressive success in engineering passage of a $1.35 trillion tax cut. Early September polls showed that his public approval rating had fallen to 51 percent. Only Gerald Ford, who alienated many voters when he pardoned Richard Nixon, had experienced lower ratings during his first eight months in office. David Frum, a Bush speechwriter at the time, probably exaggerated only slightly when he later wrote, that "on September 10, 2001, George Bush was not on his way to a very successful presidency."[1]

September 11 changed all that. Bush quickly became the most popular American president on record and the dominant political figure of the day. But in changing the course of his presidency, did the terrorist attacks change the way he viewed the world? Many of his critics, and even many of his friends, hoped at the time that it would. They thought for certain that the horror of watching the Trade Center towers collapse would turn him from an arch-unilateralist into a card-carrying multilateralist. In this line of thinking, September 11 punctured America's sense of invulnerability, introduced it to the threats that most other countries faced on a daily basis, and showed the perils of trying to go it alone in a dangerous world. Only by working closely with others to track down stateless terrorists and foil other transnational threats could the American people be made secure. It was a view shared by Bush's father, who three days after the attack predicted: "Just as Pearl Harbor awakened this country from the notion that we could somehow avoid the call to duty and defend freedom in Europe and Asia in World War II, so, too, should this most recent surprise attack erase the concept in some quarters that America can somehow go it alone in the fight against terrorism or in anything else for that matter."[2]

It soon became clear, however, that George W. Bush did not draw the lessons from September 11 that others thought he should. He instead pursued with a vengeance many of the policies they had warned against. Suddenly a new story of personal transformation took hold. As one observer put it, Bush's response to September 11 "represents a reversal of, or at least a dramatic departure from, the position he himself took during the 2000 election campaign."[3] Gone was talk of Bush as the soft isolationist who famously promised to lead a "humble nation."[4] Now he was reborn as a crusading internationalist who had embraced Woodrow Wilson's vision of a democratic world and who was willing to use America's military might to make it happen.

Such stories of human transformation have tremendous appeal. They attest to an abiding belief that a day as horrifying as September 11 changes a country and its leaders. To suggest anything else is to dishonor the memory of the three thousand people who died for no sin greater than having gone to work on a late summer day. Tragic events should produce epiphanies.

In truth, however, September 11 did more to reaffirm Bush's view of the world than to transform it. By the president's own account, terrorist attacks had been an abstract threat, not something boiling in his blood. When the unimaginable happened, he had the choice of revising his view of the way the world worked to fit the facts or interpreting the facts to fit his worldview. Like most people, Bush chose the latter. True, his previous insistence that China and Russia were the two most important foreign-policy challenges instantly looked dated, especially when Vladimir Putin became the first head of state to call the White House and pledge support in finding those responsible. Still, in many ways September 11 confirmed much of what Bush already believed: The world was a dangerous place. Terrorists bent on doing harm were not stopped by a smile and an open hand, but by grim determination and a closed fist. International agreements and institutions could not protect the American people; only the might of the American military could. As much as other countries might decry America's arrogance and unilateralism, they would rally around the United States during crises because it is a beacon of hope for all the world's people. And while terrorists might be described as "stateless," they ultimately depended on regimes like the Taliban to operate.

September 11 stirred Bush to act on those views. Foreign policy, or more precisely, the war on terrorism, became the defining mission of his presidency. Evil suddenly had a face and an identity, even a locus. Now that it was more than an abstraction, Bush and his advisers had to figure out how to deal with it. They would spend much of the next two years developing and refining their logic, determining exactly what it meant to go after "terrorists with global reach." In pursuing this agenda, Bush would encounter little resistance from Capitol Hill—or from the Democratic Party. The country had rallied around his presidency after the attacks. As long as his decisions produced success abroad, or at least did not obviously fail, Congress was not about to stand in his way.

THE DIFFERENCES THAT had divided the United States from its allies and friends before September 11 gave way to widespread solidarity and support. "*Nous sommes tous Américains*," declared the left-leaning French daily *Le Monde*. German Chancellor Gerhard Schröder offered "unlimited solidarity" to the United States. Buckingham Palace played "The Star-Spangled Banner." South Korean schoolchildren prayed outside the U.S. embassy in Seoul. Ecuadoran firefighters honored the memory of their fallen comrades in New York City. Iranians by the thousands held candlelight vigils. In the view of Bush and his advisers, this outpouring of sympathy reflected the fact that as much as other countries might dislike specific U.S. policies, they understood that the United States is a uniquely just and beneficent great power.

In the hours after the attacks, President Bush took refuge in the world's embrace. Washington turned to the United Nations, which on September 12 passed a resolution condemning "those responsible for aiding, supporting or harbouring the perpetrators, organizers and sponsors of these acts," and authorizing "all necessary steps" to respond to the attacks.[5] The administration also received support from its oldest and strongest partners in Europe. The Atlantic Alliance for the first time in its history invoked its solemn obligation to come to the defense of a fellow member under attack. It seemed inevitable that rather than lashing out alone, Bush would assemble a broad international coalition to fight the war on terrorism.

Despite the UN Resolution and NATO's invocation of Article 5, though, Washington largely shunned offers of help from its allies, with the notable exceptions of Britain and Australia, in waging the Afghanistan war. When a European leader suggested to Bush that he consult broadly, listen to what others had to say, and adapt U.S. policy to take into account their views and interests, Bush replied: "That's very interesting. Because my belief is the best way that we hold this coalition together is to be clear on our objectives and to be clear that we are determined to achieve them. You hold a coalition together by strong leadership and that's what we intend to provide."[6] In December 2001 he announced that the United States was withdrawing from the ABM Treaty. The White House blocked international efforts to strengthen the Biological Weapons Convention, even though the anthrax attacks in the fall of 2001 vividly demonstrated the dangers of biological terrorism. Throughout 2002 the administration continued and even intensified its campaign to block the International Criminal Court from having jurisdiction over American citizens.

More important, Bush unveiled a new doctrine of preemption, one that insisted on America's sovereign right to attack potential foes before they could harm the United States. So the steps Bush took in the early fall of 2001 to work through existing international institutions represented tactical responses to the September 11 attacks instead of a fundamental conversion to the multilateralist creed.

BUSH AND HIS advisers had raised the prospect of terrorist attacks before September 11, but they had never really felt the threat in their bones. They believed terrorism was "a sort of evil that you could manage but you couldn't eliminate," as Paul Wolfowitz would later say.[7]

Like most people, Bush and his advisers tended to think inside the confines of past experience. Terrorists seldom attacked the United States. When they did target American citizens or installations, they almost always did so overseas, and the human toll, while horrifying, was relatively small. The prospect that a small group of men could kill thousands on U.S. soil seemed to belong more to the scripts of Hollywood action films than to the real world of Washington. Bush and his team, like those who had preceded them in power, were guilty of a classic failure of analysis, which, as the economist Thomas Schelling once put it, is "to confuse the unfamiliar with the improbable. The contingency we have not considered seriously looks strange; what looks strange is therefore improbable; what is improbable need not be taken seriously."[8]

However, if Bush and his advisers had not anticipated the identity of the murderers, they could comfort themselves with the knowledge that they had known that there were murderers about. They had argued for years that the euphoria about the collapse of the Soviet bloc and the "end of history" had obscured the fact that America still had many enemies around the world. In retrospect, they saw the decade-long interregnum between the end of the cold war and the terrorist attacks as representing little more than what columnist George Will called a "holiday from history."[9] As Bush told the nation in an address to a joint session of Congress nine days after the attacks, September 11 had awakened America to a danger that was not new and different, but old and familiar. "We have seen their kind before. They are the heirs of all the murderous ideologies of the 20th century. By sacrificing human life to serve their radical visions—by abandoning every value except the will to power—they follow in the path of fascism, and Nazism, and totalitarianism. And they will follow that path all the way, to where it ends: in history's unmarked grave of discarded lies."[10]

Bush continued, saying that al Qaeda found America repugnant in almost all respects. "They hate what we see right here in this chamber—a democratically elected government. Their leaders are self-appointed. They hate our freedoms—our freedom of religion, our freedom of speech, our freedom to vote and assemble and disagree with each other." He went on. "These terrorists kill not merely to end lives, but to disrupt and end a way of life. With every atrocity, they hope that

America grows fearful, retreating from the world and forsaking our friends. They stand against us, because we stand in their way."[11]

Bush and his advisers believed that Osama bin Laden and his followers thought they could push the United States out of their way for a simple reason—America's lack of resolve. The dead at the World Trade Center, at the Pentagon, and in a field in rural Pennsylvania paid the price for Washington's failure to respond forcefully to previous attacks. Dick Cheney and others recalled the repeated terrorist attacks on American citizens during the 1980s and 1990s: The bombing of the U.S. embassy in Beirut in April 1983 that killed sixty-three Americans. The truck bombing six months later that killed 241 Marines stationed at Beirut's airport. The 1985 murder of the wheelchair-bound Leon Klinghoffer, who was shot and thrown off the deck of the Italian cruise ship *Achille Lauro* into the Mediterranean Sea. The 1986 bombing at a West Berlin discotheque that killed two American servicemen and wounded dozens of others. The 1988 bombing of PanAm Flight 103 over Lockerbie, Scotland. The first bombing of the World Trade Center in 1993, which had come perilously close to toppling one of the towers. The bombing of the U.S. military barracks at Khobar Towers in Saudi Arabia in 1996. The attacks on the U.S. embassies in Kenya and Tanzania in 1998. The bombing of the USS *Cole* in 2000. In all, over the course of three decades, Arab and Islamic terrorists had killed nearly 1,000 Americans. "That's four times as many as died in 1898 aboard the USS *Maine*—the ship whose destruction triggered the Spanish-American War," wrote Bush speechwriter David Frum. It's also "more than five times as many as died at the Alamo."[12]

In the view of the Bush team, Washington's response in virtually every case with the exception of the Berlin disco bombing, which prompted airstrikes against Libya, had been timid. Terrorist attacks were treated as crimes rather than acts of war. Governments and groups that sponsored or aided terrorism seldom suffered anything more than a tongue-lashing by an American ambassador or an embargo on U.S. goods that they could just as easily get from Europe or Asia. "Weakness, vacillation, and unwillingness of the United States to stand with our friends, that is provocative," argued Cheney. "It's encouraged people like Osama bin Laden . . . to launch repeated strikes against the

United States, and our people overseas and here at home, with the view that he could, in fact, do so with impunity."[13] Donald Rumsfeld had worried about the consequences of American passivity even before September 11. "I never believed that weakness was your first choice," the Pentagon chief argued in July 2001. "I have always felt that weakness is provocative, that it kind of invites people to do things that they otherwise wouldn't think about doing."[14] He had pushed this point on Bush early in the administration. "A lot of people in the world had come to conclude that the United States was gun-shy, that we were risk averse," Rumsfeld told reporters. "The President and I concluded that whenever it occurred down the road that the United States was under some sort of threat or attack, the United States would be leaning forward, not back."[15] Terrorists and their supporters, the Bush team believed, had to pay a stiff price for their actions.

At the same time, even America's friends sometimes refused to cooperate with Washington because they feared terrorist retaliation more than U.S. anger. Italy allowed the terrorists who killed Leon Klinghoffer to go free after they surrendered control of the *Achille Lauro*. When U.S. warplanes subsequently forced a plane carrying the terrorists to land at a NATO base in Italy, the Italian government prevented U.S. officials from arresting the men and allowed the two leaders of the group to go free. Saudi Arabia refused to cooperate in tracking down leads about the men responsible for the Khobar Towers bombing. To defeat terrorists, the Bush administration had to restore the credibility of American resolve with both its friends and its enemies. "How do we know the United States won't abandon us?" Pakistani General Pervez Musharraf asked Bush when the two met in New York two months after the September 11 attacks. "You tell your people," said Bush, "that the President looked you in the eye and told you that he would stick with you."[16]

The Bush administration also recognized that defeating al Qaeda would require improving homeland security within the United States and intensifying counterterrorist operations, especially cooperation with other countries on intelligence and law enforcement. Right after September 11, the White House and Congress agreed to appropriate an additional $9.8 billion for homeland security. In February 2002

Bush asked Congress to earmark $37.7 billion for homeland security in 2003, or more than twice the amount spent when he assumed office. Counterterrorism became priority number one at the CIA and the FBI.

As impressive as the spending increases on homeland security were, they fell far short of what would be needed to protect the most vulnerable targets in the United States. The administration argued that it was impossible to put up an ironclad defense. "There is not enough money in the galaxy to protect every square inch of America and every American against every conceivable threat that every hateful fanatic in the world might conjure up," said Mitchell Daniels, the director of the White House Office of Management and Budget.[17] Even as Bush submitted his plan for creating a new Department of Homeland Security, he declined to order a major review, let alone a reshuffling, of the CIA and the FBI.

Bush instead insisted on taking the battle to the terrorists. "We need to fight it overseas," he told his war council, "by bringing the war to the bad guys."[18] This reflected a simple belief: The best defense is a good offense. Just as significant, even as Bush identified al Qaeda as the specific threat, he asserted that defeating the group required targeting the states that safeguarded it and other terrorists with a global reach. "We will make no distinction between the terrorists who committed these acts and those who harbor them," he declared the night of the attacks.[19] He laid down this marker, which is now remembered as the Bush doctrine, without first consulting Cheney, or Rumsfeld, or Colin Powell.[20] Days later, Wolfowitz pledged that the United States would focus on "removing the sanctuaries, removing the support systems, ending states who sponsor terrorism."[21] The link between terrorist organizations and state sponsors became the "principal strategic thought underlying our strategy in the war on terrorism," according to Douglas Feith, the third-ranking official in the Pentagon. "Terrorist organizations cannot be effective in sustaining themselves over long periods of time to do large-scale operations if they don't have support from states."[22] This dismissal of the possibility that terrorists could operate without government support reflected a view that Bush and his advisers had held long before September 11. They believed that states remained the primary forces in world politics, notwithstanding all the talk about how globalization empowered the angry few and promoted the rise of groups capable of evading and challenging government power.

Given its overwhelming power as well as the fact that it had been attacked, the United States would lead the fight against terrorists and their state sponsors. Bush left open the possibility of working with others to track down al Qaeda. "Contrary to my image as a Texan with two guns on my side," he told Czech president Vaclav Havel, "I'm more comfortable with a posse."[23] But at the same time, Bush refused to pledge that he would act only if others agreed to follow. He had no intention of letting others dictate what the United States could do, even if that meant sacrificing support in some foreign capitals. "At some point we may be the only ones left," Bush conceded. "That's okay with me. We are America."[24]

Bush also made clear that the war on terrorism would permit no room for neutrality. "We will pursue nations that provide aid or safe haven to terrorism," he told Congress. "Every nation, in every region, now has a decision to make. Either you are with us, or you are with the terrorists."[25] The need to force countries to choose sides, even if only rhetorically, was essential. To suggest that countries could sit on the sidelines of the conflict would mean tolerating terrorism as a kind of nuisance in world politics rather than as a grave threat to free and democratic nations. "What September 11th to me said was this is just the beginning of what these bastards can do if they start getting access to so-called modern weapons," said Wolfowitz, "and that it's not something you can live with any longer."[26]

AFTER SEPTEMBER 11 foreign policy no longer played second fiddle to domestic policy. The war on terrorism became *the* priority for Bush, especially in the days immediately following the attacks, because no one knew when, where, or even if, the second shoe would fall. "We now recognize," he later observed, "that oceans no longer protect us, that we're vulnerable to attack. And the worst form of attack could come from somebody acquiring weapons of mass destruction and using them on the American people."[27] Domestic policy did not cease to matter, as Bush's effort in 2002 and 2003 to push through more tax cuts attested. However, it ceased to matter most. Karl Rove, his chief political adviser, recalled, "The President said, 'I want to pursue my domestic agenda with vigor, but you've got less of my time and less of my energy and less of my focus, because I'm necessarily spending more time on war-related issues and on homeland security related issues, and that's just the reality of it.'"[28]

In many ways, waging the war on terrorism became not just Bush's top priority, but his mission. "I'm here for a reason," Bush told Rove shortly after the attacks, "and this is going to be how we're going to be judged."[29] He told Japanese prime minister Junichiro Koizumi something similar. "History will be the judge, but it won't judge well somebody who doesn't act, somebody who just bides time here."[30] Reminiscent of his insistence that he did not go to Austin simply to put his name in the placecard holder, he committed himself to doing more than merely stopping terrorists. "I will seize the opportunity to achieve big goals," he told Bob Woodward. "There is nothing bigger than to achieve world peace."[31]

The mission that Bush envisioned went well beyond defending America's national interests. It was more fundamentally a struggle between good and evil that touched all the world's peoples. The notion of evil had always figured prominently in Bush's thinking, as it had in the thinking of the president he often sought to emulate, Ronald Reagan. "America has determined enemies, who hate our values and resent our success," Bush said in a 1999 speech. "The Empire has passed, but evil remains."[32] Nevertheless, Bush invoked the word *evil* sparingly in his public comments before the attacks in New York and Washington. This probably owed at least somewhat to the instinctual aversion of most foreign policy thinkers, including some of his advisers, to describing the world in black-and-white terms. Rice recalls that she reacted negatively to Reagan's 1982 "evil empire" speech to the British House of Commons. "I thought, 'Oh, that's incredibly undiplomatic, and I hope it doesn't provoke an incident.'"[33] The foreign policy establishment's aversion to theological rhetoric was understandable in a world in which events might turn one day's adversary into the next day's ally.

However, just as September 11 galvanized Bush to pursue his foreign policy revolution, so it also swept away any inhibition he might have felt about speaking publicly about evil. He used the term early and freely. "Today," he said in his primetime television address on the night of the attacks, "our nation saw evil."[34] He invoked the word three more times in his four-minute address. Three days later he told mourners at the National Cathedral, "Our responsibility to history is already clear:

to answer these attacks and rid the world of evil."[35] Four months later he warned the world of the "axis of evil." The Texan had always preferred blunt talk to euphemisms, and watching jetliners plow into skyscrapers on a beautiful late summer day made it hard not to believe that evil lurked in the world.

In depicting the war on terrorism as a struggle between good and evil, Bush frequently alluded to God's support for his efforts. "Even though I walk through the valley of the shadow of death, I fear no evil, for You are with me," he told the nation on the night of the attacks, quoting the well-known words of the Twenty-Third Psalm.[36] "Freedom and fear, justice and cruelty, have always been at war," he told a joint session of Congress nine days later, "and we know that God is not neutral between them."[37] Invoking the Lord's name was certainly not new in American politics. Almost every American president did. However, Bush was one of the most overtly religious occupants of the Oval Office in more than a century. "This thing about his faith—I mean, this is real for him," his father told NBC's Tom Brokaw. "Here's a man that's read the Bible through twice and it's not to make it holier than thou or not to make a political point. It's something that is in his heart."[38]

Bush's frequent references to God resonated with Americans, especially in the early days after the national tragedy. Over time, however, his obvious religiosity bothered many people at home and even more people abroad. The problem was not just that secular people were uncomfortable with the invocation of God, though many were, or that some thought that in tying America's cause to God's desires Bush was providing a mirror image of the Islamic terrorists he was trying to hunt down. Many feared that he saw his role in the war on terrorism as part of a divine mission, and that this faith would blind him to the risks inherent in his policy choices. Some, but not all, of Bush's friends and advisers told reporters privately that he saw himself as carrying out God's will. "I think, in his frame, this is what God has asked him to do," said one close friend.[39] An unnamed senior administration official later added, Bush "really believes he was placed here to do this as part of a divine plan."[40] A group of religious leaders visited the White House shortly after September 11. One of them told Bush that he was doing work that God had chosen for him. "I accept the responsibility," Bush replied.[41]

Bush denied that he ever told anyone that he believed God had chosen him to wage the war on terrorism. "It's not true," he said. "I think God sustains us, but I don't think I was *chosen*. I was chosen by the American people."[42] By the same token, however, his public statements encouraged the speculation that he believed himself the instrument of Providence. "Events aren't moved by blind change and chance," he told a gathering of religious leaders in early 2003. "Behind all of life and all of history, there's a dedication and purpose, set by the hand of a just and faithful God."[43] And Bush, like most of his predecessors in the Oval Office, openly proclaimed America to be an instrument of God's will. "As I said in my State of the Union," he told the National Religious Broadcasters' convention in early 2003, "liberty is not America's gift to the world. Liberty is God's gift to every human being in the world. America has great challenges; challenges at home and challenges abroad. We're called to extend the promise of this country into the lives of every citizen who lives here. We're called to defend our nation and to lead the world to peace, and we will meet both challenges with courage and with confidence."[44]

Journalists, psychologists, and talk-show pundits debated how Bush's faith influenced his conduct of the war on terrorism, if it did at all. The true connection in the end was probably unknowable, perhaps even to Bush himself. What was certain was that there was nothing in Christianity generally, or evangelicalism specifically, that specified strategies for pursuing al Qaeda or finding weapons of mass destruction. Evangelicals were as capable of arguing that Christianity required them to concentrate on remedying the mote in their own eye as that it required them to go forth boldly into the world to remedy injustice at the point of a sword. Jimmy Carter, the man who first introduced most Americans to the term "born again," and Bill Clinton, a Southern Baptist and regular churchgoer, approached foreign policy differently than Bush did and criticized many of his responses to September 11. Equally important, Bush's most enthusiastic supporters within his own administration did not necessarily share either his religious conviction or his religion. Indeed, a dislike for ambiguity and a lack of self-doubt—traits Bush had in abundance and that were commonly attributed to his faith—were personality characteristics that could be found among many secular-minded, indeed even irreligious, people.

However Bush's faith influenced his decision to wage war on terrorism, he still had to rethink his own foreign policy priorities. During the campaign and into his first months in office, he had been certain that great-power competition trumped all in world politics and that hostile great powers constituted the primary threat to U.S. security. Given that both Russia and China endorsed, with varying degrees of enthusiasm, America's war on terrorism, that case became difficult to make. Bush did not try to make it. If anything, he went in the other direction, suggesting that a fundamental strategic realignment among the great powers might be under way. "We have our best chance since the rise of the nation state in the 17th century to build a world where the great powers compete in peace instead of prepare for war," he told the graduating class of West Point in June 2002. "Competition between great nations is inevitable, but armed conflict in our world is not. More and more, civilized nations find ourselves on the same side—united by common dangers of terrorist violence and chaos. America has, and intends to keep, military strengths beyond challenge, thereby, making the destabilizing arms races of other eras pointless, and limiting rivalries to trade and other pursuits of peace."[45]

It is impossible to say whether Bush truly believed his own words, was trying to create a new reality by insisting that the world had changed, or was simply trying to neutralize potential rivals with sweet talk while he hunted down terrorists and tyrants. What is clear is that terrorists and tyrants replaced great powers as the focus of his foreign policy after September 11. The problem he faced, however, was how to translate his broad predispositions about how the world worked into a set of workable policies. Knowing that power matters and that evildoers must meet with swift and certain punishment in itself said little about whether the United States should work with Pakistan or isolate it. Understanding that coalitions of the willing offered practical advantages over formal international organizations still left open the question of how much operational efficiency Washington should give up if it could get the assistance or approval of international institutions such as the United Nations and NATO.

Bush and his advisers would spend much of the first two years after September 11 thinking through these questions. Because they had not thought through these issues before, they often made up responses on the fly. This at times produced claims that seemed strained. "The terrorists attacked the World Trade Center, and we will defeat them by expanding and encouraging world trade," the president told a group of California businessmen six weeks after September 11, as if flooding the Islamic world with cheap imports would undo al Qaeda.[46] At other times, the fact that Bush was developing and refining his thinking as he went along meant that his subordinates often squabbled over what he had actually decided or sought to reopen issues if they thought he had decided incorrectly. That Bush's thinking continued to evolve after September 11 is hardly remarkable, given the natural changes that come with the passage of time and the lessons of experience. What was significant was that Bush's strategy for winning the war on terrorism proceeded from principles and predispositions that were evident long before the World Trade Center towers collapsed in a cloud of smoke and debris.

IN PROVIDING BUSH with a motive to act abroad, September 11 also gave him the opportunity to do so without fear of being challenged at home. Congressional displeasure with Bush's handling of foreign policy had grown throughout the summer of 2001. Helping to fuel the criticism was the fact that control of the Senate shifted to the Democrats in June when James Jeffords of Vermont formally left the Republican Party and became an Independent. The new Senate majority leader was Tom Daschle of South Dakota, a soft-spoken liberal who could be a fierce defender of Democratic Party positions. A potential presidential candidate in 2004, he vowed early to engage "in more active involvement on international issues."[47]

Bush's problems, however, were not only with congressional Democrats. Many Senate Republicans grumbled privately that the White House's heavy-handedness was to blame for Jeffords's defection. House Republicans balked at Bush's plan to pay back dues that Washington owed to the United Nations. Some Republicans, led by Bush's 2000 campaign rival John McCain, distanced themselves from the White House on the issue of global warming. Moderates in the party questioned the wisdom of alienating many of America's traditional allies.

Congressional resistance to Bush's national security policies gave way on September 11. In a replay of a well-known phenomenon in American politics, the attacks shifted the pendulum of power away from Capitol Hill and toward the White House. On September 14, after little debate about the consequences of what they were about to do, all but one member of Congress voted to give Bush stunningly broad latitude to retaliate against those responsible for the attacks. The resolution stated that he could "use all necessary and appropriate force against those nations, organizations, or persons he determines planned, authorized, committed, or aided the terrorist attacks that occurred on September 11, 2001, or harbored such organizations or persons."[48] In effect, Congress declared war and left it up to the White House to decide who the enemy was.

Capitol Hill's newfound deference manifested itself on other issues as well. In a bid to shore up support overseas, the House quickly passed the legislation needed to pay U.S. back dues to the United Nations. Congress said nothing in September when Bush waived sanctions that had been imposed on Pakistan after its May 1998 nuclear tests. By mid-October, Congress had authorized the White House to waive other sanctions that had been placed on Islamabad over the years. Senate Democrats dropped what had been a concerted effort to slash spending on missile defense and to limit testing of any antimissile system. They also said little when Bush announced in December 2001 that the United States was withdrawing from the ABM Treaty.

Congress was even reluctant to defend its constitutional prerogatives. Just weeks before the ABM withdrawal announcement, the White House issued the Military Order of November 13. It declared that the foreign citizens the United States detained while waging its war on terrorism could be tried before military commissions. The order alarmed civil libertarians in both political parties and prompted more than three hundred law professors to sign a letter calling the commissions "legally deficient, unnecessary, and unwise."[49] Regardless of the wisdom of military commissions—they had been used many times before in American history, and a subsequent Pentagon directive addressed many, but by no means all, of the critics' complaints—the president's executive order presumably implicated Congress's constitutional authority to "define and punish . . . offenses against the law of nations" and its power to make all other laws "necessary and proper" for executing the federal government's enumerated powers. Nonetheless, Congress neither blocked the president's order nor acted to reinforce its legal basis. Nothing changed even when the Justice Department turned over Jose Padilla, an American citizen and suspected member of al Qaeda, to the Defense Department to be held as an enemy combatant, thus putting him effectively beyond the reach of the law. Few lawmakers wanted to be seen sympathizing with an alleged terrorist.

Congress was similarly silent as Bush lifted some of the restrictions on the CIA's ability to operate covertly, permitted government prosecutors to listen in on conversations between people charged with terrorism and their lawyers, approved the roundup of thousands of Arab and Muslim men, and made it more difficult to get some presidential papers made public. When Congress did act, it usually did so to ratify Bush's initiatives. Just seven weeks after the attacks, Congress passed essentially intact the administration's proposed USA Patriot Act. This mind-numbingly complex law greatly expanded federal law enforcement powers, especially in the area of electronic surveillance. The Patriot Act also defined a new crime of "domestic terrorism" so broadly that civil libertarians worried that it could be used against activist groups on the left and right that practice civil disobedience. Capitol Hill's main change to the Patriot Act was to add a sunset clause on the provisions regarding electronic surveillance, meaning that those government powers will expire in 2005 unless Congress acts to extend them.

The depth of Congress's deference partly reflected the enormity of the attacks and a principled belief that lawmakers should defer to strong presidential leadership in times of national crisis. But it also reflected a healthy dose of politics. Rather than blaming Bush for failing to anticipate the attacks, Americans rallied around him. His public approval ratings soared to 90 percent, a figure seen only once before— when his father waged the Gulf War. Whereas the elder Bush's approval ratings quickly returned to their prewar levels, the younger Bush's remained high for months. On the first anniversary of the terrorist attacks, 70 percent gave him a thumbs up for the job he was doing as president, and some 60 percent still did so in the summer of 2003. Bush's newfound popularity translated into political power. Lawmakers may ignore the pleadings of an unpopular president, but they usually heed the demands of a popular one.

The Democratic Party's lack of credibility with the American public on foreign policy further bolstered Bush's political position. For years Americans had told pollsters that they had far more confidence in Republicans than Democrats when it came to handling national security issues. September 11 only reinforced this perception. Polls showed that Americans gave the nod to Republicans over Democrats when it came to dealing with terrorism by margins as high as three to one. Democrats suddenly found themselves in a position where they risked being dismissed out of hand or accused of being unpatriotic if they criticized Bush's decisions in the war on terrorism. With only a few seats separating the two parties on Capitol Hill, most Democratic lawmakers who would have preferred to challenge the White House decided that discretion was the better part of valor and opted for silence. Bush seemed beyond challenge.

PRESIDENT BUSH AND his advisers—all of whom already had expansive views of presidential authority—happily seized on the opportunity to act without having to clear their decisions with 535 secretaries of state. They also worked hard to keep Congress, and especially congressional Democrats, on the defensive. The war on terrorism was a natural issue for Republicans to use to their advantage. "We can go to the country on this issue because they trust the Republican Party to do a better job of protecting and strengthening America's military might and thereby protecting America," Karl Rove told a Republican National Committee meeting in January 2002. "The second place we should go to the country is on protecting the homeland," he added. "We can go to the country confidently on this issue because Americans trust the Republican Party to do a better job of keeping our communities and families safe."[50]

Republicans on Capitol Hill were happy to help the White House use the terrorism issue against the Democrats. In February 2002, Daschle told reporters that the war on terrorism "has been successful" but that Bush's efforts to expand the war lacked "a clear direction" and that U.S. troops had to find Osama bin Laden and other top al Qaeda leaders "or we will have failed."[51] Daschle's comments, especially his insistence on the need to capture bin Laden, were hardly inflammatory. When Bush had been asked a week after September 11 whether he wanted Osama bin Laden dead, he replied: "I want justice. There's an old poster out west, as I recall, that said, 'Wanted: Dead or Alive.'"[52]

Republican criticism of the Senate majority leader, however, was instantaneous and vitriolic. "How dare Senator Daschle criticize President Bush while we are fighting our war on terrorism, especially when we have troops in the field?" complained Senate Minority Leader Trent Lott. "He should not be trying to divide our country while we are united." House Majority Whip Tom Delay issued a one-word press release calling Daschle's comments "disgusting." Representative Tom Davis of Virginia, chairman of the National Republican Congressional Campaign Committee, accused Daschle of "giving aid and comfort to our enemies," which happens to be the legal definition of treason.[53] These accusations did not persuade Daschle to retract or modify his comments. But it was telling that few Democratic senators came to his defense. They remained silent even though many had privately voiced the same concerns.

Politics similarly influenced Bush's decision to propose creating a new homeland security department. Democrats had pushed the idea ever since the September 11 attacks. Bush resisted the proposal for months, insisting that his decision to create an Office of Homeland Security in the White House headed by Pennsylvania governor Tom Ridge was sufficient. "Creating a cabinet post," argued White House spokesman Ari Fleischer in March 2002, "doesn't solve anything."[54] Throughout the spring of 2002, however, the Democratic proposal gained support. Meanwhile, the White House was buffeted by a string of news stories about how the CIA and the FBI had bungled leads that might have uncovered the September 11 plot. In early June Bush suddenly reversed course. On the same day that FBI agent Coleen Rowley testified before Congress on the FBI's missteps, Bush went on national television to unveil a homeland security reorganization proposal that dwarfed anything being considered on Capitol Hill. The proposed department would merge twenty-two agencies, employ nearly 170,000 workers, spend more than $35 billion annually, and become the federal government's third largest bureaucracy.

After demanding the creation of a homeland security department for months, congressional Democrats could only applaud Bush's proposal. However, his change of heart did more than just nullify the potential edge that Democrats had developed on homeland security. By its sheer scale and his insistence that Congress enact it by year's end, Bush's plan pushed almost every other major issue to the political sidelines. That was a blessing for a White House worried about the political consequences of a sluggish economy and a growing budget deficit. Some in Bush's circle couldn't help crowing about their political jujitsu. The Department of Homeland Security is "the right thing to do for the right reasons," argued Mark McKinnon, Bush's chief media consultant during the campaign. "It also throws a huge blanket over the entire domestic agenda. The domestic agenda right now is security. It's covering up everything else."[55]

Besides entirely reshaping the domestic political agenda, Bush's proposal contained what was for Democrats a poison pill—a provision that would strip workers in the new department of the civil service protections they had previously enjoyed. The Democrats faced a dilemma. They could endorse the president's proposal and alienate one of their key constituencies, organized labor, or oppose it and risk being accused of putting their party's interests ahead of the country's. The Democrats chose the latter. Republicans skillfully exploited the decision, with Bush at one point charging Senate Democrats with being "more interested in special interests in Washington and not interested in the security of the American people."[56] The charges stuck, at least with some voters. Republicans retook control of the Senate in the November elections, and a lame-duck Congress created a new homeland security department largely along the lines Bush had proposed.

Even as Bush was scoring political points at the Democrats' expense over the Department of Homeland Security, he was putting them in another political box over Iraq. His threats during the first half of 2002 to topple Saddam Hussein prompted Democrats to insist that the country could not go to war without congressional approval. The

White House initially argued that the 1991 Gulf War resolution, the September 11 resolution, and the president's inherent powers as commander in chief made that unnecessary. In early September, however, Bush called for a congressional vote. He and his advisers recognized that they faced a win-win situation. The political climate made it almost certain that Congress would vote for war. And if Democrats opposed the war, they would hand the Republicans yet another issue in the upcoming congressional elections. In this case, many Democrats decided it was better to follow the president than oppose him. Congress passed the Iraq War resolution in October 2002 by wide margins.

Besides using the war on terrorism to put and keep the Democrats on the defensive, Bush also used it to his own electoral advantage. In May 2003 he flew to the USS *Abraham Lincoln*, which was just off the coast of San Diego—not by helicopter, but by jet, which allowed television cameras to show a spectacular landing on the aircraft carrier's deck—to announce the end of major fighting in Iraq. Overnight, the man often caricatured as a little boy with big ears was seen by many Americans as a sexy fighter jock. The White House also arranged for the Republican Party to delay the start of its presidential nominating convention in New York City until the end of August 2004, so that Bush's acceptance speech would flow seamlessly into the commemorations honoring the third anniversary of September 11. And the war on terrorism took center stage in Bush's fund-raising letters for the 2004 election: "I'll be depending on friends and supporters like you to get my campaign organized and operating across our country," he wrote in May 2003. "We have no more urgent and important duty than to wage and win the War on Terrorism."[57]

Democrats complained that Bush was exploiting the war on terrorism for political gain. They wondered what happened to the man who came into office pledging to change the tone in Washington, and who said after September 11, "It's time to take the spirit of unity that has been prevalent when it comes to fighting the war and bring it to Washington, D.C."[58] September 11 certainly changed the priority that Bush gave to foreign policy. It gave him a defining mission for his presidency. But it did not blunt his political reflexes—or his determination to avoid his father's fate.

SEVEN

ONTO THE OFFENSIVE

T HE GRAVITY OF THE terrorist attacks on September 11 left no question that the United States would respond. "Terrorism against our nation will not stand," George W. Bush declared moments after the second jet slammed into the south tower of the World Trade Center.[1] CIA director George Tenet and White House counterterrorism czar Richard Clarke immediately concluded that Osama bin Laden's fingerprints were all over the attack. Bin Laden was responsible for many earlier attacks against U.S. targets, including the bombing of U.S. embassies in Kenya and Tanzania in 1998 and of the USS *Cole* in Yemen in 2000. He had often proclaimed his deep hatred for the United States and threatened to strike America at home. Beginning in 1996, bin Laden and his al Qaeda network had established a large infrastructure in Afghanistan with the full support of the Taliban, an Islamist regime that had taken power that year.

Within hours of the attack, Bush pulled together a war council—composed of himself, Dick Cheney, Colin Powell, Donald Rumsfeld, Condoleezza Rice, Andrew Card, George Tenet, and General Hugh Shelton, the chairman of the Joint Chiefs of Staff. (Shelton would be replaced by his deputy, General Richard Myers, on his retirement at the end of September.) There, talk of possible action turned quickly to action in Afghanistan. But what would be the objectives? How could these be achieved? And what, if anything, would come afterward?

These questions preoccupied Bush and his advisers that evening and in the days that followed.

Within six days, Bush made a crucial set of decisions, setting the stage for a new, global war on terrorism. America would strike against terrorist groups with global reach, starting with al Qaeda. It would hold governments that supported terrorism in any way fully accountable. Other countries were expected to join the fight and to accept America's proposed strategy for action. Military force—to defeat terrorists, destroy sanctuaries, and coerce state sponsors of terrorism to change their ways—would play a central role. Missing from the strategy, however, was any consideration of how the use of force would affect post-war stabilization efforts in countries like Afghanistan, whose very weakness had been a source of security concerns to the United States and, indeed, much of the world.

SPEAKING TO THE nation the evening after the terrorist attacks, Bush announced that the "search is underway for those who are behind these evil acts. I've directed the full resources of our intelligence and law enforcement communities to find those responsible and to bring them to justice." This would be the first step in what he called this "war against terrorism."[2] Immediately after finishing his Oval Office address, the president walked next door into the Cabinet Room for a meeting with his full National Security Council, followed later by a session with his smaller war council. The discussion focused on what to do, and when and how to do it. Powell talked about the need to get Pakistan involved, since Islamabad had the closest ties to the Taliban regime. Cheney worried about the military difficulty of bombing a country already in a shambles after a quarter century of war. Rumsfeld pointed out that the problem was larger than bin Laden and al Qaeda and included states that supported terrorism, such as Iraq. States would be the main focus of pressure—offering a choice of supporting America in its antiterrorist cause or facing the consequences. "We have to force countries to choose," Bush declared.[3] But which countries was left up in the air.

The issue was taken up again by Bush's war council the next morning, when Rumsfeld raised the question of the overall goal. "Do we focus on bin Laden and al Qaeda or on terrorism more broadly?" Powell argued that the objective should be "terrorism in its broadest sense," focusing first on those responsible for the attack. "To the extent we define our task broadly," Cheney added, "including those who support terrorism, then we get at states. And it's easier to find them than it is to find bin Laden." Bush argued that Americans expected them to focus on bin Laden. "If we succeed, we've struck a huge blow and can move forward."[4] The war against terrorism would be fought in stages, starting with those responsible for the previous day's attack. Which meant bin Laden and Afghanistan.

The U.S. military, which had contingency plans for virtually every conceivable eventuality, had no plans on the books for going after Afghanistan. Three years earlier, the United States had fired cruise missiles at several al Qaeda training camps in response to the bombing of the American embassies in Kenya and Tanzania. U.S. submarines had been on station during the later years of the Clinton presidency, ready to launch cruise missiles in the event that the intelligence community provided reliable information on bin Laden's whereabouts. But aside from these isolated military scenarios, Rice acknowledged, there was "nothing on the shelf for this kind of war."[5] So when Bush pressed Rumsfeld on what the military could do soon, the Pentagon chief admitted there was "very little, effectively." Some major strikes might take sixty days to put together.[6] Bush was not satisfied. "This is a new world," he told Shelton. "Go back to the generals for new targets. Start the clock. This is an opportunity. I want a plan—costs, time. I need options on the table," he demanded. And they would have to be real options. "I don't want to put a million-dollar missile on a five-dollar tent."[7]

Afghanistan might be an insignificant military power, but it is protected by geography. With the closest access to the sea about three hundred miles away, it was surrounded by states with which the United States had few close relations. Pakistan would be key. It curled around the eastern and southern borders of Afghanistan. It was one of three countries to have diplomatic relations with the Taliban, and its intelligence services had very close ties with the Taliban's leader, Mullah Mohammad Omar. Any military operations conducted from sea would have to cross Pakistani territory. (Iran offered a theoretical, but not a practical, alternative.)

Relations between Washington and Islamabad had taken a turn for the worse two years earlier when General Pervez Musharraf had ousted the elected government, but now Pakistan had to be brought into the fold. "Do what you have to do," Bush told Powell. And Powell did. He drew up a list of seven demands for Pakistan, ranging from granting overflight and landing rights and sharing intelligence information to breaking off diplomatic relations with the Taliban if Kabul continued to provide sanctuary to bin Laden and al Qaeda. Powell called Musharraf, telling him, "As one general to another, we need someone on our flank fighting with us."[8] Musharraf accepted each of the seven demands and offered Powell his full support.

Even with Pakistan's support, however, there was still no military plan of action against Afghanistan. Into the void stepped the Central Intelligence Agency. Tenet had feared that the president would one day need a plan of action against the Taliban and al Qaeda, and the CIA had been working on it for months. Meeting in the White House Situation Room just forty-eight hours after airplanes had brought down the twin towers, Tenet briefed the war council on the agency's ideas. He proposed that CIA paramilitary teams, which had worked with the Afghan opposition for years, be inserted into the country together with Special Operations Forces to help the opposition oust the Taliban. The key to success was the Northern Alliance, which operated in northern Afghanistan. Guided by CIA operatives and supported by Special Forces calling in air strikes against Taliban defenses, the Northern Alliance could turn the balance of power in the opposition's favor.

Tenet turned to Cofer Black, his counterterrorism chief, who had a dramatic PowerPoint presentation describing how the proposed action could destroy the al Qaeda presence in Afghanistan. "You give us the mission," Black told the president, "we'll rout 'em out." The goal, of course, would be to capture al Qaeda fighters and hand them over to law enforcement authorities, but it was Black's experience that al Qaeda men never surrendered. They would have to be killed. "When we're through with them, they will have flies walking across their eyeballs," Black said, employing an image that got everyone's attention. "How long will it take?" Bush asked. Once agents were on the ground, it would go very quickly—weeks rather than months, Black responded.[9]

Bush was impressed. The president was itching for action—and here was a plan that would engage the enemy in a hurry.

STILL, MANY DETAILS needed to be worked out. The special-ops component of the plan had to be developed. A role for coalition partners had to be devised. And the planners needed to settle on a strategy beyond Afghanistan. On Saturday, September 15, just four days after the terrorist attacks, the war council convened again at Camp David for an extended day of meetings.

Bush brought a memo from British prime minister Tony Blair suggesting ways to move forward. Blair, leader of the leftist Labour party, was an unlikely ally of the president. He had been a close friend and supporter of President Clinton, with whom he shared a deep interest in the intricacies of government policy. Together Blair and Clinton had forged a "third way" of governing that married fiscal conservatism with progressive social policy. Blair had emerged as a forceful spokesman of internationalism, arguing that foreign policy should focus on building and strengthening the institutions of the international community—a stance that was in sharp contrast to Bush's disdain for international treaties and organizations. The first meeting between Bush and Blair had gone well, but there was little of the camaraderie that had marked earlier encounters between Clinton and Blair. When asked what he and Blair had in common aside from policy, the nonplussed Bush answered that they both used Colgate toothpaste.[10] But none of this mattered after the terrorists attacked. Blair immediately made clear that Britain stood "shoulder to shoulder with our American friends in this hour of tragedy, and we, like them, will not rest until this evil is driven from our world."[11]

Blair's five-page memo, which he had sent Bush a day after the attacks, outlined his ideas for undertaking a campaign against terrorism. The prime minister argued that it would be critical to shape world opinion by publicly presenting any evidence linking bin Laden to the attacks. He proposed demanding that the Taliban hand over bin Laden and al Qaeda's leaders, shut down training camps, and allow international monitors to enter Afghanistan or face the consequences. If the Taliban resisted, the Northern Alliance would have to be a crucial part of any military campaign, and Pakistan's support would be necessary. Iran was also crucial, given its long border with and involvement in Afghanistan. It would thus be important for Washington to improve relations with Tehran. Britain, finally, would offer whatever was needed in the way of military support for operations in Afghanistan.[12] Blair's ideas—and his steadfast support for the United States—proved useful and heartening as Bush considered how to respond to the attacks.

Tenet opened the Saturday morning session at Camp David with a set of colorful slides entitled "Going to War." Each slide featured a picture of bin Laden inside a slashed red circle. He reviewed the plan Cofer Black had outlined two days earlier and put the Afghanistan action within the larger context of an expanded CIA role in the global war on terrorism. Tenet proposed that the president grant the CIA "exceptional authorities" to destroy al Qaeda around the world. He even brought along a draft presidential finding expanding the CIA's role and authority to go after terrorists wherever they might be hiding. The CIA director presented the council with a "Worldwide Attack Matrix," detailing ongoing or planned covert counterterrorism operations in eighty countries, specifying what the agency would be doing in each of the countries. It was a dazzling performance. "Great job!" Bush exclaimed, clearly pleased to be presented with a set of concrete proposals.[13]

After presentations by FBI director Robert Mueller and Attorney General John Ashcroft on the investigation into the attacks and proposed legislation to beef up law-enforcement powers, General Shelton gave a briefing on what the military could do. He had three options for Afghanistan. One was to launch cruise missiles from surface ships and submarines against terrorist training camps. Since the camps would most likely be empty, everyone realized these strikes would be merely symbolic. Another was to send manned bombers to attack fixed defensive sites of the Taliban regime. Such an attack could last three or four days, and possibly even ten, but after that the bombers would run out of targets. The final option was to add ground troops to the mixture— Special Forces and possibly Army troops and Marines. Given Afghanistan's protected location, it would take at least ten to twelve days to get any forces on the ground because Washington would have to negotiate with neighboring countries to secure basing rights for search-and-rescue troops and equipment.

The discussion next turned to the overall goal of military action. There were two main issues: What should be the objective of military action in Afghanistan, and what would come after? The military goals were relatively straightforward. Everyone agreed that pressure should be brought to bear on the Taliban to give up bin Laden and end its support for al Qaeda. Most of those present believed that the fate of the Taliban and al Qaeda were so intertwined that the removal of the latter required the ouster of the former. But what then? Who would take over? And what would be the impact on Pakistan? There was speculation, but there were no clear answers.

The other issue concerned military action beyond Afghanistan. Rumsfeld had earlier raised the question of Iraq, and now his deputy, Paul Wolfowitz, chimed in. Wolfowitz had long believed that the first Bush administration had blundered by ending the Gulf War before Saddam Hussein had been removed from power. Now he saw a chance to rectify this mistake. A war against Afghanistan was risky—American troops could get bogged down, stability would be difficult if not impossible to achieve after the Taliban was ousted, and in any case in his view the real support for terrorism lay elsewhere. Wolfowitz suggested there was a chance—anywhere from 10 to 50 percent—that Saddam Hussein was involved in September 11. Saddam's regime was brittle and could be easily overthrown. His weapons of mass destruction made him a menace both larger and more immediate than Afghanistan. He had to be dealt with at some point, so why not now?

There was little support for Wolfowitz's argument. Afghanistan would have to come first. It was the refuge of the perpetrators of the September 11 attacks, and Americans would expect their government to deliver justice there. Powell warned that the international coalition that was then forming in support of action would fall apart if the war went beyond al Qaeda. If the United States moved against Iraq right away, the coalition members would "view it as a bait-and-switch—it's not what they signed up to do." Rumsfeld countered that if the coalition would not hold, then that "argues for a different coalition." The mission should determine the coalition, not the other way around. Bush agreed. He was not about to let any other countries dictate the terms for the war on terrorism.

Having heard everyone's views, Bush thanked all for coming and told them he would let them know what he decided. The war council reconvened on September 17 in the White House, and the president was ready with specific assignments. Powell would issue an ultimatum to the Taliban—hand over bin Laden or the regime would be history. Tenet would get his exceptional authorities under a new presidential finding authorizing covert operations. His agents also were to begin providing full support to Afghan opposition forces. Shelton was told to draw up detailed plans for an attack using missiles, bombers, and ground troops. "Let's hit them hard," Bush said. "We want to signal this is a change from the past. We want to cause other countries like Syria and Iran to change their views." For now, Afghanistan would remain the focus. The Pentagon should accelerate planning for possible military action against Iraq, but, Bush said, this was a "first-things-first administration," and Afghanistan would come first.[14]

Three days later, Blair visited Bush in the White House, where they finalized their agreement on how to proceed. "I agree with you that the job in hand is al Qaeda and Taliban," Bush told Blair. "Iraq, we keep for another day."[15] That evening, Bush made his decisions public in a widely praised address to Congress and the nation. "Deliver to United States authorities all the leaders of al Qaeda who hide in your land," Bush demanded of the Taliban. "Close immediately and permanently every terrorist training camp in Afghanistan, and hand over every terrorist, and every person in their support structure, to appropriate authorities. Give the United States full access to terrorist training camps, so we can make sure they are no longer operating." There would be no negotiations or discussions. "The Taliban must act, and act immediately. They will hand over the terrorists, or they will share in their fate."[16]

TWO WEEKS OF intense diplomatic pressure failed to persuade the Taliban to meet Bush's demands. On October 7, U.S. and British forces began the Afghan war. The immediate goals were limited: "to disrupt the use of Afghanistan as a terrorist base of operations, and to attack the military capability of the Taliban regime," Bush told the nation that Sunday afternoon. The Taliban had failed to meet America's demands. "And now the Taliban will pay a price. By destroying camps and disrupting communications, we will make it more difficult for the terror network to train new recruits and coordinate their evil plans."[17]

"Pay a price," "disrupt the use of Afghanistan" for terrorist activities, "make it more difficult" to prepare terrorist attacks—these were highly circumscribed objectives for a major military operation. They suggested that Washington understood that the war might not be an easy one. Indeed, four days after the operation began, Bush offered the Taliban a second chance. "If you cough him up, and his people, today," the president said, "we'll reconsider what we're doing to your country."[18]

Military operations in Afghanistan were initially quite measured. This reflected several political and military realities. Politically, there was some reluctance to give too much support to the Northern Alliance forces, for fear that they would topple the Taliban and take Kabul. Most of the Alliance's warlords—mainly Tajiks and Uzbeks, both minorities within Afghanistan's mixture of ethnic groups—had blood on their hands from their disastrous rule of Afghanistan following the ouster of the communist government in the early 1990s. They had long been opposed by the Pashtuns, who represented a plurality of Afghans and formed the nucleus of the Taliban's support. Pakistan, which had to consider the impact of Afghan political developments on its own Pashtun population, had supported the U.S. bombing campaign (including by granting basing and overflight rights) on the condition that a post-Taliban government would be broadly representative of Afghanistan's ethnic mixture. But American CIA operatives had difficulty in identifying a viable Pashtun opposition leader, especially after Abdul Haq, a legendary Pashtun resistance fighter, was captured and executed by the Taliban in late October. As a result, John Burns of the *New York Times* reported, "American military planners are finding themselves obliged to calibrate the bombing to achieve a desired political result—establishing a stable, broadly representative government in Kabul—that has eluded Afghanistan for decades."[19]

But politics was only one reason for the slow pace of the military campaign. Lack of adequate military capabilities was another, more important reason. For all the talk of wanting to "hit them hard" and using the full spectrum of America's military capability, little of it was available the day bombing started. There were no Army troops or Marines deployed inside Afghanistan to take the fight directly to the enemy. Airpower was available in some measure, but as Shelton had warned, there were precious few fixed targets of any significance inside an impoverished country shattered by a quarter century of violence. There were cumbersome rules of engagement in place for selecting targets to minimize the risk to civilians. Lawyers had to be consulted before especially sensitive targets were hit, which resulted in sometimes costly delays—including a number of missed opportunities to kill top Taliban and even al Qaeda leaders. It took weeks to get permission from Pakistan and the central Asian states to base helicopter-borne combat search-and-rescue teams near the fighting. Without these teams, whose role was to help stranded forces, the military would not commence combat operations. And it took even longer to get U.S. Special Forces into position to assist the opposition and help target American airpower against the Taliban defenses. The first Special Forces A-team, a twelve-member contingent of Army Rangers, was not deployed in the north until October 19—more than four weeks after Bush gave the go-ahead and nearly two weeks after bombing started.[20]

But the real problem was in many ways more fundamental than the lack of adequate capabilities. The military operation lacked clarity of purpose. Was it to get Osama bin Laden? To destroy al Qaeda? Topple the Taliban? Ensure Afghanistan would never again be a terrorist haven? Send a message to other terrorist supporters? All of the above? Bush's war council had not given definitive answers to any of these questions. Bush and his advisers agreed that after the horror of September 11, some form of significant military action was necessary. "We're steady, clear-eyed and patient," the president told King Abdullah of Jordan in late September. "But pretty soon we'll have to start displaying scalps."[21] However, there were many different objectives aside from revenge—and all of these permeated the design and execution of the military strategy in Afghanistan.

There also was no clear sense, at least in the beginning, of who was in charge. The initial planning had come from Langley rather than the

Pentagon or Tampa, home of U.S. Central Command, which was responsible for military operations in south central Asia. The CIA had its own paramilitary forces operating in the area, and it even had its own firepower—unmanned Predator drones armed with Hellfire missiles. In fact, the CIA often acted as if it were actually running the war.

It was little wonder, then, that Rumsfeld felt he was not in charge of the operation. "This is the CIA's strategy," he said on October 16. "You guys are in charge. You guys have the contacts. We're just following you in. We're going where you tell us to go." The CIA objected, saying General Tommy Franks, head of Central Command, was in charge. "I think what I'm hearing is a FUBAR," said Richard Armitage, Powell's deputy and a burly former special operations officer. FUBAR is the off-color military term used for when things are Fucked Up Beyond All Recognition. Bush hated these kinds of discussions. He wanted clarity and accountability. Rice was sent to tell Rumsfeld that this was now a military operation—and that he was in charge. A few days later, Rice's deputy, Stephen Hadley, had to repeat the point. "Somebody needs to pick this up and design a strategy," he told Rumsfeld. "Quite frankly, it's yours for the taking."[22]

Which is exactly what Rumsfeld did. He pushed Franks to accelerate the deployment of Special Forces into the north in order to increase the firepower that could be brought to bear against the Taliban. He wanted tangible results on the ground—and if that meant the Northern Alliance would make progress before the contours of a post-Taliban government had been decided, so be it. On October 21, Special Forces operating in the north called in air strikes in direct support of opposition forces. It was a first. The result was a new strategy combining Afghan opposition troops on the ground, U.S. Special Forces to help direct the fight, and massive airpower to devastate Taliban defenses.

Rumsfeld was committed to the strategy, and he would frequently recount how Special Forces on horseback would accompany the Northern Alliance troops to exploit the strategic openings created by precision bombing. But even as he took charge of the strategy in late October, some of his generals harbored doubts about the course he had chosen.

Looming in the background was Afghanistan's reputation as a grave-yard of empires—for the British at the turn of the twentieth century and the Soviet Union in the 1980s. The generals worried that the United States would suffer a similar fate. Myers warned on October 21 that success, while guaranteed, might take a long time. "It may take till next spring. It may take till next summer. It may take longer than that."[23] As October wore on, the skepticism rose. Franks was especially concerned about the Northern Alliance. "I don't place any confidence in the opposition," he told Bush. A highly classified analysis by the Defense Intelligence Agency concluded that neither the northern city of Mazar-e-Sharif nor Kabul would fall by winter. Talk inside and out-side the administration increasingly turned to the need for deploying U.S. troops—fifty thousand or more was a number Bush and his war council considered.[24] Rumsfeld even spoke of possibly much larger numbers. "It is true, we do not have anything like the ground forces we had in World War II or in Korea or in the Gulf War, but nor have we ruled that out."[25]

But that was in late October. In early November, the tide in Afghanistan turned. Additional Special Forces teams directed devastat-ing strikes from bombers against Taliban and al Qaeda troops, whose defensive positions rapidly collapsed. The Northern Alliance took Mazar-e-Sharif on November 10 and the capital the next day. Fighting continued in the east, near Kunduz, and in the south, around the Tal-iban stronghold of Kandahar. But the onslaught was too much for the Taliban and al Qaeda. Its leaders abandoned Kandahar on December 7, with most fleeing into the mountains along the Afghan-Pakistan bor-der and some into other rugged parts of Afghanistan.

THE MILITARY OPERATION turned out to be a rousing success, proving all the naysayers wrong. It was possible to defeat a regime more than seven thousand miles away. Modern military technology, the tenacity and ingenuity of Special Forces, and the determination of people to be freed from dictatorial rule proved to be an unbeatable combination.

But how much had been accomplished with the Taliban's ouster from power? Osama bin Laden and many key al Qaeda leaders were still on the loose. Ensuring that Afghanistan would never again host terrorist organizations required a massive effort to stabilize a country long riven by ethnic tensions and devastated by war. These fundamental tasks were still to be completed when Washington celebrated the Taliban's defeat in early December. Furthermore, accomplishing them was made more difficult by how the war was fought. The military strategy depended on warlords who shared some American interests (like ousting the Taliban) but not others (like creating a stable, representative government that could govern the entire country). Having ousted the Taliban on the cheap, achieving these more fundamental objectives would prove costly. This became painfully clear just days later in the forbidding mountains of Tora Bora.

After the fall of Kandahar, U.S. intelligence got wind that upward of two thousand al Qaeda fighters were holed up in the mountains east of Jalalabad. Signal intercepts indicated that Osama bin Laden and several of his chief lieutenants were among the mostly Arab fighters. Here was a chance to get the man responsible for the deaths of three thousand Americans. Yet, in a decision of major strategic consequence, Franks decided to rely on local militias and the Pakistan regular army to tighten the noose around Tora Bora. Special Forces directed air strikes against the cave complexes high up in the cold mountains, and some Afghan forces moved in to search the caves after they had been struck. But after a few days of bombing it was clear that many of the fighters, including bin Laden, had fled through the rugged mountains into nearby Pakistan.

What went wrong? al Qaeda fighters bribed some of the Afghan militias to let them pass. But the most important reason for the failure was that the Afghans and Pakistani forces did not have the same incentive to get bin Laden as the United States did. The Afghanis wanted undisputed control of the area—which getting rid of al Qaeda would do. Pakistani regular army troops might do what they were told, but they were not eager to hunt down fierce Arab fighters in the middle of winter high up in the mountains. Neither cared much about what would happen to Osama bin Laden and his fighters once they had disappeared. Some may even have been sympathetic to his cause.

This, clearly, was a job for American troops—not foreign forces with little stake in the result. And American troops were available. U.S. Marines had established a base south of Kandahar. Soldiers from the 10th Mountain Division were readying for deployment into Bagram air-base north of Kabul, and thousands of additional forces were stationed in the region. As the military historian Frederick Kagan later argued, a few battalions of helicopter-borne troops could have been deployed to seal the escape routes out of the mountains.[26] Yet, despite the fact that Franks had openly doubted the Afghan opposition, he and his commanders decided to rely on local fighters rather than on American troops to accomplish this critical mission. This decision was made even though Bush had put the highest priority on capturing bin Laden, including signing a presidential finding giving the CIA authority to kill him.[27]

Many reasons have been given for the failure to send American troops. One was the fear of American casualties, a legacy of Vietnam and Somalia. This fear was misplaced. Most Americans would have supported the use of U.S. troops to get bin Laden, the man responsible for the murder of three thousand of their fellow citizens. Another fear, frequently repeated by Rumsfeld, Franks, and others, was that Afghanis would react violently to a large American military presence—just as they had to the Soviet occupation in the 1980s. However, the Soviet experience was the wrong analogy. The Red Army had been exceedingly brutal, and its occupation had no local support. The U.S. intervention, by contrast, removed a regime that most Aghanis despised. A final explanation was that it would have been difficult to deploy a large number of troops into Afghanistan quickly, given its location and the lack of adequate basing facilities in the region. However, it would not have been impossible to deploy a few thousand troops rapidly, even if doing so entailed significant risk. Tora Bora was a crucial military operation—one that surely should have justified the risk.

THE FAILURE AT Tora Bora was not the only consequence of a flawed military strategy. So was the postwar stabilization effort. During the weeks of deliberation on how to intervene in Afghanistan, the war council paid little attention to what would happen in Afghanistan after the Taliban was removed. When on October 4 Bush asked, "Who will run the country?" Rice kicked herself for not having addressed this question earlier. "Her most awful moments," recounts Bob Woodward, "were when the president thought of something that the principals, particularly she, should have anticipated."[28] Nevertheless, it speaks volumes about the decisionmaking process that three full weeks into high-level planning for a war, no one had bothered to consider how the United States would win the peace.

Part of the reason for the administration's failure to plan for postwar Afghanistan was its ideological distaste for nation-building, a reflection of the fact that the president and most of his advisers were assertive nationalists, not democratic imperialists. During the presidential campaign, Bush had frequently denigrated American involvement in efforts to rebuild other nations. Rice had scoffed at the thought of the "82nd Airborne escorting kids to kindergarten."[29] Moreover, the whole administration seemed wrapped up in the muscular notion that superpowers fight wars; they do not do windows.

This disdain for nation-building dominated the administration's Afghan policy in the early going—and limited U.S. involvement thereafter. Even after the first bombs were falling, Rumsfeld distanced himself from any U.S. responsibility for helping to forge a more stable government once the Taliban was gone. "I don't think [that] leaves us with a responsibility to try to figure out what kind of government that country ought to have," the Pentagon chief said on October 9. "I don't know people who are smart enough from other countries to tell other countries the kind of arrangements they ought to have to govern themselves. One would hope and pray that they'd end up with governments that would provide the best possible for the people of those countries."[30] Bush offered little more than hope and prayer two days later. While he acknowledged learning the lesson "from the previous engagement in the Afghan area, that we should not just simply leave after a military objective has been achieved," he suggested that it "would be a useful function for the United Nations to take over the so-called 'nation-building'—I would call it the stabilization of a future government—after our military mission is complete."[31]

It was only in mid-October that the administration began to consider what postwar political arrangements needed to be made in Afghanistan. Powell appointed Richard Haass, one of his top aides, to work with the United Nations and other governments to determine the kind of government that might emerge once the Taliban was ousted. Haass, operating in tandem with his State Department colleague James Dobbins and the UN Special Representative to Afghanistan, former Algerian foreign minister Lakhdar Brahimi, worked with Afghan opposition forces and governments of the neighboring countries to devise a political process for ensuring that a broadly representative, multi-ethnic governing structure would be formed. These efforts culminated in a major meeting held in Bonn, Germany, during late November and early December. There, a well-regarded Pashtun leader, Hamid Karzai, emerged as everyone's least controversial choice to lead a transitional administration. The Bonn meetings also set in motion a process for establishing permanent governing structures for the country. On December 22, 2001, Karzai and his transitional government took the oath of office in newly liberated Kabul.

Putting a government in place is one thing; ensuring its effective functioning is quite another. The challenges in Afghanistan were immense. Here was a country that had known little but war for more than a quarter century. It had no functioning economy to speak of—its only productive crop was the poppy, used to produce heroin. Its annual per capita gross domestic product was about $150, putting it in the same league as the poorest countries in Africa. Millions of Afghanis had fled the country over the years, with about two million living in refugee camps across the border in Pakistan and one-and-a-half million in Iran. The humanitarian situation was precarious largely because of a prolonged drought, with more than seven million people depending on food shipped in from abroad.

Bush publicly committed his administration to help get Afghanistan back on its feet. "We know that true peace will only be achieved when we give the Afghan people the means to achieve their own aspirations," Bush declared in April 2002 in a speech dedicated to remembering the contributions of George C. Marshall, chief of staff of the U.S. military in World War II and later secretary of state in the Truman administration. "Marshall knew that our military victory against enemies in World War II had to be followed by a moral victory that resulted in better lives for individual human beings."[32] But Afghanistan would receive little of the generosity that Europe had received under the recovery plan that bore Marshall's name. The United States and other countries pledged to contribute $4.5 billion over five years to help Afghanistan's rebuilding—far less than the more than $80 billion America alone spent on the Marshall Plan. The assistance to Afghanistan was also far less than the international community spent on reconstruction elsewhere over the previous decade. The annual per capita expenditure was just one-fifth of what was spent in Rwanda and East Timor and one-seventh of what was spent in the Balkans.[33] Bush's own commitment to Afghanistan was episodic. The White House's 2004 budget submission failed to include any funds for Afghan reconstruction.

Apart from financial assistance, what the twenty-three million Afghanis lacked most was security. Fighting continued in parts of the country long after the fall of Kabul, with U.S. forces and Afghan militias tracking down Taliban and al Qaeda fighters, some of whom were trying to infiltrate back into Afghanistan from their shelters in the northwest territories of Pakistan. In March 2002 a major battle erupted in the Shar-e-kot valley in eastern Afghanistan when American and allied forces launched "Operation Anaconda" to ensnare no fewer than one thousand Taliban and al Qaeda fighters who had infiltrated the area. The security vacuum created by the Taliban's ouster was filled by regional warlords—Ismael Khan in the west, Rashid Dostum in the north, Gul Agha in the south, and Karim Khalili in the center—many of whom Washington had actively supported after September 11. (The CIA estimated it spent $70 million inside Afghanistan to fight the war, which Bush considered the biggest bargain of all time.)[34] Not only did some of the warlords engage in skirmishes with one another, but all of them had their own ideas about who should control what in Afghanistan. Neither Hamid Karzai nor any other Kabul-based central government figured in their plans.

These deep divisions left Karzai controlling little more than Afghanistan's capital. Security in Kabul rested in the hands of an international peacekeeping force—the International Security Assistance Force, or ISAF—composed of some four thousand troops that were initially under British command. Bush declined to let American forces participate in ISAF. The Pentagon insisted that asking American troops to assume peacekeeping responsibilities would interfere with ongoing combat operations. Then again, Bush had no intention of using American troops for peacekeeping or nation-building. "Look," Bush told his advisers on October 12, "I oppose using the military for nation-building. Once the job is done, our forces are not peacekeepers. We ought to put in place a UN protection and leave."[35] What's more, the administration opposed expanding ISAF's writ outside Kabul, believing that the best way to ensure security in the long run would be to create an Afghan national army. "If we rely on international forces to provide security throughout the country," Cheney asserted, "that's likely to delay getting on with the business of building an Afghan Army."[36] But building a new army—especially one willing and able to take on well-armed warlords—would take a decade or more. Four thousand Afghans were trained in the first year, but some quickly left the armed forces. What to do about security in the meantime? Washington did not have an answer.

Security was the central issue Lakhdar Brahimi raised when he briefed the UN Security Council on the situation in Afghanistan in May 2003. The lack of security "casts a long shadow over the whole peace process and, indeed, over the whole future of Afghanistan," Brahimi told the Council. Even eighteen months after the Taliban was routed, the security environment continued to deteriorate because of "daily harassment and intimidation, inter-ethnic and interfactional strife, increases in the activity of elements linked to the Taliban and to Gulbuddin Hekmatyar, and the drugs economy." Moreover, the "national security institutions are perceived by many Afghans, perhaps the majority, as not serving the broad national interests of all the people of Afghanistan."[37]

Brahimi's warning came only days after Rumsfeld, on a visit to Afghanistan, declared that it was now possible to move from the combat phase of military operations to the final, stabilization phase. Yet even as Rumsfeld made his announcement, Bush, speaking from the deck of the aircraft carrier USS *Abraham Lincoln*, noted that "a Special Operations task force, led by the 82nd Airborne, is on the trail of the terrorists and those who seek to undermine the free government of Afghanistan."[38] This war, it seemed, had not yet ended. And peace was still a long way off.

EIGHT

THE BUSH STRATEGY

T HE AFGHAN WAR enjoyed broad international support. A large coalition of countries offered troops, aircraft, naval vessels, and other forms of direct military assistance. After initially rejecting many offers of help, the Bush administration eventually accepted troop contributions from nearly twenty countries. Britain supplied special forces, and one of its cruise missiles was fired in the very first volley of the war. France contributed Mirage fighter jets that bombed al Qaeda concentrations during Operation Anaconda in the battle of Shar-e-Kot. Germany, Denmark, Australia, and others sent special forces. Key Gulf states offered bases from which to fly bombing and surveillance missions. Many more countries contributed intelligence and other information. Military contributions continued after the major fighting had ended. Twenty months after the fall of Kabul, half the foreign military forces in Afghanistan were from countries other than the United States. In August 2003 command of the international peacekeeping force in the Afghan capital formally shifted to NATO.

The widespread international willingness to participate in military operations reflected the legitimacy of America's cause in Afghanistan. After September 11, no country defended al Qaeda and its Taliban supporters, and nearly all accepted America's inherent right of self-defense in striking back against those who had attacked it. But most who supported the United States in the Afghan War and its aftermath believed that military action would end there. "I am quite confident that I have understood the U.S. government correctly," a senior west European diplomat told the *Washington Post* in October 2001. "The United States government has told us at very high levels that what the president has said is . . . what we're working on: al Qaeda, bin Laden and terrorism. Full stop."[1] As a result, there was an expectation that after its success in Afghanistan, Washington would turn its attention to longer-term strategies designed to bring to justice those who had escaped and to prevent future attacks like those of September 11. In other words, many expected that the focus would now shift from overt military operations to more covert law enforcement activities.

But just as many countries had been proved wrong in their belief that U.S. foreign policy after September 11 would shift in a multilateralist direction, so they were now proved wrong in their belief (and hope) that the president's Afghanistan-first strategy was an Afghanistan-only strategy. George W. Bush had made clear from the outset that the United States was engaged in a broader enterprise—and he was not the kind of person to change his mind. "Our war on terror begins with al Qaeda," the president had declared on September 20, "but it does not end there. It will not end until every terrorist group of global reach has been found, stopped and defeated."[2] On the same day that the first bombs fell on Afghanistan, John Negroponte, Bush's ambassador to the United Nations, informed his colleagues that "further actions with respect to other organizations and other States" might be necessary.[3] However, the extent of Bush's commitment to take the war on terrorism further became clear only after the war in Afghanistan had achieved its initial successes.

EVEN AS THE fighting in Afghanistan got under way, many inside and outside the administration considered what would come next. There were many candidates for what quickly became known as Phase Two of the war on terror. Iraq was by far and away the first choice. Even after suffering a major defeat in the Gulf War and enduring twelve years of sanctions, Saddam Hussein remained defiant in the face of demands to end his quest for nuclear, chemical, and biological weapons. Other possible targets were the failing or failed states that might house al Qaeda and other terrorist cells now that the Afghan sanctuary had been eliminated. Somalia, the Sudan, Yemen, Georgia, and the Philippines were often mentioned, and in some instances Washington dispatched Special Forces to help train local armies in antiterror operations. Then there were other major terrorist groups—such as Hezbollah, Hamas, and Islamic Jihad—and their supporters in Tehran and Damascus.

While the debate raged about who or what would be next, weapons of mass destruction emerged as a major consideration. Dick Cheney, above all, worried that another, far more lethal terrorist attack using radiological, biological, or even nuclear weapons was possible. Sitting in the presidential bunker deep beneath the White House in the hours after the attacks on New York and Washington, he observed that "as unfathomable as this was, it could have been so much worse if they had weapons of mass destruction."[4] It was well known that al Qaeda had sought access to such weapons, and Cheney and others worried that rogue states might be a ready source of material and other assistance.

Three weeks after the September 11 attacks, Cheney's worst fears appeared to come true. On October 5, Robert Stevens, an editor at the *Sun*, a weekly supermarket tabloid in Boca Raton, Florida, died of inhalation anthrax. It was the first reported case of anthrax in the United States since 1976 and one of only eighteen cases in the previous century. What at first appeared to have been a fluke exposure during a hiking trip in North Carolina soon took a sinister turn. Anthrax spores were found in the *Sun's* editorial office. Over the next two weeks envelopes containing a sophisticated form of anthrax were received by news organizations and the offices of two Democratic senators. The anthrax mailings, which ultimately infected nineteen people with the disease and killed five of them, demonstrated the ease with which a highly lethal attack could be launched. The resulting panic and the extraordinary expense of cleaning up the sites in which anthrax spores were found also underscored that a small-scale biological attack, even if it failed to kill many people, could paralyze the country.

As if the anthrax mailings were not enough, by late October U.S. intelligence was also picking up rumors of another terrorist attack, this one possibly involving a so-called dirty bomb, radiological material wrapped around a conventional explosive. Although a dirty bomb would be nowhere near as lethal as a nuclear bomb, it could release significant amounts of radiation into the air. Depending on the amount and type of radiological material involved, a dirty bomb could contaminate a large part of a major city and create wholesale panic. Such an attack, Condoleezza Rice said, would "make Sept. 11 look like child's play."[5]

Where would al Qaeda get these materials? When George Tenet briefed the president on the threat in the last week of October, he noted that Iraq topped the list of countries malicious enough to help al Qaeda achieve its goal of acquiring radiological or other weapons of mass destruction. Even though the available intelligence constituted what one knowledgeable source called an "incomplete mosaic" of fact, inference, and potentially false leads, Tenet's briefing "sent the president through the roof."[6] That much became evident when a group of former White House press secretaries gathered in the White House mess just after Thanksgiving at the invitation of Bush's spokesman, Ari Fleischer. The president stopped by and spent fifteen minutes impressing on all of them the dire nature of the threat. Many left the luncheon far more worried about nuclear terrorism than when they had come.

Bush ordered his war council to give nuclear terrorism priority over every other threat to the United States. Hundreds of sophisticated sensors were deployed at U.S. border crossings and transportation choke points around Washington. A Delta Force team was put on standby alert to seize any materials the sensors might detect. But these preventive steps constituted only a passing response to what the administration saw as a serious, long-term danger. These terrorist groups "are seeking chemical, biological and nuclear weapons," Bush warned delegates at an international conference on combating terrorism in November 2001. "Given the means, our enemies would be a threat to every nation and, eventually, to civilization itself. So we're determined to fight this evil, and fight until we're rid of it." That determination would include striking first: "We will not wait for the authors of mass murder to gain the weapons of mass destruction. We act now, because we must lift this dark threat from our age and save generations to come."[7] This last statement foreshadowed what would soon become a distinguishing feature of Bush's foreign policy revolution—the willingness to strike before rather than just in response to an attack.

THE FULL EXTENT of Bush's war on terror became apparent when he delivered his first State of the Union address in January 2002. "A terrorist underworld—including groups like Hamas, Hezbollah, Islamic Jihad, Jaish-i-Mohammed—operates in remote jungles and deserts, and hides in the centers of large cities," Bush told Congress and the nation. But that was not all. The threat facing the United States extended beyond these terrorist groups to rogue states such as Iran, Iraq, and North Korea that were bent on acquiring weapons of mass destruction. "States like these, and their terrorist allies, constitute an axis of evil," Bush warned. "By seeking weapons of mass destruction, these regimes pose a grave and growing danger. They could provide these arms to terrorists, giving them the means to match their hatred. They could attack our allies or attempt to blackmail the United States. In any of these cases, the price of indifference would be catastrophic."

Then, using the most dire language heard in any presidential speech since John F. Kennedy's first State of the Union address four decades earlier, Bush declared that the United States could no longer afford to sit and wait until America was struck again. "Time is not on our side. I will not wait on events, while dangers gather. I will not stand by, as peril draws closer and closer. The United States of America will not permit the world's most dangerous regimes to threaten us with the world's most destructive weapons."[8]

The importance of Bush's address lay in clearly identifying a major new threat to the United States—the combination of terrorism, tyrants, and technologies of mass destruction. This new threat was considerably broader in scope than the terrorist groups with global reach that had been the main preoccupation of the antiterror coalition Bush had assembled immediately after September 11. Yet in highlighting this threat, Bush said nothing about how he proposed to defeat this trinity of evil. The principal elements of a strategy for dealing with the new threat emerged only in the days, weeks, and months following his speech.

The key elements of this emerging strategy, which reflected the administration's hegemonist worldview, were American power and leadership, a focus on rogue states, and the need to act preemptively. A few weeks after Bush's axis of evil speech, Cheney made clear that responsibility for meeting this threat lay squarely on America's shoulders. "America has friends and allies in this cause," the vice president told a packed gathering at the Council on Foreign Relations, "but only we can lead it. Only we can rally the world in a task of this complexity, against an enemy so elusive and so resourceful. The United States, and only the United States, can see this effort through to victory. This responsibility did not come to us by chance. We are in a unique position because of our unique assets—because of the character of our people, the strength of our ideals, the might of our military, and the enormous economy that supports it."[9]

The concern that terrorists might acquire weapons of mass destruction led the administration to focus on the states that were able and willing to help terrorists get hold of these technologies. Echoing Bush's warning about the axis of evil, Cheney promised that "we will work to prevent regimes that sponsor terror from threatening America or our friends and allies with chemical, biological or nuclear weapons—or allowing them to provide those weapons to terrorists."[10] Donald Rumsfeld left little doubt about how this goal was to be accomplished. "Defending against terrorism and other emerging 21st century threats may well require that we take the war to the enemy," he told the faculty and students at the National Defense University days after the president's axis of evil speech. "The best, and in some cases, the only defense, is a good offense."[11]

The administration pulled the main strands of its emerging strategy together in time for Bush's commencement address at West Point on June 1, 2002. Calling for new thinking to match new threats, the commander in chief told the newest generation of soldiers that the old cold war doctrines of deterrence and containment were no longer a sufficient basis for defending America. "Deterrence—the promise of massive retaliation against nations—means nothing against shadowy terrorist networks with no nation or citizens to defend. Containment is not possible when unbalanced dictators with weapons of mass destruction can deliver those weapons on missiles or secretly provide them to terrorist allies." The United States could not rely on treaties signed by tyrants. And while homeland and missile defense were clear priorities, "the war on terror will not be won on the defensive." Instead, Bush proclaimed that "we must take the battle to the enemy, disrupt his plans, and confront the worst threats before they emerge. In the world we have entered, the only path to safety is the path of action. And this nation will act." Ultimately, Bush concluded, the nation's "security will require all Americans to be forward-looking and resolute, to be ready for preemptive action when necessary to defend our liberty and to defend our lives."[12]

Bush's enunciation of what he later termed the "new doctrine called preemption" represented a major departure for American foreign policy.[13] Of course, as Colin Powell noted, the United States always had the option of using force preemptively, and there were times it even had done so.[14] But never before had a president made the case for preemption in principle, let alone in public. Following the speech, Rice tried to downplay its significance by suggesting that the concept of preemption "really means early action of some kind," and included such traditional tools as forging diplomatic coalitions among great powers. As an example of nonmilitary forms of preemption, Rice cited the Kennedy administration's decision to stop Soviet ships from reaching Cuba during the 1962 missile crisis. "They settled on a strategy that actually was pre-emptive, but didn't use military force to do it, and thereby preserved the possibility for the Soviets to back down."[15] Of course, Kennedy had opted for a blockade rather than the much more dangerous option of preemptively attacking the nuclear missiles in Cuba. Moreover, Moscow's decision to back down came only after Kennedy agreed in secret negotiations to remove U.S. missiles from Turkey after the Soviet missiles in Cuba had been dismantled.

THE FULLEST ELABORATION of Bush's strategy for defeating the terrifying combination of terrorism, tyrants, and technologies of mass destruction came in the *National Security Strategy*, a document that the White House issued annually at the behest of Congress. Bush released the strategy on september 20, 2002, just as the domestic and international debate on Iraq was heating up. The document, written in plain English so that, as Bush told his staff, "the boys in Lubbock" could read it, was the most comprehensive statement of the administration's foreign policy.[16]

Consistent with its hegemonist worldview, the administration put American power at the center of its strategy. That power derived from a combination of America's "unparalleled military strength" and its embodiment of freedom and democracy. "The great struggles of the twentieth century between liberty and totalitarianism ended with a decisive victory for the forces of freedom," Bush wrote in the introduction to the strategy. "In keeping with our heritage and principles, we do not use our strength to press for unilateral advantage." Instead, the goal of American power was to help make the world safe for freedom to flourish. "We will defend the peace by fighting terrorists and tyrants. We will preserve the peace by building good relations among the great powers. We will extend the peace by encouraging free and open societies on every continent." The essence of the Bush strategy, therefore, was to use America's unprecedented power to remake the world in America's image.

Achieving this goal required removing the obstacles and threats to liberty and freedom that existed throughout the world—"to create a balance of power that favors human freedom," as Bush put it. To foster "conditions in which all nations and all societies can choose for themselves the rewards and challenges of political and economic liberty," it was necessary to create conditions that would enable people everywhere to choose freedom, democracy, and free enterprise. The primary obstacle to people making that choice, the administration argued, "lies at the crossroads of radicalism and technology," where terrorists and tyrants were determined to acquire technologies of mass destruction. "The United States will not allow these efforts to succeed. We will build defenses against ballistic missiles and other means of delivery. We will cooperate with other nations to deny, contain, and curtail our enemies' efforts to acquire dangerous technologies. And, as a matter of common sense and self-defense, America will act against such emerging threats before they are fully formed." While Washington "will constantly strive to enlist the support of the international community, we will not hesitate to act alone, if necessary, to exercise our right of self-defense by acting preemptively" against the threat confronting the nation and, indeed, the world. "We must be prepared to stop rogue states and their terrorist clients before they are able to threaten or use weapons of mass destruction against the United States and our allies and friends."

The administration pointed out that after September 11 there could be no doubt that terrorists and the rogue states that supported them would stop at nothing in their attempts to strike America again. "Today, our enemies see weapons of mass destruction as weapons of choice. For rogue states these weapons are tools of intimidation and military aggression against their neighbors." Such weapons could enable them "to blackmail the United States and our allies to prevent us from deterring or repelling the aggressive behavior of rogue states." Deterrence by threatening retaliation would be less likely to work "against leaders of rogue states more willing to take risks, gambling with the lives of their people, and the wealth of their nations." And, of course, "deterrence will not work against a terrorist enemy whose avowed tactics are wanton destruction and the targeting of innocents."

This is why America might have to act preemptively, the strategy stated. "The United States has long maintained the option of preemptive actions to counter a sufficient threat to our national security. The greater the threat, the greater is the risk of inaction—and the more compelling the case for taking anticipatory action to defend ourselves, even if uncertainty remains as to the time and place of the enemy's attack. To forestall or prevent such hostile acts by our adversaries, the United States will, if necessary, act preemptively." The administration argued that a strong legal case could be made for preemption under these circumstances. "Legal scholars and international jurists often conditioned the legitimacy of preemption on the existence of an imminent threat—most often a visible mobilization of armies, navies, and air forces preparing to attack. We must adapt the concept of imminent threat to the capabilities and objectives of today's adversaries. Rogue states and terrorists do not seek to attack us using conventional means." Of course, force would not have to be used "in all cases to preempt emerging threats, nor should nations use preemption as a pretext for aggression. Yet in an age where the enemies of civilization openly and actively seek the world's most destructive technologies, the United States cannot remain idle while dangers gather."

Once the grave threat to liberty had been eliminated, it would be possible to extend the peace to every corner of the globe. This, indeed, was both a strategic and a moral imperative. Strategically, "the events of September 11, 2001, taught us that weak states, like Afghanistan, can pose as great a danger to our national interests as strong states. Poverty does not make poor people into terrorists and murderers. Yet poverty, weak institutions, and corruption can make weak states vulnerable to terrorist networks and drug cartels within their borders." Morally, the poverty that gripped much of the world offended American values. "A world where some live in comfort and plenty, while half of the human race lives on less than $2 a day, is neither just nor stable."

For all its focus on ways to extend the peace, the core of the Bush strategy was defeating the enemies of freedom. Not only did terrorists and tyrants most threaten the security of America and the world, but the strategy held that the core values of freedom, democracy, and free enterprise would triumph once these threats had been eliminated. "Americans," Bush told the nation in his 2003 State of the Union address, "are a free people, who know that freedom is the right of every person and the future of every nation. The liberty we prize is not America's gift to the world, it is God's gift to humanity."[17] At the very core of the Bush strategy, then, was a deeply American assumption about people all over the world—that given the chance, people everywhere would make the same choice Americans had made since gaining independence more than two hundred years ago: they would embrace freedom, democracy, and free enterprise.

THE BUSH STRATEGY represented a profound strategic innovation—less in its goals than in the way Bush proposed to achieve them. That was why the doctrine of preemption became the focal point of discussions about the strategy at home and abroad. After all, Bush effectively abandoned a decades-long consensus that put deterrence and containment at the heart of American foreign policy. "After September the 11th, the doctrine of containment just doesn't hold any water, as far as I'm concerned," Bush explained in early 2003.[18] Powell, Rice, and other officials subsequently tried to downplay the centrality of preemption. Powell argued, "There is no such strategy of pre-emption. There is an option called pre-emption that fills a couple of paragraphs in a 31-page national security document."[19] Rice insisted that the "number of cases in which it might be justified will always be small."[20] For Bush, however, preemption was not a mere option, but what *New York Times* reporter Michael Gordon called "a cardinal principle" of his foreign policy.[21] Otherwise, why call it a doctrine as the president did? Why give presidential speeches about it and place it at the heart of a public national strategy document?

Critics leveled four complaints against the preemption doctrine. First, many questioned why the administration had decided to make a public statement about something that had long been an option of U.S. policy and, in some instances, an actual policy. "It is not clear to me what advantage there is in declaring it publicly," said Brent Scowcroft, national security adviser during the Ford and first Bush administrations. "It has been common knowledge that under some circumstances the U.S. would preempt. As a declaratory policy it tends to leave the door open to others who want to claim the same right. By making it public we also tend to add to the world's perception that we are arrogant and unilateral."[22] In other words, there was much to lose and little to gain by making the doctrine public—or even turning an option into a policy.

Scowcroft's comment touched on a second objection to the preemption argument: countries would use it as a cover for settling their own national security scores. Days after the strategy's publication, Russia hinted that it might have to intervene in Georgia to go after Islamic terrorists allegedly hiding in the Pankisi Gorge. India embraced preemption as a universal doctrine. "Every nation has that right," Finance Minister Jaswant Singh said on a visit to Washington days after the strategy's publication. "It is not the prerogative of any one country. Preemption is the right of any nation to prevent injury to itself."[23] But, as Henry Kissinger argued, "it cannot be in either the American national interest or the world's interest to develop principles that grant every nation an unfettered right of preemption against its own definition of threats to its security."[24] The strategy recognized this problem by warning nations not to "use preemption as a pretext for aggression." But the administration did not identify what separated justifiable preemption from unlawful aggression. Without a bright line that could gain widespread adherence abroad, the administration ran the risk that its words would be used to justify ends it opposed.

Third, critics argued that the Bush strategy suffered from considerable conceptual confusion, which had real policy consequences. Most important, it conflated the notion of preemptive and preventive war. *Preemptive* wars are initiated when another country is clearly about to attack. Israel's decision to go to war in June 1967 against its Arab neighbors is the classic example. *Preventive* wars are launched by states against others before the state being attacked poses a real or imminent threat. "What made war inevitable," the ancient Greek historian Thucydides wrote about the Peloponnesian War, "was the growth in Athenian power and the fear this caused in Sparta."[25] The purpose of initiating war in these circumstances is therefore to stop a threat before it can arise. Israel's strike against Iraq's Osirak reactor in 1981 was one example of preventive war. Cheney's argument that Iraq needed to be struck before it acquired nuclear weapons was another.[26] Much of the Bush rhetoric—including the justification for the Iraq War—was consistent with the notion of preventive war, not preemption. Yet, while preemptive wars have had a long-recognized standing in international law as a legitimate form of self-defense, preventive wars did not. Not surprisingly, a resort to preventive war in the case of Iraq would prove highly controversial.

Finally, critics of the preemption doctrine raised significant practical concerns. "A military response poses other problems," Senators Joe Biden and Dick Lugar argued in July 2002, warning the White House not to move precipitously against Iraq. "By attacking Mr. Hussein, we might precipitate the very thing we are trying to prevent: his use of weapons of mass destruction."[27] This was an assessment the intelligence community shared. In an October 2002 letter to Congress, Tenet argued that while "Baghdad for now appears to be drawing a line short of conducting terrorist attacks with conventional or chemical and biological weapons against the United States. Should Saddam conclude that a U.S.-led attack could no longer be deterred, he probably would become much less constrained."[28] A month later, the Defense Intelligence Agency concluded that Saddam would use chemical weapons only if "regime survival was imminently threatened."[29]

FOR ALL THE criticism of the Bush strategy's core innovation, the real debate was to be a practical one about Iraq rather than a doctrinal one about preemption. In part this reflected the fact that the rhetoric surrounding the doctrine, notwithstanding, Iraq was the driving force behind its promulgation. For all the talk about an axis of evil, it was clear that at least initially the focus would be squarely on Baghdad. Just two weeks after the president warned about the axis, Powell told Congress, "There is no plan to start a war with these nations," referring to Iran and North Korea. "We want to see a dialogue. We want to contain North Korea's activities with respect to proliferation, and we are going to keep the pressure on them. But there is no plan to begin a war with North Korea; nor is there a plan to begin a conflict with Iran."[30] But neither Powell nor any other official had anything reassuring to say about Iraq. On the contrary, the administration left no doubt that it wanted Saddam Hussein gone—and sooner rather than later.

NINE

The Inevitable
Showdown

H AD TERRORISTS NOT attacked America on September 11, Iraq would likely have remained a secondary issue in American foreign policy. Before the attacks, the Bush administration had sought to strengthen the containment of Saddam Hussein through the adoption of so-called smart sanctions, which focused on preventing Iraq from importing military goods while relaxing restrictions on trade more generally. Colin Powell went as far as to claim the policy a success. "We have kept him contained, kept him in his box," he said following his first tour as secretary of state around the Middle East.[1] That was not the view of many other senior officials in the administration, but few of them cared enough to force a major change in policy during the months before the terrorists struck. During this period, George Tenet worried about stateless terrorism, Donald Rumsfeld focused on military transformation and missile defense, Dick Cheney was preoccupied with energy and other domestic issues, and Condoleezza Rice concentrated on relations with Russia.

The only senior official deeply concerned about Iraq before September 11 was Paul Wolfowitz. Wolfowitz's alarm about Iraq went back more than two decades. As a policy planner in the Carter Pentagon, he and a small team of analysts drafted a report on security threats in the Persian Gulf that first warned about the potential danger Iraq's outsized military posed to Kuwait and Saudi Arabia. By the time of the

Gulf War, Wolfowitz was the third-ranking civilian at Defense. He believed it was a mistake for the United States to have left Saddam in power. He strongly opposed allowing Saddam's forces to brutally suppress the Shiite uprising in the south, when hundreds of thousands of U.S. troops stood by just across the border. Throughout the 1990s Wolfowitz forcefully advocated a policy aimed at ousting Saddam. He believed this could be accomplished by arming and training opposition forces, backed, if necessary, by U.S. airpower. He was supported in this view by a number of other democratic imperialists, including Richard Perle, James Woolsey, William Kristol, and Robert Kagan.[2] Yet, for all the intellectual power behind this effort, it gained little traction in the first months of Bush's tenure.

All that changed after September 11. Within minutes of the attack, Wolfowitz told aides he thought Saddam Hussein was behind the strikes. Bush echoed this view. "I believe Iraq was involved," he told his war council on September 17.[3] After the attacks, many in the administration became more open to arguments about the need to move swiftly against Saddam's regime. "Dick Cheney," Wolfowitz later told *Time*, "is someone whose view of the need to get rid of Saddam Hussein was transformed by Sept. 11—by the recognition of the danger posed by the connection between terrorists and WMDs [weapons of mass destruction] and by the growing evidence of links between Iraq and al-Qaeda."[4] Soon after the attacks, Cheney immersed himself in a study of Islam and the Middle East, meeting with scholars such as Bernard Lewis and Fouad Ajami who argued that toppling Saddam would send a message of strength and enhance America's credibility throughout the Muslim world. And, of course, the attacks had a major impact on the president. "The strategic vision of our country shifted dramatically," Bush later explained, "because we now recognize that oceans no longer protect us, that we're vulnerable to attack."[5]

In the weeks immediately after the attack, the administration's attention remained focused squarely on Afghanistan and Osama bin Laden. "We ha[d] a lot of business on our plate," recalled Stephen Hadley, Bush's deputy national security adviser. There was no time to address Iraq "in any systematic way."[6] But once the Taliban was ousted from power, attention swiftly turned to Iraq. Long-standing advocates of toppling Saddam pointed to the ease of the Afghan victory to underscore the likelihood of swift success in Iraq. "There must be a Phase 2," Richard Perle argued in mid-November 2001. "At the top of the list for Phase 2 is Iraq."[7] Bush, too, began to talk about Saddam. "The leader of Iraq is an evil man," Bush reminded Americans in October. "We're watching him carefully."[8] Six weeks later, Bush escalated his rhetoric. Saddam "ought to let the inspectors back in," the president declared in reference to the long-standing UN demand that Iraq give up all its weapons of mass destruction and allow UN inspectors to verify their absence. Then, when asked what would happen if Saddam continued to refuse, Bush made a veiled threat: "He'll find out."[9]

Even as Bush publicly insisted on resuming inspections in Iraq, he was privately gearing up for a confrontation with Saddam. In December 2001, Bush met with General Tommy Franks to discuss military options for Iraq during a meeting that was originally meant to go over military developments in Afghanistan.[10] That same month, David Frum, one of Bush's speechwriters, was told to begin drafting a justification for war against Iraq for the president's State of the Union address the next month.[11]

By the new year, Bush publicly expressed what he had privately concluded—that nothing short of Saddam's ouster would suffice. In his axis of evil speech, Bush raised the importance of confronting the rogue state threat. Immediately after the speech, Bush directed the Pentagon and the CIA to start planning for Saddam's overthrow. The CIA was given between $100 million and $200 million in new funding for covert activities against Saddam's regime. The Pentagon was told to begin planning for an invasion, possibly as early as late summer.[12]

Public diplomacy soon complemented the covert activities against Iraq, with senior administration officials taking to the airwaves to make the case for regime change. On a Sunday in mid-February, Condoleezza Rice and Colin Powell blanketed the morning talk shows. Rice argued on CBS's *Face the Nation* that "the world will be much safer when the Iraqi people have a regime that they deserve, instead of the regime that they have. It is hard to imagine Saddam Hussein ever doing the kinds of things that he needs to do to make others feel secure around him."[13] Powell made the case for inspections, but added that their resumption would not be enough to satisfy the United States. "Even then," Powell told CNN's *Late Edition*, "the United States believes the Iraqi people would still be better off with a new kind of leadership that is not trying to hide this sort of development activity on weapons of mass destruction and is not of the despotic nature that the Saddam Hussein regime is."[14] By March 2002, then, there was little doubt where the Bush administration stood on Iraq.

"FUCK SADDAM. We're taking him out," Bush told Rice as he poked his head in her White House corner office in early March as she was meeting with three senators to discuss what to do about Iraq.[15] The president's determination could not have been clearer. But while the goal of regime change in Iraq was widely shared within the administration, and indeed beyond, there were significant differences over how to achieve it. Much of 2002 was given over to this debate, which pitted the administration's hawks, led by Cheney and Rumsfeld, against its doves, principally Powell.

From the outset, the hawks argued that military force would be necessary to overthrow Saddam's regime. They reached this conclusion not only because they were convinced Saddam could never be forced to change his ways, but also because they thought his ouster could be accomplished with relative ease. Flush from victory in Afghanistan, the hawks contended that the combination of precision airpower, local opposition forces supported by U.S. Special Forces, and a relatively small number of American ground troops would suffice to force Saddam from power. As Kenneth Adelman, one of many hawks on the Defense Policy Board, an informal advisory council to Rumsfeld, argued, "Demolishing Hussein's military power and liberating Iraq would be a cakewalk. Let me give simple, responsible reasons: (1) It was a cakewalk last time; (2) they've become much weaker; (3) we've become much stronger; and (4) now we're playing for keeps."[16] Though few inside the administration were prepared to go as far as Adelman and others in predicting that war against Iraq would be a "cakewalk," Rumsfeld and many Pentagon civilians were convinced that the advances in American technology and novel strategies would enable the American military to achieve a swift military victory with far fewer troops than many traditionalists believed necessary.

Powell and Tenet had a different view. Tenet worried that a war in Iraq would stimulate more terrorism and could even lead Saddam to hand over some of his weapons to terrorist organizations. Both concerns were highlighted in the National Intelligence Estimate on Iraq, which explained the intelligence community's assessment and was completed in October 2002. Powell was concerned about underestimating the difficulties of a military operation against Saddam. He had strongly supported the decision by the elder Bush to end the Gulf War well short of Baghdad, fearing that a war to oust the Iraqi strongman would, as he later recalled, have fractured the international coalition and fragmented Iraq into separate ethnic entities, outcomes that would have undermined regional stability.[17] And even after September 11 and the swift ouster of the Taliban, the former chairman of the joint chiefs of staff doubted the military efficacy of overthrowing the regime in Baghdad. "With respect to what is sometimes characterized as taking out Saddam," Powell told the *New York Times* in November 2001, "I never saw a plan that was going to take him out. It was just some ideas coming from various quarters about, Let's go bomb."[18] Instead of bombing, Powell believed containment was the best way to force regime change. Armed with a credible threat to use force and backed by a united international community, Powell maintained that Baghdad could be forced to hand over its weapons of mass destruction. That would significantly lessen the threat to American security and might ultimately weaken Saddam sufficiently to ensure his overthrow by Iraqis. This containment strategy was also supported by the U.S. military, which, like Powell, feared the common tendency of hawks, especially those who had never served in uniform, to overestimate the efficacy of military power.

Like every debate about the use of force in the previous three decades, the Iraq debate reflected the deep divisions that the Vietnam War left on the American psyche. The men who had done the fighting (and who had seen many of their friends dying) were deeply leery about military interventions of any kind—especially when the political objective was not just to defeat a military enemy, but to change an entire regime. With two tours of duty in Vietnam, Powell was this camp's standard-bearer. An entire doctrine on the use (and nonuse) of force bore his name—and reflected the Army's commitment never to repeat the Vietnam experience.

But the Powell Doctrine of using force only as a last resort, only for clearly vital interests, and then only decisively to achieve clear military objectives, was anathema to the hawks. To them, this cautious approach to using power reflected everything that had gone wrong with American foreign policy. The post-Vietnam retreat from the "imperial presidency," the reluctance to use force or engage in daring covert action, the subservience of American policy to domestic politics—all this had created a global perception of American weakness rather than strength. Cheney, Rumsfeld, and others were determined to reverse the trend. Even in his first conversation with Bush about becoming secretary of defense, Rumsfeld had urged that the president take a "forward leaning" approach to the use of force if the opportunity were to arise. Iraq offered an opportunity to finish what success in Afghanistan had started—to exorcise the ghosts of Vietnam once and for all.

ALTHOUGH IRAQ WAS destined to be a target of action, debate over how to cope with the growing violence between Israel and the Palestinians absorbed the administration's energies during the first half of 2002. Ever the diplomat, Powell wanted the administration to pursue a vigorous mediating role. Bush feared he would get sucked in and lose control of the situation. Many administration officials regarded past U.S. mediation efforts as little more than a fool's errand; some even believed Clinton's immersion in the peace process during his last year in office had only made matters worse. "I think if you go back to when the violence began," Ari Fleischer said in February 2002, "you can make the case that in an attempt to shoot the moon and get nothing, more violence resulted."[19] Yet doing nothing also had its costs, as Cheney found out when he traveled to the region in March. Originally intending to enlist Arab support for confronting Saddam, Cheney discovered that no Arab leader had any interest in talking about Iraq. All of them wanted to know what Washington proposed to do about the escalating violence, which dominated TV screens across the Arab world. The vice president returned from his eleven-day, ten-country tour convinced that the administration needed to address the escalating conflict between Israel and the Palestinians before moving on to Baghdad.

For months the administration debated what to do as terrible scenes of suicide bombings and Israeli reprisals dominated the headlines. Cheney and Rumsfeld argued that in the post–September 11 climate, the United States had to stand squarely behind an Israeli government combating terrorist bombers. Powell believed that the violence would not end until its underlying causes were addressed—and that required active U.S. diplomatic involvement. Initially, Bush sided with Powell. In April he sent his secretary of state to the Middle East and, while condemning terrorism in no uncertain terms, he called on Israel to pull back its forces from West Bank cities "without delay."[20] Israeli prime minister Ariel Sharon was not about to pull his forces back as long as terrorism continued, however. So Bush tacked the other way. In late June, he announced that any further American participation in the peace process would be possible only after the Palestinians had chosen a new leadership "not compromised by terror."[21] Arafat had to go. Nothing could be done until that had happened.

The months of debate about the Middle East had left the administration's Iraq policy adrift. There had been no follow-up to Bush's decision that Saddam had to be taken out. Even many of the administration's senior officials were in the dark. When Richard Haass, Powell's close confidant, met with Rice in July in one of their regular meetings, he wondered whether Iraq really should be front and center in the administration's foreign policy. "That decision's been made, don't waste your breath," Haass recalled Rice's saying.[22] Yet, aside from military planning, which had in one form or another been going on since mid-September 2001, the policy process on Iraq was at a standstill.

That process finally got under way in July. During a series of secretive meetings among Bush's top advisers, which appeared as "Regional Strategies Meeting" on the private schedules of the participants so as to hide their true nature, the administration began to tackle a host of critical questions.[23] What role, if any, should there be for the United Nations, which for the past twelve years had dominated Iraq policy? Should resumption of weapons inspections be a goal? What could key allies contribute? What were the military options for removing Saddam? What would come after his ouster? Should Congress be asked to authorize the use of force? The idea was to use the summer months to hash out these and other questions and to begin a rollout of Bush's policy after Labor Day. Nothing much could be done publicly because, as Karl Rove noted, "in August the president is sort of on vacation." Moreover, said Andrew Card, "from a marketing point of view, you don't introduce new products in August."[24]

However, maintaining an orderly, politically sensitive process is not the same as agreeing how to launch a new product—especially when the "product" is a major war thousands of miles from home. There were deep differences within the administration on how to proceed, with Powell and Cheney representing the competing poles in the debate. Powell, who had done yeoman's work pulling together a large and broad antiterror coalition, wanted "something approaching that level of support if we were going to do Iraq."[25] During a two-hour private dinner with Bush in early August, Powell argued that Bush should go the United Nations and seek international backing for a vigorous weapons inspection regime. The president should consider using force only if Baghdad refused to turn over its weapons of mass destruction, as demanded by sixteen successive Security Council resolutions.[26] Cheney, in contrast, feared that the UN route would once again open up the inspection trap, in which Saddam would give the weapons inspectors just enough to undermine efforts to gain international support for military action. In any case, the vice president argued, international support was not critical. "The fact of the matter is for most of the others who are engaged in this debate, they don't have the capability to do anything about it anyway."[27] Moreover, Cheney had no doubt that in the long run, after Saddam had been successfully ousted, "a good part of the world, especially our allies, will come around to our way of thinking."[28]

This internal debate burst into public view during what Powell recalled was far more "exciting an August" than he had anticipated.[29] On Capitol Hill, the Senate Foreign Relations Committee held a series of hearings that proved unexpectedly critical of a possible war against Iraq—with leading Republican members among those who questioned the wisdom of acting precipitously. Also chiming in was House Republican Majority Leader Dick Armey, who argued that it was unbecoming of America's great tradition to attack another country without provocation. "I don't believe that America will justifiably make an unprovoked attack on another nation," Armey told reporters in early August. "It would not be consistent with what we have been as a nation or what we should be as a nation." Asked what America should do about the threat Saddam posed, he said: "My own view would be to let him bluster, let him rant and rave all he wants and let that be a matter between he and his own country. As long as he behaves himself within his own borders, we should not be addressing any attack or resources against him."[30]

But the most unexpected criticism came from a number of high-ranking officials in previous Republican administrations, some no doubt encouraged by protagonists inside the administration, all of whom argued strongly for seeking a broad international coalition to support action against Iraq. James Baker, the elder Bush's close friend and his first secretary of state, argued that the president should go to the United Nations and seek another resolution in support of squeezing Saddam.[31] Henry Kissinger, while supporting the need for action against Iraq, maintained that in order to gain international support, "the objective of regime change should be subordinated in American declaratory policy to the need to eliminate weapons of mass destruction from Iraq as required by the U.N. resolutions."[32] Brent Scowcroft, the senior Bush's former national security adviser and the coauthor of his memoirs, went further. He argued that "an attack on Iraq at this time would seriously jeopardize, if not destroy, the global counterterrorist campaign we have undertaken."[33] Lawrence Eagleburger, who had replaced Baker as secretary of state, took the same position.[34]

The escalating opposition to war against Iraq from prominent Republicans left the administration's pro-war camp reeling. But not for long. In a major speech in late August before the Veterans of Foreign Wars, Cheney made the most detailed and powerful case yet for taking action against Iraq. He warned that the problem was not just that Saddam Hussein possessed chemical and biological weapons and was ready to use them. The threat was more dire still. "Many of us are convinced that Saddam will acquire nuclear weapons fairly soon," Cheney warned. "Just how soon, we cannot really gauge. Intelligence is an uncertain business, even in the best of circumstances." But the consequences of Saddam's succeeding would be grave:

Armed with an arsenal of these weapons of terror, and seated atop ten percent of the world's oil reserves, Saddam Hussein could then be expected to seek domination of the entire Middle East, take control of a great portion of the world's energy supplies, directly threaten America's friends throughout the region, and subject the United States or any other nation to nuclear blackmail. Simply stated, there is no doubt that Saddam Hussein now has weapons of mass destruction. There is no doubt he is amassing them to use against our friends, against our allies, and against us. And there is no doubt that his aggressive regional ambitions will lead him into future confrontations with his neighbors—confrontations that will involve both the weapons he has today, and the ones he will continue to develop with his oil wealth.

The answer to this threat could not be weapons inspections of uncertain effectiveness, Cheney continued. "A person would be right to question any suggestion that we should just get inspectors back into Iraq, and then our worries will be over. Saddam has perfected the game of cheat and retreat, and is very skilled in the art of denial and deception. A return of inspectors would provide no assurance whatsoever of his compliance with UN resolutions. On the contrary, there is a great danger that it would provide false comfort that Saddam was somehow 'back in his box.'"[35]

Cheney's speech elicited just the reaction he had intended. It caused an uproar all over Europe—accelerating German chancellor Gerhard Schröder's decision to make opposition to America's Iraq policy the centerpiece of his reelection campaign and leading French president Jacques Chirac to condemn "attempts to legitimize the unilateral and preemptive use of force."[36] More important, Cheney's speech blindsided Powell, who was then on vacation in the Hamptons. Bob Woodward recorded Powell's reaction when he read the front-page headline "Cheney Says Peril of Nuclear Iraq Justifies Attack" in the next day's *New York Times*. "Powell was astonished. It seemed like a preemptive attack" on the policy process.[37] Ten days earlier, Powell, Cheney, and the president's other top advisers had met with Bush and unanimously agreed to take the Iraq issue to the United Nations. Cheney's swipe at inspections was also contrary to Bush's year-long insistence that inspectors should return to Iraq, a point Powell himself had made publicly in a prerecorded BBC interview days earlier. "The president has been clear that he believes weapons inspectors should return," he had told David Frost. "Iraq has been in violation of many UN resolutions for most of the last 11 or so years. And so, as a first step, let's see what the inspectors find."[38]

With the internal debate now public, Bush was forced to choose. This he did in early September, when he essentially decided to take Powell's route to Cheney's goal. The president would go to the United Nations and challenge the members to enforce the numerous Security Council resolutions passed on Iraq over the preceding twelve years. "All the world now faces a test, and the United Nations a difficult and defining moment," Bush told the General Assembly in mid-September. "Are Security Council resolutions to be honored and enforced, or cast aside without consequence? Will the United Nations serve the purpose of its founding, or will it be irrelevant?" If meeting that challenge required the Security Council to enact new resolutions, so be it. "But the purposes of the United States should not be doubted," the president warned. "The Security Council resolutions will be enforced—the just demands of peace and security will be met—or action will be unavoidable. And a regime that has lost its legitimacy will also lose its power."[39] It was a bold speech that challenged the world community. It was nevertheless received with great relief by many countries. The United States had decided to work through the United Nations rather than to act alone.

DESPITE BUSH'S PORTENTOUS speech, the administration had no strategy for turning its challenge to the world into a workable policy. The decision to seek a new UN resolution had been made only hours before Bush ascended to the podium in the General Assembly. For days, Cheney had vigorously resisted going to the United Nations yet again on Iraq, but Bush finally decided to side with Powell on this issue, not least because Prime Minister Tony Blair had told him that Britain could support the United States in war only if the issue were enforcement of UN resolutions. Yet no one knew what such a resolution should contain. An interagency team charged with drafting a text started work only after Bush had spoken in New York. When Iraq predictably reacted to Bush's speech by announcing that UN inspectors could return "unconditionally," Washington was still trying to get its act together.

The internal policy battle that had preceded Bush's UN address now shifted to the drafting of a new resolution. There was broad agreement that any resolution would have to declare Iraq in material breach of existing UN demands to disarm, contain a tough new inspection regime that would give weapons inspectors full and unfettered access to all sites at any time, and warn that force might be used if Baghdad failed to comply. But Pentagon officials, backed by Cheney's office, wanted more. They insisted that the resolution authorize weapons inspectors to declare no-fly/no-drive zones and other exclusion zones that would be "enforced by UN security forces or member states," in effect granting the United States a right to intervene militarily in support of the inspection process. They also insisted that in case of Iraqi noncompliance, the resolution authorize "member states to use all necessary means to restore international peace and security in the area."[40]

A draft resolution containing the Pentagon's provisions was circulated in New York in late September, even though the State Department and Britain had argued that it stood no chance of being accepted by the other permanent members of the Security Council. Indeed, the draft went nowhere. France, Russia, and China were willing to consider tougher inspections (itself a major change), but rejected any preauthorization for the use of force, whether to assist the inspectors or to punish noncompliance. There could be, in the parlance of the UN negotiators, "no automaticity" with regard to any use of force.

Behind this firm stance lay the growing conviction on the part of many Security Council members that the United States had come to the United Nations under false pretenses. Many believed that Washington regarded the resolution as a prelude to war rather than as a possible alternative to it. The Bush administration provided plenty of ammunition for this view. Even as it was circulating a draft resolution demanding Iraq give up all its weapons of mass destruction, Powell told the BBC that "the U.S. continues to believe that the best way to disarm Iraq is through a regime change."[41] Subsequent clarifications by Bush and Powell—that, as Bush argued, Saddam's full compliance with UN resolutions "would also change the nature of the Iraqi regime itself"—did little to alleviate doubts about the administration's true intentions.[42]

With America as much as Iraq becoming the issue at the United Nations, there was no way a majority in the Security Council would support a resolution authorizing the use of force if the United States or anyone else aside from the Security Council itself determined Baghdad had failed to comply. To prove the point, France threatened to introduce its own draft resolution that would strengthen inspections but remain silent on consequences in case of noncompliance. Faced with a likely Security Council majority in favor of such a resolution, Washington was forced to compromise. Rather than approving an automatic authorization to use force in case Iraq failed to comply, the new resolution agreed that the Security Council would convene to "consider the situation." Separately, Baghdad was warned of "serious consequences" if it continued to violate its obligations under various UN resolutions. That formulation proved crucial. Paris, Moscow, and others had successfully resisted any automaticity. But Washington and London had successfully avoided the need to go back to the Security Council for an affirmative vote to use force.

After eight weeks of intense negotiations, the UN Security Council voted unanimously to adopt resolution 1441 on November 8, 2002. It was a remarkable victory for America—and for Powell. Three years earlier, when the Security Council last considered how to deal with Iraq's weapons of mass destruction, France, Russia, and China had abstained on a U.S.-UK resolution that in many ways proposed weakening the inspection regime from what had existed before. Now, a much stronger regime than had ever been in place received the Council's unanimous approval. As for Powell, he had won important internal battles—on whether to go to the United Nations, to seek a new resolution, and to compromise on the authorization to use force. And he had worked hard to persuade his colleagues on the Security Council to back a much more robust approach to getting Iraq into compliance with its international obligations.

Nevertheless, even as the administration savored its victory in New York, it again failed to anticipate the many pitfalls that were sure to arise once the provisions of resolution 1441 were implemented. To win agreement, Washington had had to settle for a resolution that postponed rather than resolved many of the most critical issues. For example, there was no consensus within the Security Council on how much Iraqi cooperation would be enough to avoid war—nor on how much noncooperation would provoke it. Nor was there a prescribed timeline or a clear sense of how long inspectors should probe to determine Iraqi compliance. Bush's advisers were divided on these issues. Many assumed that robust inspections fed by U.S. and British intelligence would quickly provide a "smoking gun" proving that Saddam was cheating or that he would blatantly refuse to cooperate with the inspectors. At that point everyone, including France, would support the use of force to topple the regime. Short of finding such convincing evidence, however, the administration was not prepared to deal with situations in which differing interpretations about Iraq's compliance would come to the fore.

A month after the resolution's passage, Baghdad delivered a 12,000-page declaration on its banned weapons program. The declaration was anything but the "currently accurate, full, and complete" listing of its programs that resolution 1441 required. Baghdad's failure to come clean signaled to everyone in the administration—including Powell—that Saddam had no intention of taking advantage of his final opportunity to disarm. "It should be obvious that the pattern of systematic holes and gaps in Iraq's declaration is not the result of accidents or editing oversights or technical mistakes," Powell declared. "These are material omissions that, in our view, constitute another material breach."[43] War now appeared inevitable—indeed, sooner rather than later.

But few other countries shared Washington's conclusion about the inevitability of war—though many had long believed that this had been its objective all along. French diplomats argued that a further material breach was defined by the resolution as occurring when there are "false statements or omissions in the declarations . . . *and* [not *or*] failure by Iraq at any time to comply with and fully cooperate in the implementation" of the resolution. In other words, a false declaration alone was not enough to justify force. But that, clearly, was not Washington's view, and this became abundantly clear to Paris when Chirac's diplomatic adviser,

Maurice Gourdault-Montagne, met with Rice in Washington in mid-January. Back in Paris, he told Chirac that Bush was going to war "no matter what."[44] It was a course France could not, at least not yet, support.

For Washington, then, the question was not whether to go to war, but how to ensure the broadest possible international support. And it is here that diplomacy failed most spectacularly. Blair had served notice that Britain's support hinged on further Security Council action, preferably a second resolution, a position shared by many other European countries. An opening was provided in late January, when Hans Blix, one of the chief UN weapons inspectors, bluntly criticized Baghdad's halting cooperation in his first report to the Security Council since inspections had resumed two months earlier. "Iraq appears not to have come to a genuine acceptance, not even today, of the disarmament which was demanded of it."[45] Four days after Blix's surprise statement, Blair met Bush at the White House and pressed for the introduction of a second resolution. Bush declined.

This proved to be a mistake. For in response, perhaps, to Blix's critical report, Baghdad shifted its behavior. Cooperation on inspections and other procedural matters improved, and Iraq even began to destroy more than one hundred Al-Samoud missiles that Blix declared to be in violation of the range limitations for ballistic missiles permitted by the United Nations. Blix's subsequent reports to the Security Council were far more measured in tone than his initial, unexpectedly harsh indictment of Baghdad. Blix instead stressed Iraqi cooperation on procedures and process, even if on substance many questions remained unresolved. Also, just as Cheney and others opposed to resuming inspections had predicted, the political momentum in New York shifted away from Washington toward the bloc of member states, led by France and Germany, that opposed war.

It was only on February 24 that the United States, Britain, and Spain introduced a second resolution declaring that Iraq had failed to meet its obligations. Last-minute negotiations seeking to add specific benchmarks and a timeline followed, but to no avail. Washington had little interest in being flexible—the only reason it backed another resolution was to help Britain and other friends who needed it for domestic political reasons. It expended little effort to secure the resolution's passage.

Powell worked the phones, but he did not travel to any of the critical countries to secure their vote. Nothing was done to try to woo Russia or even Germany away from France, which by early March had indicated it would veto a resolution authorizing war "regardless of the circumstances," as Chirac put it.[46] Washington even failed to put significant pressure on Mexico or Chile—two other Security Council members—to side with the United States.

On March 6 Bush made one last bravura stance. "No matter what the whip count is, we're calling for the vote," Bush told a primetime news conference. "It's time for people to show their cards, to let the world know where they stand when it comes to Saddam."[47] But it was too late. A second resolution would not only fail because of a French and likely Russian veto; there were not even the votes necessary for Washington and London to claim a moral victory. The admission of failure came at a strange summit between the leaders of Britain, Spain, and the United States in the Azores, a group of small islands in the Atlantic, on March 16. Nothing could have underscored these leaders' international isolation more graphically than this meeting in the middle of nowhere. "It was seen as a defeat," Powell later conceded, "and it was a defeat."[48]

Thus when the United States went to war against Iraq on March 19, it did so without the explicit backing of the UN Security Council. Perhaps there was nothing the Bush administration could have done to avoid this outcome. It would have been difficult to overcome the widespread presumption at the United Nations and elsewhere that Washington was bent on regime change in Baghdad, no matter what. Then again, a more vigorous diplomacy and greater tactical acumen might have succeeded in gaining the consensus of the Council—or at least of a large majority of its members. For example, had Bush agreed with Blair in late January and introduced a second resolution setting out the remaining disarmament tasks necessary for Iraq to fulfill by a clear deadline (for instance, eight weeks hence), he might have won passage of a resolution before opposition to it hardened. But even if it had proved impossible to pass such a resolution, the effort would likely have had the political benefit of isolating those who were unalterably opposed, instead of isolating Washington.

TEN

THE IRAQ WAR

A T 3:30 P.M. on March 19, George W. Bush's war council gathered in the Oval Office for a hastily called meeting. CIA director George Tenet had important information. A reliable source inside Baghdad had told the agency that Saddam Hussein, his sons, and much of the senior Iraqi leadership would be gathering that night at a private home called Dora Farms on the southern outskirts of Baghdad. Should the president give the order to strike the complex in the hope of killing Saddam even before the war against his regime had started? Only hours before, Bush and his aides had met in the White House Situation Room, and the commander in chief had given General Tommy Franks, the military commander who had joined the discussion by secure video from Qatar, the order to execute the war plan against Iraq. Now they had to weigh the pros and cons of a decapitating strike that could end the war before it began. After nearly four hours of discussion, Bush gave Franks the go-ahead to attack Dora Farms that evening.

Bush's decision to go after Saddam was fraught with risk. The intelligence information might be mistaken—and instead of hitting a command site, the bomb might obliterate a building filled with women and children. The attack on Dora Farms reflected Saddam's centrality in Bush's thinking about the war. After all, Bush had said six months earlier, this was "the guy who tried to kill my dad."[1] Perhaps more important, Bush regarded Saddam as an overriding threat, whose ouster from power had been the primary objective of American foreign policy for more than a year.

Five hours after Tenet brought Bush news of the high-level Iraqi gathering, two F-117 stealth fighters dropped four satellite-guided bombs on the structure in Baghdad. Next came a volley of Tomahawk cruise missiles launched from ships in the Persian Gulf and Red Sea. Dora Farms was heavily damaged, but a possibly wounded Saddam Hussein nevertheless escaped. The war was under way.

THE FIRST MAJOR contingent of U.S, British, and Australian Special Forces entered Iraq hours before the strike on Dora Farms. Their mission was to secure critical oil wells and pumping stations in the south and north, to take control of storage sites for weapons of mass destruction throughout the country, and to track down missile launchers in the western desert before they could launch their lethal weapons against Israel. The original plan was to give these forces a head start of forty-eight to seventy-two hours, but the attempt to bomb Saddam and his sons advanced the start of ground combat operations by two days. Twenty-four hours after U.S. missiles and bombs struck the leadership gathering in Baghdad, U.S. and British forces launched a full-scale invasion of Iraq from Kuwait. The bombing campaign that was to have "shocked and awed" the Iraqi leadership followed the next day. The war had now begun in earnest.

While British forces secured the huge Rumalia oil fields in the south, U.S. Marines and Army troops raced north into Iraq on their way to Baghdad. Despite severe sandstorms and resistance from fighters who, Bush later admitted, "were a lot fiercer than we thought,"[2] U.S. forces reached the Republican Guard's defensive lines outside of Baghdad in just ninety-six hours by bypassing the cities in the south (where the Shiite population was expected to revolt against Saddam's Baathist regime). At the same time, a devastating air bombardment of Iraqi Republican Guard divisions defending the approaches to Baghdad destroyed most of their combat power, leaving the capital largely undefended. American soldiers captured Saddam Hussein International Airport just west of Baghdad on April 5, the same day U.S. Marines entered the eastern suburbs. A daring armored thrust through the center of the city met no organized resistance. Four days later, in the heart of downtown Baghdad, the statue of Iraq's erstwhile leader was ignominiously toppled by celebrating Iraqis and American troops. "They got it down," Bush exclaimed as he and millions around the world watched the triumphant scene on television.[3] Three weeks after the war started, Baghdad had fallen, and Saddam's rule was over.

It was a stunning military victory. Of course, it helped that the adversary was both weak and incompetent. "In socioeconomic terms," Thomas Friedman later commented, "we were at war with the Flintstones."[4] Even so, military experts around the world were in awe at the superiority and sophistication of American military technology, the training and daring of the men and women doing the fighting, and the agility and cunning of the war plan. The immediate cost in American lives was even less than during the first Gulf War, when the ground war lasted only one hundred hours.

It was above all an American victory. Only Britain contributed significant firepower to the fight, deploying about 45,000 troops into the theater. Australia helped out with some 2,000 troops, and Poland provided 200 special forces. Kuwait, Qatar, and other Gulf states provided critical basing support. But that was the extent of the non-American contribution. The Bush administration somewhat desperately insisted that its military action had broad international support. In the early days, the White House released fact sheets listing nearly fifty countries that supported the war to demonstrate, as Bush put it, that the coalition was "larger than one assembled in 1991 in terms of the number of nations participating."[5] However, Bush could substantiate that claim only by including such powerhouses as Macedonia, Micronesia, the Marshall Islands, Palau, and Tonga and by ignoring that the Gulf War coalition consisted of nations that actually contributed hundreds of thousands of troops and tens of billions of dollars in treasure. Indeed, this "coalition of the anonymous, the dependent, the halfhearted, and the uninvolved," as *New York Times* columnist Bill Keller described Bush's "coalition of the willing," only helped to underscore the degree to which the United States was isolated in its quest to oust Saddam.[6]

Of course, none of this mattered when it came to the war itself. At a cost of $370 billion a year, the United States maintained armed forces strong enough to vanquish any foe anywhere with speed and certitude. No other country could come close—and very few had much to contribute to a military campaign of this kind. But where Washington's international isolation mattered was in the aftermath, which, as many of the administration's critics had predicted, would prove to be more difficult and challenging than the actual war itself. Having failed to secure broad support for the war, the United States was forced to assume most of the responsibility for managing the postwar situation in Iraq. It was an effort for which the administration proved exceptionally ill prepared.

WITHIN HOURS AFTER joyous Iraqis helped topple Saddam's statue in Baghdad, looters began to steal everything in sight—laying waste to much of the infrastructure that precision bombing had left unscathed. Many government buildings were plundered and in many cases burned to the ground. Hospitals were emptied of much needed medication and equipment. Disorder and chaos reigned throughout the capital city. "Freedom's untidy," Donald Rumsfeld commented when asked about the looting. "Free people are free to make mistakes and commit crimes and do bad things."[7] Unfortunately, the "untidiness" persisted, and the widespread availability of guns and arms created a culture of lawlessness in which looting, carjackings, and armed robberies became the norm rather than the exception.

The lack of security was aggravated by the absence of even the most basic services. For weeks, Baghdad and other major cities had no electricity—this at a time when the midday temperatures topped one hundred degrees. Water was available only sporadically, and most basic government services—from trash pickup to salary and pension payouts—has disappeared. Within the country, no single person was clearly in charge. The Iraqi government was gone, but there was nothing to replace it. Overall command was in the hands of General Franks, but, except for a brief, triumphal visit to Baghdad, he remained at his regional headquarters in Qatar—and soon moved back to Central Command's home base in Tampa. Lieutenant General David McKiernan commanded all ground forces in the country and proclaimed himself in charge. But the civilian administration was in the hands of retired Lieutenant General Jay Garner, who headed the Pentagon's Office of Reconstruction and Humanitarian Assistance. Garner, however, did not arrive in Baghdad until two weeks after the city fell to U.S. forces. The resulting power vacuum in Iraq was quickly filled by the best-organized local forces—including by the Kurds in the north, Shiite religious leaders in the south, and an assortment of thugs, criminals, and agitators in and around Baghdad.

Within weeks of winning the war, America looked as if it might be losing the peace. Failure to provide for security and basic services left an Iraqi populace that had initially welcomed the ouster of Saddam increasingly disenchanted with the American presence. While many wanted the Americans to succeed, nostalgia for the order and security of the prewar days soon returned. "At least we had power and security," a shopkeeper told *Time*. "Democracy is not feeding us."[8]

What went wrong? At its most basic, the administration repeated the same mistake it made in the Afghan campaign. It assumed that the war phase and the postwar phase could be carried out largely independent of each other—even though the Pentagon was in charge of the planning and execution of both the war and its aftermath. Very little if any thought was given to how the conduct of the war would determine the requirements of the peace.

This was most evident in the availability of troops to police postwar Iraq. While the 100,000 or so U.S. Marines and soldiers were, with the support of another 25,000 British ground troops, enough to win the war rapidly, this force fell far short of what was required once the war ended. "We consciously chose to keep our force size relatively small," Paul Wolfowitz advised Congress after the war was over. That gave the force the speed, agility, and flexibility to defeat Saddam's forces quickly. "There is no plan that could have achieved all the extraordinary speed of the plan and, at the same time, have been able to flood the country with 100,000 military policemen. Choices had to be made."[9]

But even if a small force were important for winning the war (itself a doubtful proposition, given that large forces can move just as rapidly and with more confidence, as the German blitzkrieg showed), that is no excuse for failing to have sufficient troops available for securing the peace afterward. The additional troops could have moved into Iraq on the heels of the invading forces, secured the flanks and supply lines that were dangerously exposed, and provided for basic security once the Iraqi opposition had been defeated. Indeed, that had been the advice of General Eric Shinseki, the Army's chief of staff, who had commanded NATO forces in Bosnia. When asked in February 2003 how many troops would be needed to stabilize post-Saddam Iraq, he answered, "I would say that what's been mobilized to this point, something on the order of several hundred thousand soldiers."[10]

Rumsfeld and Wolfowitz had dismissed Shinseki's suggestion as "wildly off the mark," but the reasons for their dismissal are instructive. Rather than suggesting that additional troops would interfere with the war plan, Wolfowitz told Congress that it was "hard to conceive that it would take more forces to provide stability in a post-Saddam Iraq than it would take to conduct the war itself." In fact, there were many reasons to "suggest that peacekeeping requirements in Iraq might be much lower than our historical experience in the Balkans." These included the likely contribution of troops by many other countries. "I would expect that even countries like France will have a strong interest in assisting Iraq's reconstruction," Wolfowitz explained. Then there were the Iraqis themselves. "We are training free Iraqi forces to perform functions of that kind, including command of Iraqi units, once those units have been purged of their Baathist leadership."[11] In other words, the Pentagon (or at least its civilian masters) believed a relatively small U.S. force would suffice once Saddam had been ousted. Indeed, in late April the administration was still planning to reduce the American military presence in Iraq to fewer than two divisions by the fall of 2003— some 50,000 troops in all.[12]

However, the reality on the ground proved all these optimistic assumptions wrong—and General Shinseki right. As chaos spread through much of the country, it became clear that more, not fewer, troops were needed. "We now have 150,000 coalition forces across Iraq," General McKiernan said. "Ask yourself, could you secure California all the time with 150,000 soldiers? The answer is no."[13] By early May the withdrawal of troops from Iraq had been halted, and additional forces were hastily dispatched to the region. By July 1, Bush announced, 230,000 Americans were serving in or near Iraq.[14] The non-American contribution, in contrast, was a little more than 13,000 troops—all but a handful of them British.

Returning from a visit to the Balkans in mid-May 2003, Wolfowitz argued that one lesson to be learned from the peacekeeping operations there was the need for forces "so big and strong that nobody would dare pick a fight with us. I think there may be something to the notion that the more you have at the beginning, the faster you can draw down."[15] With America's extensive experience with peacekeeping operations in the 1990s, that was a lesson that should have been learned before rather than after the Iraq War.

SEVERAL OTHER MISTAKES compounded the failure to integrate postwar considerations into war planning. The most important was the initial decision to minimize U.S. involvement in the postwar effort so as to avoid any connotation that America was occupying Arab lands, a decision that also reflected the administration's disdain for nation-building. After a very short transition (the talk was of weeks rather than months or years), authority would be handed over to an interim Iraqi administration, which would prepare the way for the establishment of a representative government. Exile groups close to the Pentagon would play a prominent role in the interim governing authorities. "I don't think it has to be expensive, and I don't think it has to be lengthy," a senior administration official said about the postwar effort. "Americans do everything very quickly."[16] This, then, would be nation-building lite.

Underlying the optimism about a rapid transition were three assumptions—all of which proved to be wrong. First, Pentagon planners assumed that the most immediate postwar need would be to provide humanitarian assistance, deal with large numbers of refugees, and limit and clean up any environmental damage from burning oil well fires—all disasters that occurred during the Gulf War. Fortunately, none of these problems materialized, in part because of the speed of the military victory. But Garner's small staff spent a disproportionate time planning for these contingencies, while ignoring other, equally important aspects of postwar operations. "This is an ad hoc operation, glued together over about four or five weeks' time," Garner told Congress in mid-May 2003. His team "didn't really have enough time to plan," even though he had been in charge of the effort since the beginning of the year.[17] Yet, like generals everywhere, postwar planners apparently assumed the next war would be like the last. Indeed, Garner had been appointed to head the postwar operation in large part because he had skillfully handled the Kurdish refugee crisis that emerged in the wake of the Gulf War.

But the Iraq War was different. Its goal was to remove a regime, and the postwar problems would all be America's. The most critical among these would be maintaining law and order, though the planning effort largely ignored these considerations. One reason was the assumption that the physical and administrative infrastructure of Iraq would be largely intact after the war. Targeting plans called for sparing much of the country's infrastructure—including to the point of leaving Iraqi television and radio on the air for much of the war. America's military technology enabled the United States to "redefine war on our own terms," Bush argued. "In this new era of warfare, we can target a regime, not a nation."[18]

With the infrastructure remaining in place, planners assumed that the administrative structures could rapidly resume work once the war was over and deliver services and necessities to the Iraqi people. "They told us to bring two suits," one of Garner's aides told the *New York Times*. "We thought we would be walking into functioning ministries, that we would fire the Baathists in the top jobs, and get the trains running again in a couple of months."[19] Police would maintain law and order, the Iraqi army would be put to work clearing rubble and building roads, and the rest of the bureaucracy would see to the needs of ordinary Iraqis. Most of this would be paid for with Iraqi assets—including oil export revenues and the return of frozen Iraqi funds. This, in short, would be different—and simpler—than other peacekeeping operations. "Iraq was a state and is a state," Deputy Secretary of State Richard Armitage explained in rejecting comparisons with much more complex and lengthy peace operations. "It's not a failed state like Afghanistan, it's not a new state like East Timor, and it's not a non-state like Kosovo."[20]

But it was naive to think that a government could function smoothly after its top layer had been removed. Saddam's regime, after all, was a dictatorship; nothing important happened in Iraq without the direct say-so of Saddam. When the regime collapsed, a large power vacuum naturally emerged. Yet the administration assumed that Garner's team of a few hundred civilian advisers could restart the machinery of government with no major hitches. None of this came to pass. Looters ransacked government offices, destroying the files and data central to governing. The police—at least those that remained—were both cowed by the widespread lawlessness and completely incapable of western-style policing, given that their previous experience consisted largely of taking bribes, directing traffic, and backing up Saddam's thugs who maintained law and order with brute and arbitrary force. Much of the army dissolved into the population at large. This left responsibility for administering Iraq in American hands—or the hands of any other organized group able and willing to take charge. Unfortunately, no one in authority had anticipated this situation—leaving the American military and civilians in Iraq without a clear sense of what to do. "We're making this up here as we go along," conceded Lieutenant General William Wallace, the V Corps commander, in mid-May.[21]

A final assumption undergirding American planning for post-Saddam Iraq was that the American presence would be welcomed throughout the country. "We will, in fact, be greeted as liberators," Cheney promised on NBC's *Meet the Press* three days before the start of war.[22] Yet the freedom Iraqi people gained through the removal of Saddam Hussein meant far less to them when there was no electricity to cool their homes and cook their food, when security was so sparse that they feared going out on the streets and children could not go to school, when there was no gasoline to fill up cars, and when the vast majority of people long dependent on the state for money and services were suddenly left high and dry. Being liberated is one thing; being able to get on with life, let alone prosper, is another.

A MONTH INTO the postwar operation, flaws in the prewar planning were obvious. Rather than sticking with a failed policy, Bush rapidly shifted gear. He appointed a new civilian administrator for all of Iraq, Paul Bremer. Garner's informality and lack of focus had undermined confidence in the American operation. Responding to criticism of the postwar effort, Garner had said: "We ought to look in a mirror and get proud, and stick out our chests and suck in our bellies and say, 'Damn, we're Americans!'"[23] This bravado failed to solve the myriad problems facing Iraq.

Bremer, a former foreign service officer with a decisive manner, immediately took charge. He banned the top 25,000 or so Baath party members, some of whom were returning to power during Garner's tenure, from any position of public office. He dismantled the army, security forces, and propaganda apparatus that had supported Saddam's regime. He ordered the confiscation of all weapons except for guns and rifles that could be kept in homes and disbanded all militia forces (except for the Kurdish *pesh merga* forces, which had fought alongside American troops against the Iraqis). And he told political leaders, including the exiles close to key American officials, that the transition to Iraqi rule would take months or years rather than the few weeks originally envisaged.

Bremer was supported in his efforts by a beefed-up and more assertive military presence in Iraq, especially in Baghdad. The Pentagon sent additional forces into Iraq in May, and Rumsfeld promised "to keep any number of troops that are appropriate and necessary in Iraq for as long as it takes to create a secure and permissive environment."[24] In June, daily patrols by American troops in Baghdad doubled, from 600 to 1,200 a day, with many conducted on foot or in Humvees rather than tanks. Instead of worrying about personal safety, the commander of the 1st Armored Division said we "must not let force protection become our overriding concern, so that we go to ground and build fortresses around ourselves and don't do the mission we came to do," which was to provide security for Iraqis.[25] In short, Bush decisively shifted the American emphasis in postwar Iraq from nation-building lite to nation-building heavy—or occupation. "Occupation is an ugly word, not one Americans feel comfortable with," Bremer said two weeks into the job, "but it is a fact."[26]

Bremer's decisive intervention may have come too late, however. Even as he was arriving on the scene, the security situation confronting American soldiers in central Iraq had begun to deteriorate. Resistance in Sunni Arab enclaves in and around Baghdad became increasingly brazen and better coordinated. Small bands of insurgents, as well as lone gunmen, attacked widely dispersed patrols and convoys, wounding scores and killing dozens. In June 2003, an average of one American or British soldier was killed in combat each day, a figure that slowly rose the following month. American troops suffered on average thirteen armed attacks every day after Bush had declared major combat operations over on May 1. The deteriorating security situation threatened the administration's postwar efforts in Iraq. "There are some who feel that the conditions are such that they can attack us there," Bush said testily July 2. "My answer is, bring 'em on."[27] His taunt might have been unwise. The next day, two more American soldiers were killed in combat and nineteen wounded.

In the early summer of 2003 it was still too early to tell whether the United States confronted a full-scale insurgency or was dealing with the last gasps of a dying regime. The failure to capture or kill Saddam Hussein encouraged some of his former supporters to believe that killing American troops would force Washington to cut and run. Saddam appeared to be banking on just that, issuing calls for a jihad against the occupiers in recorded messages from his secret hideaway. Even if Saddam were found, though, it was not clear that this would put an end to the attacks. Three months into the occupation, many Iraqis (not just Saddam loyalists) wanted American troops to leave—and saw attacks on them as the quickest route to bringing this about.

A way had to be found to stop the escalating violence that was derailing the American postwar effort in Iraq. More troops were needed to hunt down and intimidate the attackers. Yet with more than a third of the U.S. Army already tied down in Iraq, and much of the remainder committed to Afghanistan, the Balkans, Korea, and other pressing contingencies, only a large-scale call-up of the Reserves or the deployment of more foreign troops could fulfill that requirement. After the war, the administration sought foreign contributions. Of the seventy countries asked to send troops, about half responded positively—though most with a commitment of only a few hundred troops. Two non-American divisions—one led by British forces, the other by Poles—would be ready for deployment by September 2003. But these troops would at best be additions to, not replacements for, the 145,000 or so American soldiers in Iraq. The American force commitment, Franks announced, would have to remain there for the "foreseeable future."[28]

At best, then, Bush had bought the United States a major, and costly, commitment in Iraq. Rumsfeld estimated the cost of just the troop deployments in Iraq at nearly $4 billion a month—or almost $50 billion a year (Afghanistan costs another $10 billion per year). The reconstruction and humanitarian costs added billions of dollars more to the overall cost of the operation. In time, this investment might stabilize and reform Iraq and offer its people the much better life Bush had promised. But there was a worse possibility—that the security situation inside Iraq would collapse, attacks on American troops would become more organized and lethal, and the occupation would become a quagmire.

THERE WERE MANY reasons for going to war against Iraq. The most important were Saddam Hussein's possession of chemical and biological weapons and his active pursuit of nuclear weapons. "For reasons that have a lot to do with the U.S. government bureaucracy," Wolfowitz explained after the war, "we settled on the one issue that everyone could agree on which was weapons of mass destruction as the core reason."[29] Baghdad's failure to comply with its obligations to give up these weapons and their associated production facilities also provided the legal justification for using force to remove Saddam's regime from power. Without that justification there would have been no international or even congressional support for war. "We have had to operate within the context of international law," Blair argued once the war started. "And the logic of that position has been somewhat uncomfortable, frankly for me and for others, that if Saddam had voluntarily disarmed he could have remained in place."[30]

Iraq's weapons of mass destruction dominated every public justification of war by Bush and other administration officials. Indeed, starting in late summer 2002, the Bush administration embarked on a concerted campaign to persuade the American people and the world of the extent and urgency of the threat posed by Iraq's weapons of mass destruction.

The campaign started with Cheney's speech to the Veterans of Foreign Wars in late August. "Many of us are convinced that Saddam will acquire nuclear weapons fairly soon," Cheney warned. "There is no doubt that Saddam Hussein now has weapons of mass destruction. There is no doubt he is amassing them to use against our friends, against our allies, and against us."[31] Two weeks later, Bush took the case to the United Nations, declaring that Iraq "likely maintains stockpiles of VX, mustard and other chemical agents," and was expanding and improving facilities capable of producing chemical and biological weapons. The president also warned: "Iraq has made several attempts to buy high-strength aluminum tubes used to enrich uranium for a nuclear weapon. Should Iraq acquire fissile material, it would be able to build a nuclear weapon within a year."[32]

In early October, as Congress was considering authorizing the president to use force against Iraq, Bush traveled to Cincinnati to deliver a prime-time address on the scale of the Iraqi threat. "It possesses and produces chemical and biological weapons. It is seeking nuclear weapons," Bush declared without qualification. "Some ask how urgent this danger is to America and the world. The danger is already significant, and it only grows worse with time. If we know Saddam Hussein has dangerous weapons today—and we do—does it make any sense for the world to wait to confront him as he grows even stronger and develops even more dangerous weapons?" Bush answered his own question. "America must not ignore the threat gathering against us. Facing clear evidence of peril, we cannot wait for the final proof—the smoking gun—that could come in the form of a mushroom cloud."[33]

Having secured congressional authorization for a war against Iraq and unanimous UN support for returning inspectors to Iraq to determine Baghdad's full and complete compliance with its obligation to disarm, Bush made Iraq's weapons of mass destruction the centerpiece of his State of the Union address in January 2003. He made a special point of zeroing in on Saddam Hussein's putative nuclear weapons program.

The International Atomic Energy Agency confirmed in the 1990s that Saddam Hussein had an advanced nuclear weapons development program, had a design for a nuclear weapon and was working on five different methods of enriching uranium for a bomb. The British government has learned that Saddam Hussein recently sought significant quantities of uranium from Africa. Our intelligence sources tell us that he has attempted to purchase high-strength aluminum tubes suitable for nuclear weapons production. Saddam Hussein has not credibly explained these activities. He clearly has much to hide.

Bush concluded by announcing that the United States would ask the UN Security Council to convene a special session on February 5 "to consider the facts of Iraq's ongoing defiance of the world." There, the secretary of state would present information and intelligence about "Iraq's illegal weapons programs, its attempt to hide those weapons from inspectors, and its links to terrorist groups."[34]

Powell put together a presentation on the Iraqi threat with the deliberateness and care that has become his hallmark. He spent the better part of four days and nights at CIA headquarters going over all the intelligence information on Iraqi weapons programs and possible links to terrorism, including al Qaeda. The initial basis for Powell's presentation was a forty-five-page script produced by the White House staff. The guts of the script came from a briefing that Lewis Libby, Cheney's chief of staff, had given a few days earlier in the White House Situation Room. The script was a powerful indictment of Saddam Hussein. Much of it, however, was based on sources of questionable integrity, defectors who had been presented to the American intelligence community by Iraqi opposition groups, and other data of uncertain reliability. "I'm not reading this," Powell said, tossing several pages of the Libby script into the air. "This is bullshit."[35]

After carefully vetting every fact and making sure he had solid sources for every statement, Powell felt comfortable with only a third of Libby's original allegations.[36] Powell went over them again and again, making sure that he could stand by every single statement in his text. He knew that in making this presentation before the eyes of the world his own credibility was very much at stake—as was the president's and that of the nation. And he made sure George Tenet's reputation was on the line as well, insisting that the CIA director sit right behind him, clearly visible over his shoulder, as he presented the best of the agency's case to the world.

Powell's bill of indictment on Saddam's weapons programs was precise and unambiguous:

There can be no doubt that Saddam Hussein has biological weapons and the capability to rapidly produce more, many more. And he has the ability to dispense these lethal poisons and diseases in ways that can cause massive death and destruction. . . .

Our conservative estimate is that Iraq today has a stockpile of between 100 and 500 tons of chemical weapons agent. That is enough to fill 16,000 battlefield rockets. . . . Saddam Hussein has chemical weapons. Saddam Hussein has used such weapons. And Saddam Hussein has no compunction about using them again. And we have sources who tell us that he recently has authorized his field commanders to use them. He wouldn't be passing out the orders if he didn't have the weapons or the intent to use them. . . .

Saddam Hussein already possesses two out of the three key components needed to build a nuclear bomb. He has a cadre of nuclear scientists with the expertise and he has a bomb design. Since 1998, his efforts to reconstitute his nuclear program have been focused on acquiring the third and last component: sufficient fissile material to produce a nuclear explosion. . . . Saddam Hussein is determined to get his hands on a nuclear bomb. He is so determined that he has made repeated covert attempts to acquire high-specification aluminum tubes from 11 different countries, even after inspections resumed. . . .

Numerous intelligence reports over the past decade from sources inside Iraq indicate Saddam Hussein retains a covert force of up to a few dozen Scud-variant ballistic missiles. . . . Iraq has programs that are intended to produce ballistic missiles that fly over 1,000 kilometers. . . .

There is ample intelligence that Iraq has dedicated much effort to developing and testing spray devices that could be adapted for UAVs [unmanned aerial vehicles]. . . . According to Iraq's December 7th declaration, its UAVs have a range of only 80 kilometers. But we detected one of Iraq's newest UAVs in a test flight that went 500 kilometers nonstop on autopilot.

Powell's presentation was a tour de force. Forcefully and directly, but without theatrical flourishes, the former soldier methodically ticked off the facts, played intercept tapes, and showed surveillance photographs of Iraqi weapons sites. "This is evidence, not conjecture," Powell concluded. "This is true. This is all well documented."[37]

"It was a spectacular performance," the liberal columnist William Raspberry gushed, "and by the time Colin Powell was finished, I was a complete convert."[38] The American public agreed. Seventy-one percent of those who watched Powell's presentation thought he had made a persuasive case. And 56 percent of those who had watched him believed that Powell had "presented hard evidence *proving* that Iraq has weapons of mass destruction" (compared with 21 percent of those who had not watched him).[39] Even France was moved to confirm it had evidence of Iraq's "capacity to produce VX [and] the possible possession of significant stocks of anthrax and botulism toxin, and possibly a production capability."[40]

After Powell's presentation, the Bush administration ratcheted up the rhetoric in a final attempt to persuade the American public and the world of the necessity for swift military action. Days after Powell's UN appearance, Tenet argued, "we will find caches of weapons of mass destruction, absolutely."[41] Delivering a final, forty-eight-hour ultimatum to Saddam Hussein on March 17, Bush said, "intelligence gathered by this and other governments leaves no doubt that the Iraq regime continues to possess and conceal some of the most lethal weapons ever devised."[42]

The drumbeat continued even after the fighting started. On March 21, Ari Fleischer said, "There is no question" chemical and biological weapons would be found, reminding reporters, "this was the reason that the President felt so strongly that we needed to take military action."[43] The next day, Franks declared, "the regime of Saddam Hussein possesses weapons of mass destruction . . . and as this operation continues, those weapons will be identified, found, along with the people who have produced them and who guard them. And of course there is no doubt about that."[44] The reason for this confidence, Rumsfeld explained on ABC's *This Week* on March 30, was that "we know where they are. They're in the area around Tikrit and Baghdad and east, west, south and north somewhat."[45]

EVEN BEFORE THE war started on March 19, a covert Army unit of Delta Force soldiers flew deep into Iraqi territory to find and capture Saddam Hussein's weapons of mass destruction. Task Force 20, as the unit was known, surveyed all the known sites, gathered hundreds of weapons samples, and seized many of the scientists on the U.S. target list. But despite having access to the best intelligence information and being deployed with the most advanced military equipment for its quick, covert operations, Task Force 20 failed to find any hard evidence of illegal weapons.[46]

A similar fate befell the 75th Exploitation Task Force, which was put in charge of the U.S. effort to search, seize, and destroy the weapons of mass destruction Saddam Hussein was known to possess. The contingent of special forces soldiers, biologists, chemists, arms controllers, nuclear operators, and computer and document experts visited many of the sites that intelligence agencies had pinpointed before the war as likely locations where weapons were being stockpiled and produced. Six weeks after commencing their efforts with high hopes, the 75th was called back home, having failed to find a single artillery shell, missile warhead, barrel of chemicals, or liter of biological agent. "We came to bear country, we came loaded for bear," a member of the task force said, "and we found out the bear wasn't here."[47]

The soldiers and marines rapidly moving north on their way to Baghdad, each one with gas masks and hoods at the ready, were convinced that Saddam's forces at one point or another would "slime" their path with chemical or biological weapons. "What the regime was intending to do in terms of its use of the weapons, we thought we understood," observed Lieutenant General James Conway, commander of the First Marine Expeditionary Force, which attacked Baghdad along the eastern route. "We were simply wrong." That became clear to Conway and his troops when no weapons caches were found along the way. "It was a surprise to me then, it remains a surprise to me now, that we have not uncovered weapons . . . in some of the forward dispersal sites. Again, believe me, it's not for lack of trying. We've been to virtually every ammunition supply point between the Kuwaiti border and Baghdad, but they're simply not there."[48]

The only potential evidence of an illicit Iraqi weapons program turned up during the first one hundred days was the discovery of two mobile laboratories and a third truck that bore a striking resemblance to the biological weapons production vehicles Powell had described in his UN presentation. Close examination failed to reveal even a trace of any biological agent within the vehicles, which had been decontaminated, and some key American intelligence officials expressed doubt about their capacity to produce biological weapons. British intelligence was not prepared to accept the American judgment that these were production facilities and some considered it possible that the trailers were used to produce hydrogen-filled target balloons for artillery practice.[49] Nevertheless, having dismissed any alternative explanation and determined that the vehicles were very similar to the ones described by Iraqi defectors, the CIA concluded in late May that the trailers constituted "the strongest evidence to date that Iraq was hiding a biological warfare program."[50]

Relieved to finally have found evidence of an illicit weapons program, the White House rushed to publicize the CIA's finding. "We found the weapons of mass destruction," Bush declared. "And we'll find more weapons as time goes on. But for those who say we haven't found the banned manufacturing devices or banned weapons, they're wrong. We found them."[51] Of course, there was no evidence of any weapons ever having been produced in the trailers, and soon the president and the rest of the administration talked not of weapons, but of a weapons program. "Iraq had a weapons program," Bush later clarified. "Intelligence throughout the decade showed they had a weapons program. I am absolutely convinced with time we'll find out that they did have a weapons program."[52] But administration officials acknowledged that it would take time to reveal all. "I am confident that we will eventually be able to piece together a fairly complete account of Iraq's WMD programs," Douglas Feith, the undersecretary of defense for policy, told a House committee in mid-May 2003, "but the process will take months and perhaps years."[53]

IT REMAINED POSSIBLE that the United States would eventually find the thousands of liters of anthrax and botulinum toxin, the tons of VX, the tens of thousands of chemical artillery shells, the dozens of long-range missiles, and the uranium enrichment program that the Bush administration assured the world were stashed inside Iraq. But after months of futile searching, even administration insiders conceded that something had gone wrong. There were at least three possible explanations.

The most likely possibility was that more than a decade of deception enabled Saddam to hide any evidence of weapons stocks and production facilities. Much of the production capacity might have been concealed within facilities that had legitimate purposes. Weapons stocks might have been widely dispersed and concealed in places yet to be located and searched. With time, and debriefings of many of the scientists and other people associated with Saddam's weapons program, the truth about these capabilities might come to light and unambiguous proof might be discovered. Given the massive amount of money and time Saddam Hussein spent on acquiring these weapons capabilities and keeping them from the prying eyes of UN inspectors and various other intelligence agencies, it seemed quite plausible that he could have found choice hiding places in a country about the size of California.

The most frightening possibility was that the weapons were stolen or transferred to another country or even a terrorist group. There was no evidence of any deliberate transfer, but plenty of concern that materials could have been stolen before American troops were able to secure the sites where weapons were believed to have been stored. By the time American forces entered many of these sites, including many of Iraq's nuclear complexes, Iraqi citizens and perhaps organized gangs already had pillaged much of value that was inside. In some cases, people stole things for personal use. For example, barrels storing radioactive materials in the Tuwaitha nuclear complex were taken to haul water for drinking and bathing. But in other instances, dangerous materials might have been taken for nefarious purposes. In the chaos of war, one of the great risks was that weapons or materials might go missing, with the possibility of frightening consequences. Yet there was no evidence that the Pentagon ever seriously considered this eventuality. It certainly did not deploy enough troops to make sure that the ninety or so sites that were believed to contain dangerous weapons would be rapidly secured to prevent looting.

The most consequential possibility was that the intelligence on Iraq's weapons programs was not as definitive as the president and other administration officials said. Some public statements clearly over-reached. Rumsfeld's declaration on March 30—"we know where [the weapons] are"—obviously proved wrong. Bush's claims about the extent of Saddam's nuclear program in his 2003 State of the Union address were also based on disputed evidence. Intelligence analysts at the Energy and State Departments concluded that the aluminum tubes Bush cited as evidence for a new uranium enrichment program were more likely to be used for producing conventional artillery systems. Claims that Baghdad had sought to purchase uranium from Niger had proved to be unfounded many months earlier—not least since part of the evidence consisted of a blatantly forged document.[54] These assessments were shared by the International Atomic Energy Agency, which was charged with conducting nuclear weapons–related inspections in Iraq. The agency's director general reported to the UN Security Council on March 7. "To date," the inspectors have "found no evidence or plausible indication of the revival of a nuclear weapons programme in Iraq."[55]

The president and his advisers, possibly including officials in the intelligence community, clearly hyped the threat. An internal CIA panel, while affirming the judgment of intelligence analysts about Iraq's programs before the war, concluded that there had been no new or hard evidence to prove the existence of Iraqi weapons after inspectors left Iraq in 1998. Instead, intelligence assessments after that time had to rely on circumstantial or "inferential" information.[56] Rumsfeld later admitted as much, acknowledging that the administration "did not act in Iraq because we had discovered dramatic new evidence of Iraq's pursuit of weapons of mass murder. We acted because we saw the existing evidence in a new light, through the prism of our experience on September 11th."[57]

The fact that evidence on Iraqi capabilities was not very good was underscored by a Defense Intelligence Agency assessment of the Iraqi

chemical warfare program—by far its most advanced weapons program—which was completed in September 2002. The summary of that
assessment, released only in June 2003, concluded:

> [We] believe Iraq retained production equipment, expertise and
> chemical precursors and can reconstitute a chemical warfare pro-
> gram *in the absence of an international inspection regime*. . . . There
> is *no reliable* information on whether Iraq is producing and stock-
> piling chemical weapons, or where Iraq has—or will—establish its
> chemical warfare agent production facilities. Unusual munitions
> transfer activity in mid-2002 *suggests* that Iraq is distributing CW
> munitions in preparation for an anticipated U.S. attack. . . .
> Although we *lack any direction information*, Iraq *probably* possesses
> CW agent in chemical munitions, *possibly* including artillery
> rockets, artillery shells, aerial bombs, and ballistic missile war-
> heads. Baghdad also *probably* possesses bulk chemical stockpiles,
> primarily containing precursors, but that also *could* consist of
> some mustard agent or stabilized VX. [Emphases added.][58]

Read quickly and without the emphases, this summary suggests that
Iraq had an extensive chemical weapons capability. The qualifiers, however, underscored the limits of what the intelligence community actually knew. In September 2002 the Defense Intelligence Agency had "no
reliable information" on whether Iraq was producing or stockpiling
chemical weapons. Lacking "any direct information," the best it could
come up with were guesses of what Iraq might have.

However, there was no doubt in Bush's mind—or in the mind of any
other top official—that Saddam possessed chemical and biological
weapons, and most also believed that he was seeking nuclear weapons.
Saddam was evil, and there was no question he had long pursued
weapons of mass destruction. Indeed, during the 1990s UN inspectors
had found and destroyed critical components and facilities for making
weapons-grade nuclear materials, 50 long-range missiles and warheads
(some filled with anthrax), 40,000 chemical warfare munitions, 690 tons
of chemical warfare agents, 3,000 tons of precursor chemicals, and significant quantities of chemical and biological warfare production equipment.[59] And the inspectors still had not resolved the many discrepancies

involving Iraq's past production of anthrax, botulinum toxin, and VX. To Bush, there was no question that Saddam was hiding these capabilities and no question that the Iraqi dictator had exploited the four-year absence of UN inspectors to reconstitute his weapons programs. "There's no doubt in my mind," Bush said in July 2003, "when it's all said and done, the facts will show the world the truth. There's absolutely no doubt in my mind."[60]

Lack of doubt may in fact have been part of the problem—and not only Bush's lack of doubt, but that of virtually everyone with any knowledge of Iraq's weapons program. The belief that Saddam Hussein was actively pursuing weapons of mass destruction was so pervasive that any piece of information, however questionable the source or uncertain its meaning, was presumed to reconfirm what was already known to be true. This was true not just of Bush, but also of his senior advisers, of the American intelligence community, of members of the Clinton administration, of the American media and opinion makers, and, indeed, of many foreign leaders. No one seriously considered that Saddam might have destroyed most or all his weapons in the early to mid-1990s. The possibility simply did not enter anyone's calculation.

But why, if Saddam no longer had any weapons, did he not resolve the outstanding questions about his past capabilities and thereby avoid a war and his ouster from power? Why lie about something that was not true? There are a number of possible reasons. Saddam may have decided to destroy his weapons in the hope that UN inspectors, unable to find any stocks, would return to New York and argue that Baghdad was in fact meeting its international obligations, thus undermining the case for war. This would help explain why, when confronted with the charge that the Al-Samoud 2 missile exceeded the allowable 150-kilometer range, Saddam agreed to destroy the inventory of these missiles. But even if he had destroyed his weapons, Saddam had powerful incentives to leave his neighbors and the United States in the dark. For one thing, the ruse would create the impression that he remained a significant regional power. For another, Saddam may have believed that acceding to the wishes of the UN inspectors—and, in effect, the United States—would be a humiliation that would weaken his hold on power.

In the eyes of the public and future historians, whether weapons of mass destruction were found would determine whether Bush's preemptive war was justified. Bush's ex post facto justification for the war—that the Iraqi people were much better off without Saddam—ignored the basic but highly salient fact that there would not have been a war without his argument that Iraq's weapons of mass destruction posed an unacceptable threat that was both immediate and serious. While Saddam's regime was undeniably evil, even Wolfowitz agreed that that by itself was "not a reason to put American kids' lives at risk."[61]

Whether or not stores of weapons were found, one thing was clear—the threat Iraq's mass destruction capabilities posed was not imminent. Indeed, Rice admitted as much after the war. Speaking to critics who accused the president of hyping the threat posed by Iraq's weapons of mass destruction, she conceded in July 2003 that the administration did not have much new evidence on these programs before the war began. Instead, Rice argued, "The most telling and eye-catching point in the judgment of five of the six intelligence agencies [asked to render an assessment] was that if left unchecked, Iraq would most likely have a nuclear weapon in this decade. The president of the United States could not afford to trust Saddam's motives or give him the benefit of the doubt."[62] Leaving aside the fact that the State Department's intelligence arm said there was no compelling case for this conclusion, the possibility that Iraq would acquire a nuclear weapon sometime in the next eight years hardly constituted evidence of an imminent threat—one that had to be addressed in spring 2003, not the following summer or fall.

The glaring discrepancy between what administration officials from the president on down claimed about Iraq's weapons programs before the war and what was found after raised troubling questions. If it involved the willful distortion of evidence, that would be an issue of the highest political order. If the reason were inaccurate intelligence, that would be of great strategic significance, because one of the main precepts of the Bush revolution—the doctrine of preemption—stands or falls on accurate intelligence. "Preemption presupposes the ability to *know* things," George Will has rightly observed, "to know about threats with a degree of certainty not requisite for decisions less momentous than those for waging war."[63] For whatever reason, the

Bush administration did not know what it thought it knew about Iraq's weapons program. America's ability to preempt future, and perhaps graver, threats might therefore have been seriously harmed.

MANY PROPONENTS OF the war within and outside the Bush administration believed that the decisive defeat of Saddam Hussein would benefit American diplomacy in the Middle East, including giving it leverage to deal with the Israeli-Palestinian conflict. It was a view the president shared. "We meet here during a crucial period in the history of our nation, and of the civilized world," Bush declared three weeks before the war. "Part of that history was written by others; the rest will be written by us." In the president's view, the history still to be written would have to include the critical region of the Middle East. "America will seize every opportunity in pursuit of peace. And the end of the present regime in Iraq would create such an opportunity." After Iraq, the focus would turn to resolving the Israeli-Palestinian conflict by way of the so-called road map to peace developed by the United States and other nations. "It is the commitment of our government—and my personal commitment—to implement the road map and to reach that goal."[64]

Before the Iraq War, Bush had refused to engage himself or his administration in the long-standing and often vexing effort to forge a peace in this conflict-ridden region. Clinton had invested much of the last year of his presidency in the pursuit of a final peace between Israelis and Palestinians, and he had come up empty handed. The violence that ensued after Clinton's failure was a reminder to Bush that the risks of getting involved were very great and the likelihood of success very small. After September 11, moreover, Bush and other top officials believed it vital to stand shoulder to shoulder with Israel as it was engulfed by a wave of suicide bombers. Washington could hardly be fighting its own war against terrorism while it sought to halt or condemn Jerusalem's war against terrorism.

Bush believed that the Palestinian leadership, especially Yasser Arafat, was a major part of the problem in the region and therefore could not be part of any solution. For nearly ten years, the United States and the rest of the world had relied on Arafat to deliver the Palestinians in negotiations over a final peace settlement. But as the talks at Camp David during the summer of 2000 had shown, Arafat had no interest in peace—at least not on terms that would be remotely acceptable to the Israelis. Instead, Bush was convinced that Arafat had aided and abetted, if not actually directed, terrorist attacks against Israel in the years after Camp David. "You can't make a peace deal with that guy," Bush exclaimed at a dinner in 2002. "He screwed President Clinton."[65]

Rather than pursuing a policy of active engagement in the Middle East as many of his predecessors had done, Bush called for a change in the Palestinian leadership as a precondition for American involvement. "Peace requires a new and different Palestinian leadership, so that a Palestinian state can be born," Bush declared in a Rose Garden speech in June 2002. "I call on the Palestinian people to elect new leaders, leaders not compromised by terror. I call upon them to build a practicing democracy, based on tolerance and liberty. If the Palestinian people actively pursue these goals, America and the world will actively support their efforts."[66]

By putting the power of America behind the idea of democratic regime change in the Palestinian territories, Bush believed a new leadership was bound to emerge. It was not a perspective shared by many others—especially in Europe and the Arab world—who very much doubted that the Palestinian people could be persuaded to elect a new leadership when Arafat had been their overwhelming choice for president in the 1996 elections. Bush recalled French president Jacques Chirac telling him, "We have to deal with Arafat because he's the only legitimate interlocutor for the Palestinian people." Bush was dismissive. "Then *you* do a peace deal with him. What do you need us for?"[67] Such comments only added to the widespread sense that Bush's call for a Palestinian leadership change was little more than an excuse to remain on the sidelines while the conflict in the region raged on.

In fact, though, Bush's demand for a new leadership produced changes in the Palestinian Authority. In March 2003, under pressure from the United States and others, Arafat agreed to appoint Mahmoud Abbas, a relative moderate, as prime minister of a Palestinian government with real executive authority. That paved the way for the publication of the road map. It set forth the critical steps Israelis and

Palestinians needed to take in phases to achieve a two-state resolution of their conflict by 2005. Once the Palestinians and, more conditionally, the Israelis had accepted the road map, Bush committed his administration to seeking its full implementation.

After major combat operations in Iraq had ended, Bush traveled to the Middle East to meet first with Arab leaders in Egypt and then with Israeli prime minister Ariel Sharon and the newly installed Palestinian prime minister Mahmoud Abbas in Aqaba, Jordan. "I'm the kind of person who, when I say something, I mean it," Bush assured the moderate Arab leaders assembled in the Red Sea resort town of Sharm el-Sheikh. "I mean that the world needs to have a Palestinian state that is free and at peace. And, therefore, my government will work with all parties concerned to achieve that vision."[68] The Arab leaders assembled at the resort were both pleased and impressed by Bush's performance. "He spoke without notes, without help from his aides, and he really knew the details," said a member of an Arab delegation. "The difference between now and a year ago is amazing."[69]

In the meeting with Sharon and Abbas, Bush told both leaders what their responsibilities were in implementing the road map and moving toward peace. It was an opportunity, Bush later told reporters aboard Air Force One, "to observe the interplay between the two; did they have the capacity to relax in each other's presence, for starters. And I felt they did. In other words, it was—the body language was positive. There wasn't a lot of hostility or suspicion." The role of the United States, Bush said, was to "lay out the vision, encourage people to accept the vision, and then help implement the vision. In this case, we call it a road map to achieve the vision. And that's exactly what we're going to do. We can be stewards of accountability." He promised he would "ride herd" on the diplomatic process to make sure both sides continued to meet their responsibilities. All in all, Bush concluded, "I'm pleased with the last two days. We have made a good beginning."[70]

Bush's first foray into the Middle East thicket was soon followed by the familiar and more depressing reality of violence. Palestinian terrorist groups responded to the Aqaba summit by launching a coordinated series of attacks against Israelis in the occupied territories. Israel responded with an attempted assassination of a top Hamas leader. A suicide bomber in Jerusalem blew up a bus. Within a week of Bush's meeting, sixty people had been killed and hundreds more injured.

The violence was a painful reminder that the situation in the Middle East remained unchanged in important ways even after Saddam's ouster and Bush's personal engagement in regional diplomacy. While Bush believed that he "changed the whole paradigm over there," it would take more than speeches and informal get-togethers to achieve peace in this deeply divided land.[71] Much would depend on Bush's staying power—on his willingness to spend his political capital to push and cajole the parties, including Sharon, into taking the steps necessary for making progress. Success would require more than riding herd on the leaders; it might well require the deployment of significant American capabilities—from more money to troops—to push the two sides together and end the bloodshed.

ELEVEN

WHO'S NEXT?

W HEN COLIN POWELL was asked where foreign policy would be heading after the Iraq War, the secretary of state answered that rebuilding Iraq and resuming the Middle East peace process would come first. "What we will do beyond that is to fully engage again on the President's agenda, [going] back to his emphasis on free trade agreements, his emphasis on creating communities and democracies around the world, continuing to build the relationship that we have with Russia and China." And there were other important issues to address: "HIV/AIDS, famine, climate, obviously, we're not going to join Kyoto, but we have some ideas that we think we can present to the world that they would find attractive, . . . working with African nations not only on HIV/AIDS and infectious diseases, but economic development, the Millennium Challenge Account."[1]

But if Powell thought the administration would revert to a pre-September 11 foreign policy agenda after Iraq, George W. Bush had a different idea. In his speech declaring an end to the war, the president focused on the threat that drove his foreign policy revolution. "Any outlaw regime that has ties to terrorist groups and seeks or possesses weapons of mass destruction," Bush told five thousand cheering sailors aboard the aircraft carrier *Abraham Lincoln*, "is a grave danger to the civilized world—and will be confronted."[2] Bush and other senior administration officials left little doubt which regimes they had in mind. There were the other two charter members of the axis of evil—Iran and North

Korea—as well as states such as Syria, Libya, and Cuba—the "junior varsity axis of evil," in the words of one official.[3] Every one of these regimes would in one way or another have to be confronted.

IN NOVEMBER 2001, Richard Perle argued that taking out the Taliban in Afghanistan and Saddam Hussein's regime in Iraq would send an unmistakable signal to other outlaw regimes. "We could deliver a short message, a two-word message," Perle said. "'You're next.'"[4] After the war with Iraq, the Bush administration began to deliver precisely this message to Syria. The expectation was that Damascus would take America's hint and change its ways.

The coordinated effort began even before the fighting in Iraq ended. Donald Rumsfeld was the first to raise the specter of military action against Syria. In late March, he accused Damascus of "a hostile act" by shipping military supplies to Iraq.[5] When told about Rumsfeld's threat by one of his aides, Bush smiled and responded with just one word: "Good."[6] Two days later, Powell weighed in. Damascus "faces a critical choice," he told a staunchly pro-Israel audience. "Syria can continue direct support for terrorist groups and the dying regime of Saddam Hussein, or it can embark on a different and more hopeful course. Either way, Syria bears the responsibility for its choices, and for the consequences."[7] Paul Wolfowitz traveled to Capitol Hill a few days later to deliver the starkest warning yet. The Syrians were behaving badly and they "need to be reminded of that, and if they continue, then we need to think about what our policy is with respect to a country that harbors terrorists or harbors war criminals or was in recent times shipping things to Iraq."[8]

The administration's indictment of Syria contained both new and long-standing accusations. The latter included the possession of chemical weapons and an active biological weapons program. (There was no suggestion that Damascus was attempting to acquire nuclear weapons.) For more than a quarter century, moreover, Syria had exercised de facto control over much of Lebanon—including the Beka'a Valley, which was home to an amalgam of terrorist groups waging war on Israel. Finally, Syria itself had long-standing ties to terrorist groups. Hezbollah, Hamas, and other terror organizations had offices in the Syrian capital, though ostensibly only to support their media and public relations efforts. And Damascus, according to the State Department's annual terrorism report, "continued to permit Iranian resupply, via Damascus, of Hezbollah in Lebanon."[9]

But it was new developments that incensed the administration. The Pentagon and the White House were livid about reports that Syria might have provided material support to Iraqi forces, including night-vision goggles. Syria also had allowed Hezbollah and other Islamist fighters to cross its border into Iraq to fight the American "infidels." Anywhere from three hundred to three thousand fighters apparently filtered into Iraq from Syria during the three weeks of fighting. Most upsetting, finally, was evidence that Damascus had let members of Saddam's regime, including possibly some close family members, come into or pass through Syria. The Syrians must not "allow for Baath Party members or Saddam's families or generals on the run to seek safe haven and find safe haven there," Bush declared. "We expect them to do everything they can to prevent people who should be held to account from escaping in their country. And if they are in their country, we expect the Syrian authorities to turn them over to the proper folks."[10]

In response to these developments, Rumsfeld reportedly ordered the military to review contingency plans for a possible war against Syria. The Pentagon's two staunchest advocates of forceful action against Iraq and elsewhere in the Middle East, policy chief Douglas Feith and his Middle East hand, William Luti, were assigned to write a briefing paper making the case for war against Syria.[11] At the White House, Bush's spokesman, Ari Fleischer, said, "Syria is indeed a rogue nation."[12] He warned Damascus not to harbor Iraqi fugitive leaders, read from a CIA report to Congress detailing Syria's extensive efforts to acquire ever more deadly chemical and biological weapons, and reminded reporters that Syria had long been included on the U.S. list of states that sponsor terrorism. "Syria," Fleischer suggested, "needs to seriously ponder the implications of their actions."[13]

For all the bluster coming from administration officials, Bush never really intended to go to war against Syria. "I have no specific operation in mind at this point in time," Bush told a small group of reporters on April 22. "I can't think of a specific moment or a specific incident that would require military action."[14] The idea, in other words, was to use tough rhetoric to pressure Syria to change its ways. The success of such a rhetorical policy was undoubtedly enhanced by the fact that Damascus must have been acutely aware that, with Saddam's fall, it was now surrounded on virtually all sides by countries either occupied by the United States or allied with it.

Syria no doubt paid close attention to what Washington was saying. By late April, it had closed its borders with Iraq and handed over to U.S. authorities Iraqi fugitives who had entered the country. Following Powell's visit to Damascus in early May, Syria took a more positive attitude toward efforts to negotiate an Israeli-Palestinian peace. It closed some terrorist offices in Damascus and dropped the anti-American rhetoric that had dominated its public pronouncements before the Iraq War. Rather than voting against a UN resolution recognizing U.S. authority in Iraq, Syrian officials skipped the meeting, allowing the resolution to pass 14-0. Internally, there were growing stirrings for liberalization of what for decades had been brutal dictatorial rule. In short, Damascus was not about to put Bush's rhetoric to the test. Rather than risking the Taliban's or Saddam's fate, Syria's leaders decided it would be much better to accede to U.S. demands. As a result, Washington, though still concerned about Syria's support for terrorism and programs to make weapons of mass destruction, turned its attention to more immediate—and graver—dangers.

NORTH KOREA WAS in many ways the odd member of the axis of evil. Its links to terrorism were tenuous, amounting to little more than the possible sale of some weapons to terrorist groups and offering safe haven decades ago to several members of the Japanese Red Army faction. It was not terrorism, though, that justified Pyongyang's inclusion in the axis of evil, but rather its extensive efforts to produce weapons of mass destruction. (The fact that it was a non-Muslim country may also have had a role, given the administration's desire to make clear that its war on terrorism was not a war on Islam.) North Korea had large stockpiles of chemical and biological weapons and the most advanced nuclear weapons program of all the rogue states. Most disturbingly, Pyongyang seemed willing to sell anything it made to the most unsavory regimes.

North Korea's nuclear program was of most immediate concern. In the late 1980s, it had produced nuclear material sufficient to build one, or possibly two, nuclear weapons. It also had enough material stored in nuclear waste sites that, if reprocessed, would allow the building of an additional half-dozen weapons in a matter of months. The Clinton administration had spent much of its first eighteen months in office trying to negotiate an end to the North's nuclear activities. In July 1994 Washington concluded the Agreed Framework with Pyongyang, which effectively froze North Korea's plutonium program in return for international assistance with its energy needs. Under the agreement, however, the North's nuclear infrastructure would remain in place until new reactors less suitable for building nuclear weapons had been constructed. Financial and, above all, political obstacles in Washington prevented the Clinton administration from completing the construction of these reactors on schedule, so that by the time Bush entered office North Korea still possessed a significant capability for producing nuclear weapons.

The Bush administration arrived in Washington convinced that Clinton's policy toward North Korea and the wider region had been deeply flawed. Bush and most of his advisers thought Clinton had been too soft on the North and too hard on America's allies, Japan and South Korea. They faulted the Agreed Framework on several grounds. It failed to eliminate the North's nuclear program; it encouraged Pyongyang to believe it could blackmail Washington into giving it political and economic benefits by threatening to produce nuclear weapons; and it had ignored allied concerns. Any approach to the North, they argued, would have to be based on a trilateral understanding on how to proceed. In East Asia, as elsewhere, America's allies must come first.

The problem with this critique, of course, was that it was never easy to balance relations with key allies with the need to deal with the North Korean nuclear threat. As Clinton had discovered, a tough approach toward Pyongyang engendered deep anxiety in Seoul and also in Tokyo, while a more lenient approach triggered their fears that the United States might abandon them. Bush discovered the difficulty of balancing these two policy imperatives within weeks of coming to office, when South Korea's president, Kim Dae Jung, visited him in Washington.

Speaking to reporters a day before the meeting, Colin Powell said that the administration wanted "to make sure that our North Korea policy is totally synchronized with what our South Korean friends are doing. They have the lead."[15] Kim Dae Jung's preferences with regard to the North were no secret. He had won the Nobel Peace Prize the previous December for his efforts to thaw North-South relations as part of his so-called sunshine policy. The South Korean leader wanted Washington to engage Pyongyang directly. Knowing that, Powell pledged "to pick up where President Clinton and his administration left off" with regard to negotiations on missiles and nuclear weapons.[16]

That, however, was not Bush's message to the South Korean leader the next day. Bush told Kim Dae Jung that he did not trust the North Korean leader. "Part of the problem in dealing with North Korea, there's not very much transparency. We're not certain as to whether or not they're keeping all terms of all agreements. And that's part of the issue that the President and I discussed, is when you make an agreement with a country that is secretive, how do you—how are you aware as to whether or not they're keeping the terms of the agreement."[17] While the two leaders met in the Oval Office, Powell was sent out to talk to the press to underscore the administration's belief that North Korea constituted "a threat" and that any future dialogue with Pyongyang would have to await the conclusion of a policy review. "We're coming up with policies unique to the administration and the other things we want to see put on the table. And in due course, when our review is finished, we'll determine at what pace and when we will engage with the North Koreans."[18]

In being offered the choice between deferring to allies and confronting a perceived threat, Bush had left no doubt what he would do. Kim Dae Jung left Washington deeply embarrassed by Bush's public rebuff, which had fatally undermined his sunshine policy. The South Korean president was not the only casualty of the meeting, however. Powell had learned in no uncertain terms who was boss. It would take a few more months for Powell to regain his bearings on U.S. policy toward North Korea, and even then he would have to settle for something far different from his earlier inclination to start where the Clinton administration had left off.

The Korea policy review concluded in June 2001 with an offer to restart a dialogue with Pyongyang, as Powell (and America's key allies) had wanted. But the agenda for such talks would have to be far broader than Clinton's agenda, which had focused narrowly on seeking to end the North's missile development and transfers. "I have directed my national security team," Bush announced, "to undertake serious discussions with North Korea on a broad agenda to include: improved implementation of the Agreed Framework relating to North Korea's nuclear activities; verifiable constraints on North Korea's missile programs and a ban on its missile exports; and a less threatening conventional military posture."[19]

What followed was months of internal debate over whether North Korea's acceptance of the agenda was a condition for opening talks and what, if anything, Washington would be willing to offer Pyongyang if it agreed to any or all parts of the agenda. Powell and the State Department insisted that negotiations should start as soon as possible, and they favored offering the North substantial economic and political concessions in return for serious and verifiable commitments. Hard-liners in the Pentagon opposed any talks, which in their view would only encourage Pyongyang to ask for more and give less. Moreover, they argued, North Korea was the kind of country that signed agreements with no intention of abiding by their terms. Washington had no confidence in its ability to detect cheating by North Korea, the most secretive society on earth. All the more reason, the hardliners reasoned, not to negotiate agreements in the first place.

This debate went on for the better part of a year. September 11, Afghanistan, Iraq, and the war on terrorism intervened to keep North Korea policy sidelined. It briefly reappeared when Bush made Pyongyang a charter member of the axis of evil, but even then policymakers could not reach a consensus on how to proceed. Until, that is, new intelligence surfaced in the summer of 2002 that North Korea had a secret program to enrich uranium. This would enable it to build two or more nuclear weapons a year without having to restart the plutonium production facilities that had been frozen by the 1994 Agreed Framework. Powell was stunned. "You're kidding," he recalled thinking when he first heard the news. "They're putting all of it at risk—you know, the opening to Japan, the trains going through the DMZ, the soccer games in the South? They're putting all this at risk for another nuclear weapons program, after we bottled up the first one."[20]

All of a sudden there was a renewed urgency to engage North Korea. Working with America's partners in the region, the administration developed what it later termed a "bold approach" to improving relations with Pyongyang in the hope of heading off the new nuclear program. Washington was now prepared to offer significant political and economic benefits, "provided the North were dramatically to alter its behavior across a range of issues," including its nuclear and missile activities, threats to neighbors, support for terrorism, and human rights.[21]

Assistant Secretary of State James Kelly traveled to North Korea in early October 2002 to present Pyongyang with Bush's new initiative. He told his interlocutors that Washington had many concerns, not least information that Pyongyang had embarked on a secret uranium enrichment program. To Kelly's surprise, the North Koreans admitted that this was true. The admission constituted a clear violation of the Agreed Framework and left Kelly with little choice but to return home and report on his conversations. The administration kept Pyongyang's admission secret for nearly two weeks, in part because it did not want the issue to interfere with the congressional debate on whether to authorize the war against Iraq. Shortly after the Iraq vote was won in both houses on October 10 and 11, news of the North's secret program began to leak out.

But with Iraq standing front and center, the issue was left on the back burner. "We do not need another crisis now," Bush told his aides.[22] The bold initiative was shelved. Talks with Pyongyang could not resume until after the North came into complete compliance with its previous obligations. It is "hard to see how we can have conversations with a government that has blatantly violated its agreements," Undersecretary of State John Bolton said.[23] The administration made clear it would not give in to blackmail by announcing that the Agreed Framework was no longer operative and suspending the monthly shipments of heavy fuel oil required by the agreement.

North Korea, predictably, responded by escalating the confrontation. Having itself declared the Agreed Framework "null and void," it next moved to dismantle all other constraints on its nuclear program. In December it removed seals and surveillance equipment from the plutonium production facilities that had been installed as part of the Agreed Framework and ordered three international inspectors to leave. A month later, Pyongyang withdrew from the nuclear Non-Proliferation Treaty, under which it was barred from producing or possessing nuclear weapons. Then, in late January 2003, Washington received intelligence that North Korea was moving spent fuel rods from cooling ponds, possibly for reprocessing into plutonium. The rods contained enough fissile material for about six nuclear bombs. In February Pyongyang restarted the nuclear reactor capable of producing weapons grade plutonium. In March or April, it started up the reprocessing plant. And in July it claimed to have reprocessed 8,000 fuel rods. All in all, North Korea completely abrogated its commitments and became all but a declared nuclear power.

Bush and many of his supporters remained strangely quiet during this period. Administration officials insisted that they were not going to play by North Korea's rules by responding to its provocations. In late December 2002, Powell went on the Sunday talk shows to dismiss the notion that Pyongyang's actions constituted a crisis or much of a threat. "Yes, they have had these couple of nuclear weapons for many years," he told Tim Russert on NBC's *Meet the Press*, "and if they have a few more, they have a few more, and they could have them for many years."[24] It was a remarkably blasé attitude. This, after all, was North Korea Powell was talking about—the Hermit Kingdom, sealed off from the outside world but obviously up to no good. The country was run by a "pygmy" Bush said he loathed and one whose mental stability had often been questioned.[25] For more than half a century, Washington had opposed the proliferation of nuclear weapons, especially to countries like North Korea, a rogue state by any definition. But here was Powell, dismissing the threat. "You can't eat plutonium," he said dismissively.[26] Of course, you can *sell* plutonium and use the hard currency earned to buy food to eat, but somehow that appeared to have been lost on the administration.

Why the apparent contradiction in America's policy toward an unstable regime with nuclear weapons? One reason, clearly, was Iraq, which was taking all of the administration's energy and time during the fall of 2002 and winter of 2003. Another reason, though, was that Bush's stark rhetoric, and the principles that underlay his foreign policy revolution, now pointed him in a direction he feared to go.

Unlike Iraq, there were no good military options for dealing with North Korea. Quite apart from the possibility that Pyongyang might decide to go nuclear in response to a U.S. attack, its million-man army and tens of thousands of artillery pieces sat within easy range of Seoul, a city of more than ten million people. A war on the Korean Peninsula could cost hundreds of thousands—perhaps even a million—lives. Pyongyang seemed prepared to respond to U.S. military action against its nuclear facilities by turning Seoul into "a sea of fire," as it once threatened to do—even if it were convinced that the result would be the end of its own regime.[27] Little wonder, then, that even the hawks in the administration and their intellectual soul mates spoke softly even while putting down their big stick. One hawkish columnist, Charles Krauthammer, counseled a policy of at least temporary appeasement. Another, William Kristol, displayed a new-found faith in deterrence and containment. "We hawks," Karen Elliott House of the *Wall Street Journal* wrote in defense of the do-nothing approach, "believe it or not, understand the difference between using military force to preclude a future nuclear conflict and initiating military action that might spark one."[28]

Faced with this unpleasant military reality, Bush could have swallowed his fears about giving into blackmail and sought a deal with North Korea. Yet even if the president had abandoned his guiding principles, there was no guarantee Washington could strike a bargain with Pyongyang.

So instead of taking responsibility for dealing with North Korea, the Bush administration tried to shift responsibility onto the shoulders of others. In words that sounded strange coming from an administration insistent on exercising American power, Korea became for Bush a "regional issue" that was best handled within multilateral forums—ad hoc groups, the International Atomic Energy Agency, and the UN Security Council.[29] If only China and Russia would tell North Korea that it had to give up its nuclear weapons program and exert real pressure on Pyongyang, then things would be all right, so the argument went. The ball, in other words, was in someone else's court.

When China secured North Korea's agreement to talks with the United States in a multilateral setting (Beijing would participate as the meeting's convener), Bush allowed Powell one more stab at diplomacy. But the Beijing talks in April 2003 ended on the first day when the North's chief negotiator took James Kelly aside and told him that his country in fact had nuclear weapons. As Powell later recounted, the North Koreans said that "with these nuclear weapons, we can display them, we can make more, or we can transfer them."[30] Administration hard-liners immediately pointed out that this was the inevitable consequence of negotiating with renegades like the North Koreans. The president appeared to agree. "Yes," he told NBC's Tom Brokaw, "they're back to the old blackmail game."[31]

And so Bush accepted the new reality. North Korea was now a nuclear power, and its capacity to expand the size of its arsenal would no longer be a focus of American policy. Instead, the goal shifted to preventing Pyongyang from transferring any weapons or material to other countries or terrorist groups. "The president said that the central worry is not what they've got, but where it goes," a senior official told the New York Times. "He's very pragmatic about it, and the reality is that we probably won't know the extent of what they are producing. So the whole focus is to keep the plutonium from going further."[32] Powell announced the new policy publicly on NBC's Meet the Press in early May 2003. Asked what would happen if Washington discovered North Korea had more nuclear weapons, Powell said, "They have a bigger problem than they have now. Their nuclear weapons are not going to purchase them any political standing that will cause us to be frightened or to think that somehow we now have to march to their tune, march to their drummer." And would we let them sell or transfer those weapons? "Absolutely not."[33]

In June 2003, the Bush administration launched its new Proliferation Security Initiative designed to enlist other nations in an effort to interdict shipments of weapons or materials. North Korea was to be the immediate focus of what the New York Times's David Sanger called the policy of "pre-emptive pre-emption."[34] Yet, how this new policy would ensure that no plutonium, let alone a nuclear weapon, would ever find its way out of North Korea remained a mystery. A small suitcase could hold a significant amount of plutonium. North Korea was so poor that in the late 1990s upward of 10 percent of its population—roughly two million people—died from starvation. Aside from missiles and weapons, it produced nothing of value for export. As a result, Pyongyang's temptation to sell one of the world's most highly valued commodities to the highest bidder remained strong

In his axis of evil speech, Bush pointed to the nexus between terrorists, tyrants, and technologies of mass destruction. His nightmare— everyone's nightmare—was that Osama bin Laden might get his hands on a nuclear weapon. In North Korea, Bush faced the possibility of this nightmare's coming true. But in this case, Bush appeared to have been more frightened by the implications of his tough talk—that he would do anything to prevent countries like North Korea from acquiring nuclear weapons—than the possibility that his fears would become reality. Not that there was a plausible policy that would have enabled Bush to have avoided this difficult choice. But in not making the choice—and in not living up to the principles of his own foreign policy revolution—he may have let those who would do America harm make the choice for him.

WITH SYRIA RESPONDING positively to American pressure and North Korea deliberately pushed to the backburner, Iran moved to center stage. The immediate cause for Washington's increased concern about Iran was intelligence reports that al Qaeda operatives inside Iran might have directed the bombing on May 12, 2003, of residential compounds in Riyadh, Saudi Arabia, that killed thirty-four people, including nine Americans. The White House sent a strong message through British and UN diplomatic channels to Tehran demanding that it arrest and hand over any al Qaeda operatives on its territory. "Countries that are harboring those terrorist networks and providing a haven for them," Rumsfeld pointedly warned, "are behaving as terrorists by doing so."[35]

Even before reports of an active al Qaeda presence on Iranian soil surfaced in May, concern about Iranian behavior had been mounting inside the Bush administration. In December 2002, an opposition group revealed that Iran had surreptitiously constructed two nuclear facilities to enrich uranium and produce heavy water. Once completed, these would provide Iran with the capacity to produce weapons-grade uranium and plutonium. Inspectors from the International Atomic Energy Agency (IAEA) who visited the sites in February were surprised by the scale of the Iranian nuclear program: Iran had already built more than one hundred centrifuges to enrich uranium and planned to build fifty thousand in all. Tehran also revealed that it had failed to inform the IAEA it had imported nearly two tons of uranium in 1991. These revelations caused great concern. To Washington, they were proof of Iran's nuclear ambitions. "The intelligence community in the United States and around the world currently assess that Iran does not have nuclear weapons," Rumsfeld announced in June 2003. "The assessment is that they do have a very active program and are likely to have nuclear weapons in a relatively short period of time."[36] To the IAEA, "the number of failures by Iran to report the material, facilities and activities" were at the very least "a matter of concern."[37]

Compounding worries about Iran's apparent link to al Qaeda and the accelerated effort to acquire nuclear weapons were indications that Tehran, which otherwise had welcomed the overthrow of Saddam Hussein, was actively encouraging an Islamic fundamentalist takeover of Iraq. The power vacuum left in Saddam's wake was quickly filled by well-organized Shiite groups, which had formed the backbone of the internal opposition to Saddam's rule. Some of these groups, notably the Supreme Council for the Islamic Revolution in Iraq, had close ties with the Iranian government, which supported and funded many of their activities. "We have made clear to Iran that we would oppose any outside organization's interference in Iraq," Fleischer stated in late April.[38] "Iran should be on notice," Rumsfeld warned. "Efforts to try to remake Iraq in Iran's image will be aggressively put down."[39]

Many hawks had long agitated for increasing pressure on Tehran, which in many ways was the poster child of Bush's axis of evil. In its annual review of global terrorism, the State Department consistently emphasized that Iran was "the most active state sponsor of terrorism."[40] It was the primary supporter of anti-Israeli terrorist organizations, including Hezbollah and Palestinian rejectionist groups such as Hamas, Palestine Islamic Jihad, and Ahmad Jibril's Popular Front for the Liberation of Palestine–General Command. It had provided them with funding, safe haven, training, and weapons. And while Iran had arrested and transferred some al Qaeda members to other countries (including Saudi Arabia), its overall record on supporting the American war on terrorism was decidedly mixed. Initial cooperation in Afghanistan, for example, had quickly reverted to open support for elements inside Afghanistan that were bent on undermining the new government in Kabul.

What made Iran especially threatening, of course, was that its close ties to terrorism were linked to its active pursuit of weapons of mass destruction—nuclear as well as chemical and biological. The possibility that revolutionary elements within the Iranian government might transfer such capabilities to terrorists appeared less far-fetched with Iran than with any other country, including Iraq. For those itching for the next fight, Iran was therefore the logical candidate. "Take a number," is how one senior official responded when asked what message he thought Saddam's ouster would send to Tehran.[41] Many of Bush's hawkish supporters outside the administration similarly began to agitate for making Iran the next target in the war on terrorism. "The next great battle," William Kristol editorialized in the *Weekly Standard*, "will be for Iran," which he maintained "is the tipping point in the war on proliferation, the war on terror, and the effort to reshape the Middle East."[42]

Although Kristol talked about using "measures ranging from diplomacy to covert operations" and hoped that it would not come to a military confrontation with Iran, what was most notable about the Iran debate in Washington in mid-2003 was the lack of clarity on what to do. At one point, Bush drew a clear red line, declaring, "We will not tolerate the construction of a nuclear weapon. Iran would be dangerous if they have a nuclear weapon."[43] Yet he had early ruled out military action. When Tom Brokaw asked whether Iran would come after Iraq, Bush responded: "No, we just expect them to cooperate, and we will work with the world to encourage them to cooperate. We have no military plans."[44]

Instead, the Bush administration began to advance a strategy that encouraged the Iranian people to take matters into their own hands. In July 2002 Bush had issued a statement noting that "the vast majority of the Iranian people voted for political and economic reform. Yet their voices are not being listened to by the unelected people who are the real rulers of Iran. Uncompromising, destructive policies have persisted, and far too little has changed in the daily lives of the Iranian people." America's fight was with these rulers, not with the people of Iran—more than 50 percent of whom were born after the mullahs took power in 1979. "There is a long history of friendship between the American people and the people of Iran. As Iran's people move towards a future defined by greater freedom, greater tolerance, they will have no better friend than the United States of America."[45] In explaining the release of the statement, one senior official commented that the administration had given up on the ability of the popular Iranian president Mohammad Khatami to deliver reforms in the face of the ruling clique's determination to thwart him. "We have made a conscious decision to associate with the aspirations of Iranian people," this official told the *Washington Post*. "We will not play, if you like, the factional politics of reform versus hard-line."[46]

Left unresolved was the crucial question of how the Iranian people were to be encouraged. Would Iran's international isolation through continued sanctions and Washington's refusal to deal directly or indirectly with anyone in the government bring about the desired change? Or was American engagement on practical aspects of common concern the best way to break down the barriers? This central strategic question was debated almost from the first day the Bush administration entered office. Isolation had been the stated American policy for the better part of two decades, but it had not produced any significant changes in Iran's behavior. Similarly, tentative efforts at engagement—as happened in the wake of September 11 to coordinate policy on Afghanistan and before the Iraq War—produced only limited cooperation, but no lasting changes. Informal cooperation on the formation of a post-Taliban government ended when Iranian activities in support of Ismael Khan, a notorious warlord who controlled a large swath of southwestern Afghanistan, soured U.S. officials on continuing the effort. Similarly, informal talks in Geneva with Iranian officials before and during the Iraq War at first resulted in Tehran's commitment to close its borders with Iraq to fleeing members of Saddam's regime. However, this cooperation came to an abrupt end when Washington learned about an al Qaeda presence inside Iran.

What was lacking in Bush's policy toward Iran was a clear strategy for dealing with the most immediate threats the regime posed— notably its support of terrorism and its accelerating nuclear weapons program. Military action remained a last resort, though surgical strikes against known facilities would only temporarily derail Tehran's nuclear program. Aside from using force, Washington could do little on its own. Concerted pressure on Iran to open up its territory to more intrusive international inspections and to halt its material and financial support for terrorism required the agreement of other countries, notably the Europeans and Russia. They had continued to do business with Tehran even as Washington had sought to isolate it. Forging a cooperative strategy that would unite the major powers on Iran required the kind of intensive diplomatic effort that the Bush administration had shunned. Yet countering the threat Tehran posed ultimately demanded nothing less.

THE PERILS OF POWER

C HINESE LEADER Chou En-lai was once asked what he
thought of the French Revolution. "It's too early to tell," he
replied. The same could be said of the Bush revolution. It was tempt-
ing to call it a smashing success after impressive military victories
against the Taliban and Saddam Hussein. However, the ultimate question was not whether it worked in the short run, but whether it
enhanced the security, prosperity, and liberty of the American people in
the long run. Were Americans better off with or without the Bush
revolution?

George W. Bush was hardly alone in understanding that America
possessed unrivaled power—especially military power. What made him
revolutionary was his willingness to use it—even over the strenuous
objections of America's friends and allies. He used American power to
set the international agenda. Think the war on terrorism. He used it to
compel others to follow—or at least to accept—his chosen course.
Think Iraq. He used it to sideline those leaders America preferred not
to deal with. Think Mullah Omar, Saddam Hussein, and Yasser Arafat.
In these and other instances, Bush moved decisively to take the initiative. Rather than debate issues endlessly, he chose to act. And his decisions more often than not reflected his convictions rather than Washington's conventional wisdom.

But while Bush understood that American muscle could shape
events, he overestimated what the unilateral exercise of its power could

achieve. America was not omnipotent. To achieve most of its goals it still required the cooperation of others. Washington's ability to rally them to its side depended on identifying and pursuing common interests, not just national ones. Yet, during the first two-and-half years of Bush's presidency, people around the world lost trust in the United States, doubting that it had much interest in them or their problems. They feared that an America unbound had taken the tyrant's motto as its own: *Oderint dum metuant*—"Let them hate as long as they fear." And they became more reluctant to cooperate with Washington. America suddenly faced the possibility that it would end up standing all alone—a great power unable to achieve its most important goals.

"AMERICA," *New York Times* columnist Bill Keller observed, "is a feet-and-Fahrenheit power in a metric world."[1] From the start, Bush insisted that the rest of the world be measured by America's standard, not the other way around. This attitude infused Bush's language, his polite but cursory treatment of other world leaders, and his lack of concern for their interests and their advice. Bush's approach struck many as an arrogance born of power, not principle. And they resented it deeply.

After September 11, George Bush painted the world in black and white, while others, particularly overseas, painted it in shades of gray. He distinguished between those who were "evil" and those who were "good," between those who were "for us" and those who were "against us," between those who "love freedom" and those who "hate the freedom we love." The war on terrorism was a "crusade." Osama bin Laden had to be found "dead or alive." And Bush was "sick and tired" of the games Saddam Hussein played. This rhetoric helped galvanize Americans to support Bush's assertive and often audacious policies abroad. But it was alien to most foreigners, who, because of America's unquestioned supremacy, were as much a part of Bush's audience as the American people. Not accustomed to the blunt language and locutions of west Texas, many people outside the United States saw Bush's words as proof that their views did not matter.

Bush and his advisers did not try to dispel such perceptions. Instead, they frequently expressed their contempt for opinions different from their own. When Gerhard Schröder used his opposition to a war against Iraq to squeeze out a narrow reelection victory in Germany, Bush refused to place the customary congratulatory phone call. Condoleezza Rice spoke of the "poisoned" state of U.S.-German relations.

Donald Rumsfeld had a particular knack for twisting a knife in open wounds. He dismissed France and Germany as "old Europe" for failing to support a war against Iraq. To punish France for its opposition, he banned high-level U.S. military participation in the annual Paris Air Show, lobbied defense industry executives not to attend the show, disinvited France from a major military exercise, and sought to exclude the chief of the French air staff from a U.S.-hosted conference of air force commanders. He lumped Germany with Cuba and Libya as countries unwilling to help the United States in its war against Iraq—even though, in addition to granting overflight and basing rights, Germany deployed hundreds of troops to Kuwait, where they manned advanced chemical and biological warfare detection vehicles; hundreds more were in Turkey as part of a NATO commitment to defend the Turks against Iraqi retaliation; and still thousands more protected U.S. bases in Germany against terrorist attacks. When Rumsfeld traveled to Germany in June 2003, he thanked the Poles, Romanians, and Albanians for contributing to the wars in Iraq and Afghanistan. He said nothing about the larger and far more significant German military contribution to both these efforts.

France and Germany were not alone in feeling insulted by Bush and his advisers. "Most officials in Latin American countries today are not anti-American types," said Jorge Castañeda two months after resigning as Mexico's foreign minister. "We like and understand America. But we find it extremely irritating to be treated with utter contempt."[2] Castañeda's anger was unusual only in that he spoke openly about it. Most of his counterparts believed it was the better part of wisdom to seethe silently.

It was not just Washington's words that stoked this resentment but also its actions. After September 11, Bush made clear that only a country's support for the war on terror mattered much to the United States. Just as he had reoriented America's foreign policy agenda to focus single-mindedly on defeating terror, so Bush expected every other country to reorient its foreign policy as well. But the rest of the world had more to worry about than the terrorist attacks on the United States. Unspeakable poverty beset much of sub-Saharan Africa. Deadly conflicts raged in many parts of the world—from Chechnya to Colombia, Israel and the occupied territories to the Congo and west Africa. HIV/AIDS and other infectious diseases continued to infect and kill millions of people all over the globe. Bush spoke to some of these concerns and occasionally promised American aid. "We're not only a powerful nation," Bush proclaimed in Botswana in July 2003. "We're also a compassionate nation."[3] However, these lofty words were seldom matched by equivalent deeds. Bush's interest in the subject usually faded once the speech was delivered or the trip abroad completed.

Bush's pledge to step up efforts to combat HIV/AIDS was a case in point. Despite promising in his 2003 State of the Union address to "commit $15 billion over the next five years, including nearly $10 billion in new money," he requested only $1.9 billion in his 2004 budget submission to Congress.[4] Much of this money came from cutting spending on other international health-care programs.

Even issues that were once held to be priorities in the Bush White House fell by the wayside. Bush had come to office committed to placing Mexico at the center of America's foreign policy—and to paying far more attention to Latin America than his predecessors. "I will look south," he insisted on the campaign trail, "not as an afterthought, but as a fundamental commitment to my presidency."[5] Bush's first visit abroad was to Mexico, whose newly elected president, Vicente Fox, had ended more than seventy years of one-party rule. Fox shared Bush's commitment to a reinvigorated U.S.-Mexican relationship, and he was willing to make major changes to accomplish this goal. Early in his administration, Bush signaled that he was willing to work with Fox on the issue most important to Mexico—immigration. But Mexico disappeared from Bush's list of priorities after September 11. Fox felt betrayed—so much so that he saw no reason to support the United States in the Security Council on the question of Iraq.

Mexico was not alone in feeling ignored. The Bush administration acted as if the world had entered a post-diplomatic age—where making speeches and issuing ultimatums took the place of give-and-take negotiations. Once America's position was clear, others were expected to follow. Compare the run-up to the Gulf War with what preceded the Iraq War. James Baker visited forty-one countries on five continents in the months before the Gulf War. Colin Powell, by contrast, seldom traveled in the six months preceding the Iraq War, and never for the sole purpose of securing foreign support for a military undertaking that was far more challenging and controversial. His brief trips to China, Mexico, and Russia—three of the fourteen other members of the UN Security Council—all focused on issues unrelated to Iraq. Powell flew to Switzerland in early January 2003 to deliver an impassioned speech defending the administration, but he pointedly declined to stop in France and Germany, two countries whose opposition to Washington's Iraq policy proved most damaging.

Powell pointed to "the power of modern technology, the use of e-mail and telephones" as his preferred means for the conduct of diplomacy.[6] But diplomacy is best conducted in person, not over the telephone. It is not just that being willing to travel shows respect to others and helps earn their trust. It is that in an increasingly democratic world, effective diplomacy requires speaking directly to foreign publics as well as to their leaders. That can almost never be done from the confines of the White House or Foggy Bottom.

Bush's disregard for the views of others extended to international treaties. The president often acted as if America were a law unto itself. Within a few short months of coming to office, he withdrew the United States from or otherwise obstructed work on no fewer than five major international agreements—including the ABM Treaty, the Kyoto Protocol, and the treaty establishing the International Criminal Court. In most cases, Bush announced his decision with little concern for the international consequences. The ABM Treaty was an exception. Before withdrawing from the treaty, he launched an intense diplomatic effort to minimize the costs of his decision. He sent top aides to consult with friends and allies, spoke publicly of his desire to establish a cooperative relationship with Russia, and conducted new arms talks with Moscow.

Bush did not repeat this diplomatic deftness in other instances. The campaign against the International Criminal Court was a particularly egregious example of his disdain for international treaties. Bush was not satisfied with unsigning a treaty that had yet to be ratified. He also

threatened to veto UN peacekeeping missions unless soldiers participating in them were explicitly exempted from the court's jurisdiction.
He browbeat countries around the world into signing bilateral agreements forbidding the prosecution of Americans under any circumstances. He even cut off military assistance to dozens of countries that
refused to sign these agreements—even though such aid served important American interests. "Bullying is reprehensible in any circumstances," the *Financial Times* editorialized. "But simultaneously
shooting oneself in the foot looks like incompetence."[7] Though few
Americans noticed Bush's heavy-handed diplomacy on this and other
issues, it was front-page news in much of the rest of the world.

When Bush did negotiate with others, he sought agreements that
would leave America unconstrained. He endorsed a new round of multilateral trade talks, but spent no political capital on making them
succeed. He instead struck bilateral deals that did more to sustain
America's immediate economic advantage than to promote free trade
and America's long-term economic interests. The one arms control
agreement Bush negotiated was an assertive nationalist's dream.
Just three pages in length, the Moscow Treaty committed the United
States and Russia to deploy no more than 2,200 strategic nuclear
weapons by December 31, 2012—the very same day the treaty was
scheduled to expire. Nor did it require the two countries to destroy any
weapons, leaving open the possibility that the reductions could be
reversed. "What we have now agreed to do under the treaty is what we
wanted to do anyway," a senior administration official told the *New
York Times* after the agreement was signed in May 2002. "That's our
kind of treaty."[8]

"IF WE'RE AN arrogant nation, they'll resent us," Bush observed about
other countries during his second presidential debate with Al Gore. "If
we're a humble nation, but strong, they'll welcome us."[9] It was a wise
observation that Bush and much of his administration somehow forgot.
Resentment, not respect, best characterized how most other countries
reacted to the Bush revolution. Early evidence came during the 2002
elections in Germany and South Korea. In both countries, the results
turned on opposition to U.S. policy.

Foreign opinion about America increasingly soured in the weeks leading up to the Iraq War. Of the eight largest European countries polled in March 2003, only in Poland did even 50 percent hold a favorable view of the United States. Britain came a close second, with 48 percent holding a favorable view. In Italy and France, only a third did; in Germany and Russia only a quarter did; and in Spain and Turkey barely 10 percent did.[10] By the early summer of 2003, with the Iraq debate mostly past, America's image had recovered slightly—but it still was far less favorable than it had been in 2000 or even 2002.

In much of the rest of the world few people viewed the United States favorably—and their numbers were dwindling. The antagonism was especially pronounced in the Arab and Islamic world. In Jordan, Indonesia, Morocco, Pakistan, and among the Palestinians, near majorities believed that Osama bin Laden would do the right thing in world affairs. By contrast, overwhelming majorities said they had no confidence in Bush's leadership.[11]

The president and his advisers worried little about America's unfavorable image abroad. On the contrary, they expressed surprise at foreign resentment—or even growing fear—of American power. "There were times that it appeared that American power was seen to be more dangerous than, perhaps, Saddam Hussein," Rice told European journalists months after the Iraq War. "I'll just put it very bluntly: We simply didn't understand it."[12] Bush and his advisers were perplexed by hostile foreign reactions to their policies because of their deeply held conviction that America was a uniquely just nation and was seen abroad as being so. "I'm amazed that there is such misunderstanding of what our country is about," Bush said in October 2001. "Like most Americans, I just can't believe it. Because I know how good we are."[13] Bush's worldview simply made no allowance for others' doubting the purity of American motives.

Confronted with news that his policies stirred anger abroad, Bush's reaction was to insist that he was not elected to do what was popular. When asked in February 2003 about large antiwar protests in England, he responded: "First of all, you know, size of protest, it's like deciding, well, I'm going to decide policy based upon a focus group. The role of a leader is to decide policy based upon the security—in this case, the security of the people."[14] To a point, Bush was right. He could not run foreign policy as if it were a popularity contest. That did not mean, however, that the United States could afford to ignore how others viewed it from abroad. Like American presidents, foreign leaders had to take account of their own publics. When those publics opposed Bush's policies, that became a problem not just for their leaders, but for Washington as well.

The Iraq experience underscored that *how* America led mattered as much as *whether* it led. Too often America under Bush behaved like the "SUV of nations," as the journalist Mary McGrory put it. "It hogs the road and guzzles the gas and periodically has to run over something—such as another country—to get to its Middle Eastern filling station."[15] The cumulative effect of such behavior was substantial. It angered even America's closest allies, many of whom came to see their role not as America's partner but as a brake on the improvident exercise of its power. It weakened their support for American actions. And it undermined their willingness to cooperate in dealing with those challenges that were common to them all.

ALTHOUGH BUSH'S IMPERIOUS style entailed great costs for American foreign policy, that was not the only shortcoming in his revolution. To be sure, Bush would have been wiser to have shown what the Declaration of Independence called "a decent respect to the opinions of mankind." But more grace by itself would not have been enough to allay the fears of its friends and allies. The deeper problem was that the fundamental premise of the Bush revolution—that America's security rested on an America unbound—was mistaken.

This premise would have been right if the unilateral exercise of American power could have achieved America's major foreign policy goals. But the most important foreign policy challenges America faced—whether defeating terrorism, reversing weapons proliferation, promoting economic prosperity, safeguarding political liberty, sustaining the global environment, or halting the spread of killer diseases—could not be solved by Washington alone. They required the active cooperation of others.

The question was how best to secure that cooperation. Bush maintained that far from impeding cooperation, unilateralism would foster it. If the United States led, others would follow. They would join with America because they shared its values and interests. To be sure, some countries might object to how Washington intended to lead. But Bush was convinced they would come around once the benefits of American action became clear.

The flaw in this thinking became painfully obvious in Iraq. No doubt many countries, including all members of the UN Security Council, shared a major interest in making sure Iraq did not possess nuclear and other horrific weapons. But for most that common interest did not translate into active cooperation in a war to oust Saddam Hussein from power—or even into support for such a war. A few countries actively tried to stop the march to war, and many others simply sat on the sidelines.

Little changed after the toppling of Saddam Hussein's statue in Firdos Square. Although many countries believed that stabilizing postwar Iraq was vitally important—for regional stability, international security, and their own national safety—they did not rush to join the reconstruction effort. In mid-2003, American troops constituted more than 90 percent of all forces supporting the Iraq operation—at an annual cost to the American taxpayer of $50 billion. Britain provided most of the other forces. The remaining foreign contributions were insignificant. Hungary, for instance, agreed to provide 133 truck drivers. In other cases, countries agreed to contribute troops only after Washington agreed to help pay for them.

The lesson of Iraq, then, was that sometimes, when you lead, few follow. This, ultimately, was the real danger of the Bush revolution. America's friends and allies might not be able to stop Washington from doing as it wished, but neither would they necessarily be willing to come to its aid when their help was most needed. Indeed, the more others questioned America's power, purpose, and priorities, the less influence America would have. If others sought to counter the United States and delegitimize its power, Washington would need to exert more effort to reach the same desired end—assuming it could reach its objective at all. If others stepped aside and left Washington to tackle common problems as it saw fit, the costs would increase. That risked undermining not only what the United States could achieve abroad but also domestic support for its engagement in the world. The American public, always wary of being played for a sucker, might balk at paying the price of unilateralism. Americans could rightly ask, if others were not willing to bear the burdens of meeting tough challenges, why should they? In that respect, an unbound America would be a less secure America.

But Bush's way was not America's only choice. In fact, Washington had chosen differently before. When America emerged from World War II as the predominant power in the world, it could have imposed an imperium commensurate with its power—and no one could have prevented it. But Franklin Roosevelt and Harry Truman chose not to. They recognized that American power would be more acceptable and thus more effective and lasting if it were folded into alliances and multilateral institutions that served the interests and purposes of many countries. So they created the United Nations to help ensure international peace and security, set up the Bretton Woods system to help stabilize international economic interactions, and spent vast sums of money to help rebuild countries (including vanquished foes) that had been devastated by the war. It was not just America's victory in war, but also its magnanimity in peace, that made the twentieth century the American century.

Throughout the cold war, international institutions were a crucial means to exert America's authority. They bound everyone else into a U.S.-run world order. They in effect constituted what a British journalist called "America's secret empire."[16] Bush preferred to build his empire on American power alone rather than on the greater power that comes with working with friends and allies. His reliance on American military power proved extraordinarily effective in defeating foes, but far less effective in building a lasting basis for peace and prosperity. The United States could decisively defeat the Taliban and Saddam Hussein, but rebuilding Afghanistan and Iraq would have been best accomplished by working with others. The lesson was clear. Far from demonstrating the triumph of unilateral American power, Bush's wars demonstrated the importance of basing American foreign policy on a blend of power and cooperation.[17]

As Bush traveled to Europe and the Middle East in June 2003, many commentators thought they detected a change in both his demeanor and the message he was conveying. On many foreign policy issues, Bush seemed to be walking away from—or at least modifying key precepts of—the foreign policy revolution he had started. The president appeared to understand that more than overwhelming power was necessary to get things done. Diplomacy, active engagement by Bush himself, and a commitment to work within cooperative structures were needed to reach solutions in the Middle East, Iran, North Korea, and elsewhere.

On the Middle East, Bush seemed to realize that progress required his personal engagement. Rice, who was often Bush's weathervane in such matters, suggested that Clinton had set the right example. "President Clinton did a great service to the world in trying to make this work in Camp David," she told a London audience in June 2003. "Everyone in our Administration admires what he did."[18] Bush committed his administration to following in Clinton's path. He would be personally engaged in the diplomacy. Rice would be his personal representative to the peace process. And Powell would do as his predecessors had done—travel to the region frequently to move the process along.

The comeback of diplomacy in the Middle East was followed by a renewed dedication to multilateralism in dealing with the nuclear threat posed by Iran and North Korea, the other issue that dominated Bush's post-Iraq world tour. Bush turned to the International Atomic Energy Agency—the same UN body he had derided months earlier for its naïveté over Iraq's nuclear weapons program—to make sure that Iran's program remained in a box. With its European allies, Washington pushed for the conclusion of an additional inspection protocol between Tehran and the IAEA to give the agency the right to visit any suspect facilities in Iran. On North Korea, Bush argued for a regional approach that would bring South Korea, Japan, China, Russia, and the United States into multilateral talks with Pyongyang. Though what such a multilateral forum might accomplish was unclear given Washington's belief that negotiating with Pyongyang would be tantamount to giving in to blackmail, Bush at least made clear that in this case there would be no going it alone by Washington.

Why the change? Was Bush acknowledging that too much bluster and not enough attention to cooperative arrangements had been counterproductive—that the time had come to discard some of the revolutionary excesses? Or did he realize that these problems were far more complicated and required a different, more cooperative approach than Afghanistan and Iraq—that now was the time for pragmatism rather than standing on principle? Or, finally, did the coming reelection campaign mean, as he told Mahmoud Abbas, that the time for solving the Middle East conflict was now, before his focus had to turn elsewhere?[19]

All these factors were to some extent at work. By mid-2003, the Bush revolution was losing some of its zeal. "We want multilateral solutions," Rice reassured a European public, even while reminding them that problems like weapons proliferation had to be solved.[20] Iran and North Korea, though in many ways more threatening and urgent than Iraq, also were far more difficult problems to tackle unilaterally. With military force all but ruled out, a cooperative effort represented the least-bad option. And election years are a time for moderating the extremes in order to attract the average voter, a time for steady progress rather than for daring gambits.

But it was wrong to conclude that the Bush revolution had run its course—that foreign policy had begun reverting to the norm. It was not just that Bush was proud of his leadership style. "I have not looked back on one decision I have made and wished I had made it a different way," he said. "I don't spend a lot of time theorizing or agonizing. I get things done."[21] It was that at heart, Bush was a revolutionary. Everything he did in his first thirty months as president suggested that he would be audacious rather than cautious, proactive rather than reactive, and risk-prone rather than risk-averse.

ON INDEPENDENCE DAY 2003, Bush dispelled any notion that he was backtracking from his revolution. "Without America's active involvement in the world, the ambitions of tyrants would go unopposed, and millions would live at the mercy of terrorists. With Americans' active involvement in the world, tyrants learn to fear, and terrorists are on the run," Bush told twenty-five thousand cheering Americans at Wright Patterson Air Force Base in Dayton, Ohio. "The United States will not stand by and wait for another attack, or trust in the restraint and good intentions of evil men. We are on the offensive against terrorists and all who support them. We will not permit any terrorist group or outlaw regime to threaten us with weapons of mass murder. We will act whenever it is necessary to protect the lives and the liberty of the American people."[22]

NOTES

CHAPTER ONE

1. *The Writings of George Washington,* vol. 35, ed. John C. Fitzpatrick (Government Printing Office, 1940), p. 234.

2. Ibid., p. 236.

3. John Quincy Adams, "Address of July 4, 1821," in Walter LaFeber, ed., *John Quincy Adams and American Continental Empire: Letters, Papers, and Speeches* (Chicago: Quadrangle Books, 1965), p. 45, emphasis in original.

4. Quoted in Howard Jones, *Quest for Security: A History of U.S. Foreign Relations,* Volume I to 1913 (McGraw-Hill, 1996), p. 236.

5. Theodore Roosevelt, "Annual Message to Congress," *Congressional Record,* December 6, 1904, p. 19.

6. Quoted in Graham Evans, "The Vision Thing: In Search of the Clinton Doctrine," *World Today,* vol. 53 (August/September 1997), p. 216.

7. *The Papers of Woodrow Wilson,* vol. 37, ed. Arthur S. Link (Princeton University Press, 1981), pp. 213–14.

8. Woodrow Wilson, "Annual Address to Congress," *Congressional Record,* December 7, 1915, p. 96.

9. Woodrow Wilson, "Address to Congress," *Congressional Record,* April 2, 1917, p. 120.

10. Woodrow Wilson, "Address to Congress," *Congressional Record,* January 18, 1918, pp. 680–81.

11. Quoted in C. Howard Ellis, *The Origin, Structure and Workings of the League of Nations* (London: George Allen & Unwin, 1928), p. 489.

12. Quoted in Robert H. Ferrell, *American Diplomacy,* 3d ed. (Norton, 1975), p. 496; and Jones, *Quest for Security,* vol. 2, p. 340.

13. Quoted in Thomas G. Paterson, J. Garry Clifford, and Kenneth J.

Hagan, *American Foreign Relations: A History since 1895,* vol. 2, 4th ed. (Lexington, Mass.: D. C. Heath, 1995), p. 112.

14. Quoted in William L. Langer and S. Everett Gleason, *The Challenge of Isolation* (Harper and Bros., 1952), p. 144.

15. Quoted in Paterson, Clifford, and Hagan, *American Foreign Relations,* p. 28.

16. *Public Papers of the Presidents of the United States: Harry S. Truman, 1947* (Government Printing Office, 1963), pp. 178–79.

17. Quoted in Stephen E. Ambrose, *Rise to Globalism: American Foreign Policy since 1938,* 6th rev. ed. (Penguin, 1991), p. 133.

18. John Lewis Gaddis, *Russia, the Soviet Union, and the United States: An Interpretive History,* 2d ed. (McGraw-Hill, 1990), p. 216.

19. Charles Krauthammer, "The New Unilateralism," *Washington Post,* June 8, 2001, p. A29.

20. Quoted in Thom Shanker, "White House Says the U.S. Is Not a Loner, Just Choosy," *New York Times,* July 31, 2001, p. A1.

21. *The National Security Strategy of the United States,* Washington, D.C., September 2002 (www.whitehouse.gov/nsc/nss.pdf [accessed July 2003]).

22. Dick Cheney, NBC's *Meet the Press,* Washington, D.C., March 16, 2003 (www.mtholyoke.edu/acad/intrel/bush/cheneymeetthepress.htm [accessed July 2003]).

23. Jason Epstein, "Leviathan," *New York Review of Books,* May 1, 2003, p. 13.

24. Michael Lind, "The Weird Men behind George W. Bush's War," *New Statesman,* April 7, 2003, p. 12.

25. Joseph R. Biden Jr., "The National Dialogue on Iraq + One Year," Brookings Institution, Washington, D.C., July 31, 2003 (www.brook.edu/comm/events/20030731.htm [accessed August 2003]).

Chapter Two

1. Quoted in "Bush No Whizz on Foreign Quiz," BBC News, November 6, 1999 (http://news.bbc.co.uk/1/hi/world/americas/506298.stm [accessed July 2003]); and Glen Johnson, "Bush Fails Quiz on Foreign Affairs," Associated Press, November 4, 1999 [www.beloit.edu/~belmag/spring00/html/popquiz.html [access June 2003]).

2. Quoted in Johnson, "Bush Fails Quiz on Foreign Affairs."

3. Frank Bruni, *Ambling into History: The Unlikely Odyssey of George W. Bush* (HarperCollins, 2002).

4. Quoted in Dan Balz, "Bush Takes Soft Line on Abortion Stance of Running Mate," *Washington Post,* June 24, 1999, p. A7.

5. Quoted in Bruni, *Ambling into History,* p. 56.

6. Maureen Dowd, "A Baby Sitter for Junior," *New York Times*, July 26, 2000, p. A23.

7. Quoted in Tucker Carlson, "Devil May Care," *Talk Magazine*, September 1999, p. 108.

8. Nicholas Lemann, "Without a Doubt," *New Yorker*, October 14 and 21, 2002, pp. 170–71.

9. Quoted in Jacob Heilbrunn, "Condoleezza Rice: George W.'s Realist," *World Policy Journal*, vol. 16 (Winter 1999/2000), p. 51.

10. Quoted in Elaine Sciolino, "Compulsion to Achieve," *New York Times*, December 18, 2000, p. A1.

11. Quoted in ibid.

12. Quoted in Strobe Talbott, *Deadly Gambits* (Knopf, 1984), p. 16.

13. Quoted in Vernon Loeb, "Not Just Writing Checks for the Military," *Washington Post*, January 2, 2002, p. A11.

14. James A. Baker III, *The Politics of Diplomacy* (G. P. Putnam's Sons, 1995), p. 32.

15. Quoted in Jay Nordlinger, "Star-in-Waiting," *National Review*, August 30, 1999, p. 37.

16. Nicholas Lemann, "The Redemption," *New Yorker*, January 31, 2000, p. 56.

17. George W. Bush, *A Charge to Keep* (William Morrow, 1999), p. 97.

18. Governor George W. Bush, "A Distinctly American Internationalism," Ronald Reagan Library, Simi Valley, California, November 19, 1999 (www.mtholyoke.edu/acad/intrel/bush/wspeech.htm [accessed July 2003]).

19. Bush, *A Charge to Keep*, p. 123.

20. Ibid., p. 97.

21. "Transcript of President-Elect Bush's News Conference Naming Donald Rumsfeld as His Nominee to Be Secretary of Defense," Washington, D.C., December 28, 2000 (www.washingtonpost.com/wp-srv/onpolitics/elections/bushtext122800.htm [accessed July 2003]).

22. Quoted in Maureen Dowd, "Freudian Face-Off," *New York Times*, June 16, 1999, p. 29.

23. "Transcript of President-Elect Bush's News Conference Naming Donald Rumsfeld as His Nominee to Be Secretary of Defense."

24. "The First 2000 Gore-Bush Presidential Debate: October 3, 2000," University of Massachusetts, Boston (www.debates.org/pages/trans2000a.html [accessed July 2003]).

25. Bush, *A Charge to Keep*, p. 123.

26. Quoted in Sam Tanenhaus, "Bush's Brain Trust," *Vanity Fair*, no. 515 (July 2003), p. 168.

27. Quoted in James Bennet, "C.E.O., U.S.A.," *New York Times Magazine*, January 14, 2001, p. 27.

CHAPTER THREE

1. Quoted in Maureen Dowd, "Freudian Face-Off," *New York Times*, June 16, 1999, p. A29.

2. Governor George W. Bush, "A Distinctly American Internationalism," Ronald Reagan Library, Simi Valley, California, November 19, 1999 (www.mtholyoke.edu/acad/intrel/bush/wspeech.htm [accessed July 2003]).

3. Ibid.

4. Ibid.

5. Ibid.

6. Ibid.

7. Governor George W. Bush, "A Period of Consequences," The Citadel, South Carolina, September 23, 1999 (www.citadel.edu/pao/addresses/pres_bush.html [accessed July 2003]).

8. "The Second 2000 Gore-Bush Presidential Debate: October 11, 2000," Wake Forest University, Winston-Salem, N.C. (www.debates.org/pages/trans2000b.html [accessed July 2003]).

9. "Interview with George W. Bush," ABC's *This Week*, January 23, 2000.

10. Bush, "A Period of Consequences."

11. Bush, "A Distinctly American Internationalism."

12. Ibid.

13. Ibid.

14. Ibid.

15. Bush, "A Period of Consequences."

16. Ibid.

17. Quoted in Frank Bruni, "Bush Has Tough Words and Rough Enunciation for Iraqi Chief," *New York Times*, December 4, 1999, p. A12.

18. "The Second 2000 Gore-Bush Presidential Debate."

19. "Excerpts from Pentagon's Plan: 'Prevent the Re-Emergence of a New Rival,'" *New York Times*, March 8, 1992, p. A14; and Patrick E. Tyler, "U.S. Strategy Plan Calls for Insuring No Rivals Develop," *New York Times*, March 8, 1992, p. A1.

20. Quoted in Bob Woodward, *Bush at War* (Simon & Schuster, 2002), p. 137.

21. George W. Bush, *A Charge to Keep* (William Morrow, 1999), p. 239.

22. Bush, "A Distinctly American Internationalism."

23. See for instance Nicholas Lemann, "The Quiet Man," *New Yorker*, May 7, 2001, pp. 56–71.

24. "Bush Senior Foreign Policy Adviser Condoleezza Rice," Council on Foreign Relations: Live from the Convention, August 9, 2000 (www.foreignpolicy2000.org/convention/archives/t_rice.html [accessed July 2003]).

25. "Entretien avec Condoleezza Rice," *Politique Internationale*, no. 10 (Winter 2000–01), p. 30.

26. Condoleezza Rice, "Promoting the National Interest," *Foreign Affairs*, vol. 79 (January/February 2000), p. 62.

27. Ibid.

28. Quoted in Dowd, "Freudian Face-Off," p. A29.

29. Bush, "A Period of Consequences."

30. Bush, "A Distinctly American Internationalism."

31. Rice, "Promoting the National Interest," p. 47.

32. Paul Wolfowitz, "Remembering the Future," *National Interest*, no. 59 (Spring 2000), p. 41.

33. Paul Wolfowitz, "Re-building the Anti-Saddam Coalition," *Wall Street Journal*, November 18, 1997, p. A22.

34. Quoted in Tyler, "U.S. Strategy Plan."

35. Richard N. Haass, *The Reluctant Sheriff: The United States after the Cold War* (New York: Council on Foreign Relations, 1997).

36. Rice, "Promoting the National Interest," pp. 47–48.

37. Bush, "A Distinctly American Internationalism."

38. Ibid.

39. Rice, "Promoting the National Interest," p. 62.

40. Quoted in Johanna McGeary, "Odd Man Out," *Time*, September 10, 2001, p. 28.

41. Quoted in Michael Hirsh, "Our New Civil War," *Newsweek*, May 12, 2003, p. 32.

42. Rice, "Promoting the National Interest," p. 47.

43. "Excerpts from Pentagon's Plan."

44. Rice, "Promoting the National Interest," p. 47.

45. Bush, "A Distinctly American Internationalism."

46. "The Second 2000 Gore-Bush Presidential Debate."

CHAPTER FOUR

1. Frank Bruni, *Ambling into History: The Unlikely Odyssey of George W. Bush* (HarperCollins, 2002), p. 197.

2. Bill Keller, "Reagan's Son," *New York Times Magazine*, January 26, 2003, p. 29.

3. George W. Bush, *A Charge to Keep* (William Morrow, 1999), p. 97.

4. Quoted in Bob Woodward, *Bush at War* (Simon & Schuster, 2002), p. 12.

5. "President-Elect George W. Bush Holds News Conference to Name Colin Powell Secretary of State Designate," Washington, D.C., December 16, 2000 (www.usembassy.it/file2000_12/alia/a0121502.htm [accessed July 2003]).

6. Quoted in Elaine Sciolino, "Compulsion to Achieve—Condoleezza Rice," *New York Times*, December 18, 2000, p. A1.

7. Quoted in Mike Allen, "Bush Taps Rice for Security Adviser," *Washington Post*, December 18, 2000, p. A1.

8. Quoted in Henry Kissinger, *Years of Renewal* (Simon & Schuster, 1999), p. 842.

9. "Bush Names Rumsfeld Defense Secretary," Washington, D.C., December 28, 2001 (www.presidency.ucsb.edu/docs/transition2001/bush_rumsfeld_1228.php [accessed July 2003]).

10. Quoted in Woodward, *Bush at War*, p. 2.

11. Quoted in James Carney and John F. Dickerson, "Inside the War Room," *Time*, December 31, 2001/January 7, 2002, p. 114.

12. "President-Elect George W. Bush Holds News Conference to Name Colin Powell Secretary of State Designate."

13. Michael Hirsh and John Barry, "Leader of the Pack," *Newsweek*, December 25, 2000/January 1, 2001, p. 38; and James Traub, "W.'s World," *New York Times Magazine*, January 14, 2001, p. 31.

14. Johanna McGeary, "Odd Man Out," *Time*, September 10, 2001, p. 28.

15. Quoted in Bill Keller, "The World according to Powell," *New York Times*, November 25, 2001, p. 65.

16. James Fallows, "The Unilateralist," *Atlantic Monthly*, vol. 289 (March 2002), p. 26.

17. Kissinger, *Years of Renewal*, p. 176.

Chapter Five

1. Governor George W. Bush, "A Period of Consequences," The Citadel, South Carolina, September 23, 1999 (www.citadel.edu/pao/addresses/pres_bush.html [accessed July 2003]).

2. Dick Cheney, "Dick Cheney's Acceptance Speech," Philadelphia, August 2, 2000 (www.2000gop.com/convention/speech/speechcheney.html [accessed July 2003]).

3. Quoted in Paul Krugman, "Guns and Bitterness," *New York Times*, February 4, 2001, sect. IV, p. 17.

4. Bush, "A Period of Consequences."

5. George W. Bush, "Remarks by the President to Students and Faculty at National Defense University," Fort Lesley J. McNair, Washington, D.C., May 1, 2001 (www.whitehouse.gov/news/releases/2001/05/20010501-10.html [accessed July 2003]).

6. Quoted in Patrick E. Tyler, "Moscow Says Remarks by U.S. Resurrect 'Spirit of Cold War,'" *New York Times*, March 21, 2001, p. A4.

7. Quoted in Barry Schweid, "International News," Associated Press, March 22, 2001.

8. "Press Conference by President Bush and Russian Federation President Putin," Brdo Pri Kranju, Slovenia, June 16, 2001 (www.whitehouse.gov/news/releases/2001/06/20010618.html [accessed July 2003]).

9. Quoted in Alan Sipress, "Powell Vows to Consult Allies on Key Issues," *Washington Post*, February 28, 2001, p. A22.

10. "Presidents Exchange Toasts at State Dinner," Washington, D.C., September 5, 2001 (www.whitehouse.gov/news/releases/2001/09/20010906-1.html [accessed July 2003]).

11. Quoted in Jeffrey Kluger, "A Climate of Despair," *Time*, April 9, 2001, p. 30.

12. Quoted in Alan Sipress, "Bush Retreats from U.S. Role as Peace Broker," *Washington Post*, March 17, 2001, p. A1.

13. Quoted in John Lancaster, "Clinton Rules out a Visit to North Korea," *Washington Post*, December 29, 2000, p. A26.

14. "Remarks by the President and Prime Minister Blair in Joint Press Conference," Camp David, Md., February 23, 2001 (www.whitehouse.gov/news/releases/2001/02/20010226-1.html [accessed July 2003]).

15. Albert R. Hunt, "A Feckless Foreign Policy?" *Wall Street Journal*, April 19, 2001, p. A19.

16. Quoted in Nancy Gibbs, Michael Duffy, and Mitch Frank, "Saving Face," *Time*, April 16, 2001, p. 28.

17. George W. Bush, "Statement by the President," Washington, D.C., April 3, 2001 (www.whitehouse.gov/news/releases/2001/04/20010403-3.html [accessed July 2003]).

18. Quoted in Evan Thomas and Melinda Lu, "A Crash in the Clouds," *Newsweek*, April 16, 2001, p. 30.

19. Quoted in Gibbs, Duffy, and Frank, "Saving Face," p. 35.

20. "Letter from Ambassador Prueher to Minister of Foreign Affairs Tang," April 11, 2001 (www.whitehouse.gov/news/releases/2001/04/20010411-1.html [accessed July 2003]).

21. Quoted in Neil King Jr., "Bush Leaves Taiwan Policy in Confusing Straits," *Wall Street Journal*, April 26, 2001, p. A3.

22. George W. Bush, "Statement by the President Renewing Normal Trade Relations Status for China," Washington, D.C., June 1, 2001 (www.whitehouse.gov/news/releases/2001/06/20010601-5.html [accessed July 2003]).

23. Robert Kagan and William Kristol, "A National Humiliation," *Weekly Standard*, April 16/23, 2001, pp. 12–14.

24. Quoted in Evan Thomas and John Barry, "The Conflict to Come," *Newsweek*, April 23, 2001, p. 24.

25. Tom Donnelly, "Cheap Hawks," *Weekly Standard*, June 11, 2001, p. 14.

26. Rich Lowry, "It's Not Personal, Mr. Bush," *Washington Post*, July 1, 2001, p. B1.

27. Robert Kagan and William Kristol, "Clinton's Foreign Policy (cont.)," *Weekly Standard*, March 12, 2001, p. 11.

28. "Remarks by the President and German Chancellor Schroeder in Photo Opportunity," Washington, D.C., March 29, 2001 (www.whitehouse.gov/news/releases/2001/03/20010329-2.html [accessed July 2003]).

29. David E. Sanger, "Leaving for Europe, Bush Draws on Hard Lessons of Diplomacy," *New York Times*, May 22, 2002, p. A1.

30. "Remarks by President Bush and President Kim Dae-Jung of South Korea," Washington, D.C., March 7, 2001 (www.whitehouse.gov/news/releases/2001/03/20010307-6.html [accessed July 2003]).

31. Dominique Moisi, quoted in James Traub, "W.'s World," *New York Times Magazine*, January 14, 2001, p. 32.

32. George W. Bush, "President Bush Discusses Climate Change," Washington, D.C., June 11, 2001 (www.whitehouse.gov/news/releases/2001/06/20010611-2.html [accessed July 2003]).

33. David Frum, *The Right Man* (Random House, 2003), p. 240.

34. George W. Bush, "Inaugural Address," Washington, D.C., January 20, 2001 (www.whitehouse.gov/news/inaugural-address.html [accessed July 2003]).

35. Quoted in "Old Friends and New," *Economist*, June 1, 2002, p. 28.

36. Quoted in John F. Harris and Dan Balz, "A Question of Capital," *Washington Post*, April 29, 2001, p. A1.

37. Quoted in Peggy Noonan, "A Chat in the Oval Office," *Wall Street Journal*, June 25, 2001, p. A18.

38. Quoted in Johanna McGeary, "Odd Man Out," *Time*, September 10, 2001, p. 30.

39. Quoted in Barton Gellman, "A Strategy's Curious Evolution," *Washington Post*, January 20, 2002, p. A16.

40. Quoted in ibid., p. A16.

41. Quoted in Bob Woodward, *Bush at War* (Simon & Schuster, 2002), p. 34.

42. Quoted in Daniel Benjamin and Steven Simon, *Age of Sacred Terror* (Random House, 2002), p. 328.

43. Ibid., p. 336.

44. Ibid., p. 334.

45. Quoted in Gellman, "A Strategy's Curious Evolution," p. A16.

46. Quoted in Benjamin and Simon, *Age of Sacred Terror*, p. 335.

47. Quoted in Gellman, "A Strategy's Curious Evolution," p. A16. See also Judith Miller, Jeff Garth, and Dan Van Natta, "Planning for Terror but Failing to Act," December 30, 2001, p. B5.

48. Quoted in Woodward, *Bush at War*, p. 39.

49. Quoted in James Carney and John F. Dickerson, "Inside the War Room," *Time*, December 31, 2001/January 7, 2002, p. 116.

CHAPTER SIX

1. David Frum, *The Right Man* (Random House, 2003), p. 272.

2. Quoted in Patrick Tyler and Jane Perlez, "World Leaders List Conditions on Cooperation," *New York Times*, September 19, 2001, p. A1.

3. Edward Rhodes, "The Imperial Logic of Bush's Liberal Agenda," *Survival*, vol. 45 (Spring 2003), p. 140.

4. "The Second 2000 Gore-Bush Presidential Debate: October 11, 2000," Wake Forest University, Winston-Salem, N.C. (www.debates.org/pages/trans2000b.html [accessed July 2003]); and George W. Bush, "Inaugural Address," Washington, D.C., January 20, 2001 (www.whitehouse.gov/news/inaugural-address.html [accessed July 2003]).

5. *UN Security Council Resolution 1368 (2001)*, adopted September 12, 2001.

6. Quoted in Bob Woodward, *Bush at War* (Simon & Schuster, 2002) p. 281.

7. Paul Wolfowitz, "Interview with Sam Tanenhaus of *Vanity Fair*," May 9, 2003, Washington, D.C. (www.defenselink.mil/transcripts/2003/tr20030509-depsecdef0223.html [accessed July 2003]).

8. Thomas C. Schelling, "Introduction," in Roberta Wohlstetter, *Pearl Harbor: Warning and Decision* (Stanford University Press, 1962), pp. vii–ix.

9. George F. Will, "The End of Our Holiday from History," *Washington Post*, September 11, 2001, p. A27.

10. George W. Bush, "Address to a Joint Session of Congress and the American People," Washington, D.C. September 20, 2001 (www.whitehouse.gov/news/releases/2001/09/20010920-8.html [accessed July 2003]).

11. Ibid.

12. Frum, *The Right Man*, p. 142.

13. Dick Cheney, NBC's *Meet the Press*, Washington, D.C., March 16, 2003 (www.mtholyoke.edu/acad/intrel/bush/cheneymeetthepress.htm [accessed July 2003]).

14. Quoted in Bill Gertz, "Rumsfeld Says U.S. Presence in Asia Is Vital," *Washington Times*, July 25, 2001, p. A1.

15. Quoted in James Carney and John F. Dickerson, "Inside the War Room," *Time*, December 31, 2001/January 7, 2002, p. 116.

16. Quoted in ibid., p. 117.

17. "Press Briefing on the Budget by OMB Director Mitch Daniels," Washington, D.C., February 3, 2002 (www.whitehouse.gov/omb/speeches/daniels_04budget.html [accessed July 2003]).

18. Quoted in Woodward, *Bush at War*, p. 281.

19. George W. Bush, "Statement by the President in His Address to the Nation," Washington, D.C., September 11, 2001 (www.whitehouse.gov/news/releases/2001/09/20010911-16.html [accessed July 2003]).

20. Woodward, *Bush at War*, p. 30.

21. "DoD News Briefing—Deputy Secretary Wolfowitz," Pentagon, September 13, 2001 (www.defenselink.mil/news/Sep2001/t09132001_t0913dsd.html [accessed July 2003]).

22. Quoted in Nicholas Lemann, "After Iraq," *New Yorker*, February 17 and 24, 2003, p. 72.

23. Quoted in Elisabeth Bumiller, "Bush, at NATO Meeting, Firms Up His 'Posse,'" *New York Times*, November 22, 2002, p. A12.

24. Quoted in Woodward, *Bush at War*, p. 81.

25. Bush, "Address to a Joint Session of Congress and the American People."

26. Wolfowitz, "Interview with Sam Tanenhaus."

27. "President Bush Meets with Prime Minister Blair," Washington, D.C., January 31, 2003 (www.whitehouse.gov/news/releases/2003/01/20030131-23. html [accessed July 2003]).

28. "The Bush Presidency: Transition and Transformation," American Enterprise Institute, Washington, D.C., December 11, 2001 (www.aei.org/events/eventID.14/transcript.asp [accessed July 2003]).

29. Quoted in Woodward, *Bush at War*, p. 205.

30. Ibid., pp. 281–82.

31. Ibid., p. 282.

32. Governor George W. Bush, "A Distinctly American Internationalism," Ronald Reagan Library, Simi Valley, California, November 19, 1999 (www.mtholyoke.edu/acad/intrel/bush/wspeech.htm [accessed July 2003]).

33. Quoted in Jay Nordlinger, "Star-in-Waiting," *National Review*, August 30, 1999, p. 36.

34. Bush, "Statement by the President in His Address to the Nation."

35. George W. Bush, "President's Remarks at National Day of Prayer and Remembrance," Washington, D.C., September 14, 2001 (www.whitehouse.gov/news/releases/2001/09/20010914-2.html [accessed July 2003]).

36. Bush, "Statement by the President in His Address to the Nation."

37. Bush, "Address to a Joint Session of Congress and the American People."

38. Quoted in interview with Tom Brokaw, NBC's *Nightly News*, September 27, 2001.

39. Quoted in Frank Bruni, "For President, A Mission and a Role in History," *New York Times*, September 22, 2001, p. A1.

40. Quoted in Michael Hirsh, "America's Mission," *Newsweek: Special Edition*, December 2002–February 2003, p. 10.

41. Quoted in Frank Bruni, *Ambling into History: The Unlikely Odyssey of George W. Bush* (HarperCollins, 2002), p. 256.

42. Quoted in Howard Fineman and Martha Brant, "'This Is Our Life Now,'" *Newsweek*, December 3, 2001, p. 29, emphasis added.

43. George W. Bush "President Bush Addresses the 51st Annual Prayer Breakfast," Washington, D.C., February 6, 2003 (www.whitehouse.gov/news/releases/2003/02/20030206-1.html [accessed July 2003]).

44. George W. Bush, "Remarks by the President at the 2003 National Religious Broadcasters' Convention," Nashville, Tennessee, February 10, 2003 (www.whitehouse.gov/news/releases/2003/02/20030210-5.html [accessed July 2003]).

45. George W. Bush, "Bush Delivers Graduation Speech at West Point," West Point, New York, June 1, 2002 (www.whitehouse.gov/news/releases/2002/06/20020601-3.html [accessed July 2003]).

46. George W. Bush, "President Outlines War Effort," Sacramento, California, October 17, 2001 (www.whitehouse.gov/news/releases/2001/10/20011017-15.html [accessed July 2003]).

47. Quoted in Miles A. Pomper, "Daschle Determined to Weigh in on International Issues," *CQ Weekly*, July 28, 2001, p. 1829.

48. S.J. Res 23, "Authorization for Use of Military Force," September 14, 2001.

49. Quoted in Katharine Q. Seelye, "A Nation Challenged: The Military Tribunals," *New York Times*, December 8, 2001, p. B7.

50. Quoted in Thomas B. Edsall, "GOP Tout War as Campaign Issue," *Washington Post*, January 19, 2002, p. A2.

51. Quoted in Todd Purdum, "Democrats Starting to Fault President on the War's Future," *New York Times*, March 1, 2002, p. A1.

52. George W. Bush, "Guard and Reserves 'Define Spirit of America,'" Pentagon, September 17, 2001 (www.whitehouse.gov/news/releases/2001/09/20010917-3.html [accessed July 2003]).

53. Quoted in Helen Dewar, "Lott Calls Daschle Divisive," *Washington Post*, March 1, 2002, p. A6.

54. Ari Fleischer, "Press Briefing," Washington, D.C., March 19, 2002 (www.whitehouse.gov/news/releases/2002/03/20020319-7.html [accessed July 2003]).

55. Quoted in Elisabeth Bumiller and Alison Mitchell, "Bush Aides See Political Pluses in Security Plans," *New York Times*, June 15, 2002, p. A1.

56. George W. Bush, "Remarks by the President at Anne Northup for Congress Luncheon," Louisville, Kentucky, September 5, 2002 (www.whitehouse.gov/news/releases/2002/09/20020905-5.html [accessed July 2003]).

57. Quoted in Anne E. Kornblut, "Bush '04 Fund-Raising Cites War on Terrorism," *Boston Globe*, May 25, 2003, p. A1.

58. George W. Bush, "President Holds Town Hall Forum on Economy in California," Ontario, California, January 5, 2002 (www.whitehouse.gov/news/releases/2002/01/20020105-3.html [accessed July 2003]).

Chapter Seven

1. George W. Bush, "Remarks after Two Planes Crash into the World Trade Center," Sarasota, Fla., September 11, 2001 (www.whitehouse.gov/news/releases/2001/09/20010911.html [accessed July 2003]).

2. George W. Bush, "Statement by the President in His Address to the Nation," September 11, 2001, Washington, D.C. (www.whitehouse.gov/news/releases/2001/09/20010911-16.html [accessed July 2003]).

3. Dan Balz and Bob Woodward, "America's Chaotic Road to War," *Washington Post*, January 27, 2002, p. A13.

4. Quoted in Bob Woodward and Dan Balz, "'We Will Rally the World,'" *Washington Post*, January 28, 2002, p. A10.

5. Quoted in James Carney and John F. Dickerson, "Inside the War Room," *Time*, December 31, 2001/January 7, 2002, p. 117.

6. Bob Woodward, *Bush at War* (Simon & Schuster, 2002), pp. 43, 32.

7. Quoted in Dan Balz, Bob Woodward, and Jeff Himmelman, "Afghan Campaign's Blueprint Emerges," *Washington Post*, January 29, 2002, p. A11.

8. Quoted in Woodward, *Bush at War*, pp. 58–59.

9. Quoted in ibid., pp. 50–52.

10. "Press Conference by the President and Prime Minister Blair in Joint Press Conference," Camp David, Md., February 23, 2001 (www.whitehouse. gov/news/releases/2001/02/20010226-1.html [accessed July 2003]).

11. Prime Minister Tony Blair, "Statement in Response to Terrorist Attacks in the United States," London, September 11, 2001 (www.number-10.gov. uk/output/Page1596.asp [accessed July 2003]).

12. Dan Balz and Bob Woodward, "A Pivotal Day of Grief and Anger," *Washington Post*, January 30, 2002, p. A12.

13. Quoted in Bob Woodward and Dan Balz, "At Camp David, Advise and Dissent," *Washington Post*, January 31, 2002, pp. A13–14.

14. Quoted in Woodward, *Bush at War*, pp. 98, 223.

15. Quoted by Christopher Meyer, Britain's ambassador to Washington, in a background interview for "Blair's War," PBS's *Frontline*, March 18, 2003 (www.pbs.org/wgbh/pages/frontline/shows/blair/interviews/meyer.html [accessed July 2003]).

16. George W. Bush, "Address to Joint Session of Congress and the American People," Washington, D.C., September 20, 2001 (www.whitehouse.gov/ news/releases/2001/09/20010920-8.html [accessed July 2003]).

17. George W. Bush, "Address to the Nation," Washington, D.C., October 7, 2001 (www.whitehouse.gov/news/releases/2001/10/20011007-8.html [accessed July 2003]).

18. George W. Bush, "Prime Time News Conference," Washington, D.C., October 11, 2001 (www.whitehouse.gov/news/releases/2001/10/20011011-7. html [accessed July 2003]).

19. John F. Burns, "Afghan Region's Politics Snarl U.S. War Plan," *New York Times*, October 12, 2001, p. A1.

20. Frederick W. Kagan, "Did We Fail in Afghanistan?" *Commentary*, vol. 115 (March 2003), p. 39.

21. Quoted in Woodward, *Bush at War*, p. 168.

22. Quoted in ibid., pp. 243–44, 246.

23. General Richard Myers on ABC's *This Week*, Washington, D.C., October 21, 2001 (www.defenselink.mil/news/Oct2001/t10222001_t1021jcs.html [accessed July 2003]).

24. Quoted in Woodward, *Bush at War*, pp. 291, 268. See also John S. McCain, "There Is No Substitute for Victory," *Wall Street Journal*, October 26,

2001, p. A14; William Kristol, "The Wrong Strategy," *Washington Post*, October 30, 2001, p. A21; Charles Krauthammer, "Not Enough Might," *Washington Post*, October 30, 2001, p. A21; and Ivo H. Daalder and Michael O'Hanlon, "Bush and Powell Need to Remember the Lessons of Kosovo," *International Herald Tribune*, November 1, 2001, p. 6.

25. Donald Rumsfeld, "Press Conference with British Defense Secretary Geoffrey Hoon," Pentagon, October 30, 2001 (www.defenselink.mil/news/Oct2001/t10302001_t1030sd.html [accessed July 2003]).

26. Kagan, "Did We Fail in Afghanistan?" pp. 39–45.

27. John H. Cushman Jr., "New Orders Spur C.I.A. Hunt for bin Laden," *New York Times*, October 22, 2001, p. B5.

28. Woodward, *Bush at War*, p. 195.

29. Quoted in Michael R. Gordon, "Bush Would Stop U.S. Peacekeeping in Balkan Fights," *New York Times*, October 21, 2000, p. A1.

30. Donald Rumsfeld, "Press Briefing on Afghanistan," Pentagon, October 9, 2001 (www.defenselink.mil/news/Oct2001/t10092001_t1009sd.html [accessed July 2003]).

31. Bush, "Prime Time News Conference," October 11, 2001.

32. See George W. Bush, "Remarks at the George C. Marshall ROTC Award Seminar on National Security," Virginia Military Institute, Lexington, Va., April 17, 2002 (www.whitehouse.gov/news/releases/2002/04/20020417-1.html [accessed July 2003]).

33. Edward Luce and Victoria Burnett, "Afghanistan's Slow Progress," *Financial Times*, July 17, 2003, p. 11.

34. Woodward, *Bush at War*, p. 317.

35. Ibid., p. 237.

36. Quoted in Eric Schmitt, "Top General Defends Raids in Which 16 Afghans Died," *New York Times*, February 26, 2002, p. A17.

37. United Nations Security Council, *The Situation in Afghanistan*, S/PV.4750, May 6, 2003 (www.un.org/Depts/dhl/resguide/scact2003.htm [accessed July 2003]).

38. George W. Bush, "Remarks from the USS *Abraham Lincoln*," San Diego, May 1, 2003 (www.whitehouse.gov/news/releases/2003/05/iraq/20030501-15.html [accessed July 2003]).

Chapter Eight

1. Quoted in Karen DeYoung, "Allies Are Cautious on 'Bush Doctrine,'" *Washington Post*, October 16, 2001, p. A10.

2. George W. Bush, "Address to a Joint Session of Congress and the American People," Washington, D.C., September 20, 2001 (www.whitehouse.gov/news/releases/2001/09/20010920-8.html [accessed July 2003]).

3. "Letter from the Permanent Representative of the United States of America to the United Nations addressed to the President of the Security

Council," New York, October 7, 2001 (www.un.int/usa/s-2001-946.htm [accessed July 2003]).

4. Quoted in Glenn Kessler, "U.S. Decision on Iraq Has Puzzling Past," *Washington Post*, January 12, 2003, p. A1.

5. Carla Anne Robbins and Jeanne Cummings, "How Bush Decided That Hussein Must Be Ousted from Atop Iraq," *Wall Street Journal*, June 14, 2002, p. A1.

6. Barton Gellman, "Fears Prompt U.S. to Beef Up Nuclear Terror Detection," *Washington Post*, March 3, 2002, p. A1.

7. George W. Bush, "Remarks to the Warsaw Conference on Combatting Terrorism," Warsaw, Poland, November 6, 2001 (www.whitehouse.gov/news/releases/2001/11/20011106-2.html [accessed July 2003]).

8. George W. Bush, "State of the Union Address," Washington, D.C., January 29, 2002 (www.whitehouse.gov/news/releases/2002/01/20020129-11.html [accessed July 2003]).

9. Dick Cheney, "Speech to the Council on Foreign Relations," Washington, D.C., February 15, 2002 (www.whitehouse.gov/vicepresident/news-speeches/speeches/vp20020215.html [accessed July 2003]).

10. Ibid.

11. Donald Rumsfeld, "21st Century Transformation of U.S. Armed Forces," National Defense University, Washington, D.C., January 31, 2002 (www.defenselink.mil/speeches/2002/s20020131-secdef.html [accessed July 2003]).

12. George W. Bush, "Remarks at the 2002 Graduation Exercise of the United States Military Academy," West Point, N.Y., June 1, 2002 (www.whitehouse.gov/news/releases/2002/06/20020601-3.html [accessed July 2003]).

13. George W. Bush, "Remarks at Texans for Rick Perry Fundraiser," Houston, June 14, 2002 (www.whitehouse.gov/news/releases/2002/06/20020614-8.html [accessed July 2003]).

14. Glenn Kessler and Peter Slevin, "Preemptive Strikes Must Be Decisive, Powell Says," *Washington Post*, June 15, 2002, p. A16; "Colin L. Powell: Juggling the Demands of Diplomacy and a Different Kind of War," *New York Times*, September 8, 2002, p. 26.

15. Quoted in David E. Sanger, "Bush to Formalize a Defense Policy of Hitting First," *New York Times*, June 17, 2002, p. A1.

16. Quoted in David E. Sanger, "Bush to Outline Doctrine of Striking Foes First," *New York Times*, September 20, 2002, A1. Unless otherwise noted, all quotations are from the text of the strategy and accompanying introduction. *The National Security Strategy of the United States*, Washington, D.C., September 2002 (www.whitehouse.gov/nsc/nss.pdf [accessed July 2003]).

17. George W. Bush, "State of the Union Address," Washington, D.C., January 28, 2003 (www.whitehouse.gov/news/releases/2003/01/20030128-19.html [accessed July 2003]).

18. "Press Conference with Prime Minister Tony Blair," Washington, D.C., January 31, 2003 (www.whitehouse.gov/news/releases/2003/01/20030131-23. html [accessed July 2003]).

19. Quoted in James Kitfield, "'We Act with Patience and Deliberation,'" *National Journal*, February 1, 2003, p. 373.

20. Condoleezza Rice, "Wriston Lecture on the National Security Strategy," New York, October 1, 2002 (www.whitehouse.gov/news/releases/2002/ 10/20021001-6.html [accessed July 2003]).

21. Michael R. Gordon, "Serving Notice of a New U.S., Poised to Hit First and Alone," *New York Times*, January 27, 2003, p. A1.

22. Ibid., p. A11.

23. Quoted in Ramtanu Maitra, "U.S.-India Ties: An Adept Adaptation," *Asia Times*, October 8, 2002 (www.atimes.com/atimes/South_Asia/ DJ08Df07.html [accessed July 2003]).

24. Henry A. Kissinger, "Consult and Control: Bywords for Battling the New Enemy," *Washington Post*, September 16, 2002, p. A19.

25. Thucydides, *The History of the Peloponnesian War*, translated by Rex Warner (Penguin Books, 1954), p. 49.

26. For Cheney's argument, see his speech at the Veterans of Foreign Wars 103rd National Conventions, Nashville, Tenn., August 26, 2002 (www. whitehouse.gov/news/releases/2002/08/20020826.html [accessed July 2003]).

27. Joseph Biden and Richard Lugar, "Debating Iraq," *New York Times*, July 31, 2002, p. A19.

28. "CIA Letter to Congress on Baghdad's Intentions," *New York Times*, October 9, 2002, p. A12.

29. Quoted in James Risen, "Word That U.S. Doubted Iraq Would Use Gas," *New York Times*, June 18, 2003, p. A 12.

30. U.S. Senate Budget Committee, *Hearing with Secretary of State Colin Powell on the President's Fiscal Year 2003 Budget Proposal*, 107 Cong. 2 sess., February 12, 2002 (www.fnsg.com [accessed July 2003]).

Chapter Nine

1. Colin Powell, "Press Briefing en Route to Cairo, Egypt," February 23, 2001 (www.state.gov/secretary/rm/2001/931.html [accessed July 2003]).

2. They, together with thirteen others, signed a January 1998 letter to President Clinton urging him to make the overthrow of Saddam Hussein a policy priority. A copy of the letter can be found on the website of the Project for the New American Century (www.newamericancentury.org/iraqclintonletter. htm [accessed July 2003]).

3. Bob Woodward, *Bush at War* (Simon & Schuster, 2002), p. 99.

4. Quoted in Michael Elliott and James Carney, "First Stop, Iraq," *Time*, March 31, 2003, p. 177.

5. George W. Bush, "Press Conference with Prime Minister Tony Blair," Washington, D.C., January 31, 2003 (www.whitehouse.gov/news/releases/2003/01/20030131-23.html [accessed July 2003]).

6. Quoted in Michael Dobbs, "Old Strategy on Iraq Sparks New Debate," *Washington Post*, December 27, 2001, p. A1.

7. Richard Perle, "Next Stop, Iraq," Remarks at the Foreign Policy Research Institute, Philadelphia, November 14, 2001 (www.fpri.org/transcripts/annualdinner.20011114.perle.nextstopiraq.html [accessed July 2003]).

8. George W. Bush, "Prime Time News Conference," Washington, D.C., October 11, 2001 (www.whitehouse.gov/news/releases/2001/10/20011011-7.html [accessed July 2003]).

9. George W. Bush, "Remarks in Welcoming Aid Workers Rescued from Afghanistan," Washington, D.C., November 26, 2001 (www.whitehouse.gov/news/releases/2001/11/20011126-1.html [accessed July 2003]).

10. Fred Barnes, "The Commander," *Weekly Standard*, June 2, 2003, p. 23.

11. David Frum, *The Right Man* (Random House, 2003), p. 224.

12. Susan Page, "Iraq Course Set from Tight White House Circle," *USA Today*, September 11, 2002, pp. 5A–6A; Woodward, *Bush at War*, p. 329; and Evan Thomas, "Bush Has Saddam in His Sights," *Newsweek*, March 4, 2002, p. 21.

13. Condoleezza Rice, CBS's *Face the Nation*, February 17, 2002.

14. Colin Powell on CNN's *Late Edition*, Washington, D.C., February 17, 2002 (www.state.gov/secretary/rm/2002/8072.htm [accessed July 2003]).

15. Quoted in Elliott and Carney, "First Stop, Iraq," p. 173.

16. Ken Adelman, "Cakewalk in Iraq," *Washington Post*, February 13, 2002, p. A27.

17. Colin Powell, *My American Journey* (Random House, 1995), pp. 526–28.

18. Quoted in Keller, "The World according to Powell," *New York Times Magazine*, November 25, 2001, p. 63.

19. Quoted in Elisabeth Bumiller, "Bush Aide Attacks Clinton on Mideast, Then Retracts Remark," *New York Times*, March 1, 2002, p. A10.

20. "Remarks by President Bush and Prime Minister Tony Blair in Joint Press Availability," Crawford, Texas, April 6, 2002 (www.whitehouse.gov/news/releases/2002/04/20020406-3.html [accessed July 2003]).

21. George W. Bush, "Address on New Palestinian Leadership," Washington, D.C., June 24, 2002 (www.whitehouse.gov/news/releases/2002/06/20020624-3.html [accessed July 2003]).

22. Quoted in Nicholas Lemann, "How It Came to War," *New Yorker*, March 31, 2003, p. 39.

23. Eric Schmitt and David E. Sanger, "Bush Has Received Pentagon Option on Attacking Iraq," *New York Times*, September 21, 2002, pp. A1, A11.

24. Quoted in Elisabeth Bumiller, "Bush Aides Set Strategy to Sell Policy on Iraq," *New York Times*, September 7, 2002, p. A6, A1.

25. Colin Powell, "Interview with Richard Wolffe of *Newsweek*," Washington, D.C., March 13, 2003 (www.state.gov/secretary/rm/2003/18766pf.htm [accessed July 2003]).

26. Powell's meeting with Bush is detailed in Woodward, *Bush at War*, pp. 331-34.

27. Dick Cheney, NBC's *Meet the Press*, Washington, D.C., March 16, 2003 (www.mtholyoke.edu/acad/intrel/bush/cheneymeetthepress.htm [accessed July 2003]).

28. Dick Cheney, CBS's *Face the Nation*, Washington, D.C., March 16, 2003 (www.cbsnews.com/stories/2003/03/17/ftn/main544228.shtml [accessed July 2003]).

29. Powell, "Interview with Richard Wolffe of *Newsweek*."

30. Quoted in Eric Schmitt, "Iraq Is Defiant as G.O.P. Leader Opposes Attack," *New York Times*, August 9, 2002, p. A6.

31. James A. Baker III, "The Right Way to Change a Regime," *New York Times*, August 25, 2002, sect. IV, p. 9.

32. Henry A. Kissinger, "Our Intervention in Iraq," *Washington Post*, December 8, 2002, p. A15.

33. Brent Scowcroft, "Don't Attack Saddam," *Wall Street Journal*, August 15, 2002, p. A12.

34. "Interview with Lawrence Eagleburger," Fox's *News Sunday*, Washington, D.C., August 18, 2002.

35. Dick Cheney, "Remarks to the Veterans of Foreign Wars 103rd National Convention," Nashville, Tenn., August 26, 2002 (www.whitehouse.gov/news/releases/2002/08/20020826.html [accessed July 2003]).

36. Quoted in Richard A. Oppel Jr. with Julia Preston, "Administration Seeking to Build Support in Congress on Iraq Issue," *New York Times*, August 30, 2002, p. A1.

37. Woodward, *Bush at War*, p. 344.

38. Quoted in Dana Milbank, "No Conflict on Iraq Policy, Fleischer Says," *Washington Post*, September 3, 2002, p. A14.

39. George W. Bush, "Address to the UN General Assembly," New York, September 12, 2002 (www.whitehouse.gov/news/releases/2002/09/20020912-1.html [accessed August 2003]).

40. Text of U.S.-U.K. Draft Resolution, September 26, 2002. See also Michael R. Gordon, "U.S. Plan Requires Inspection Access to All Iraqi Sites," *New York Times*, September 28, 2002, p. A1; and Karen DeYoung, "For Powell, a Long Path to Victory," *Washington Post*, November 10, 2002, p. A14.

41. Quoted in Patrick E. Tyler, "U.S. and Britain Drafting Resolution to Impose Deadline on Iraq," *New York Times*, September 26, 2002, p. A14.

42. George W. Bush, "Address on the Iraqi Threat," Cincinnati, October 7, 2002 (www.whitehouse.gov/news/releases/2002/10/20021007-8.html [accessed July 2003]).

43. Colin Powell, "Press Conference on Iraq Declaration," Washington, D.C., December 19, 2002 (www.state.gov/secretary/rm/2002/16123.htm [accessed July 2003]).

44. Marc Champion and others, "How the Iraq Confrontation Divided the Western Alliance," *Wall Street Journal*, March 27, 2003, p.1; and Quentin Peel and others, "War in Iraq: How the Die Was Cast before Transatlantic Diplomacy Failed," *Financial Times*, May 27, 2003, p. 11.

45. Hans Blix, "An Update on Inspection," Report of the Executive Chairman of UNMOVIC to the United Nations Security Council, New York, January 27, 2003 (www.un.org/Depts/unmovic/recent%20items.html [accessed July 2003]).

46. Jacques Chirac, "Interview Given to 'TF1' and 'France 2,'" Paris, March 10, 2003 (www.diplomatie.gouv.fr/actu/bulletin.gb.asp?liste=20030311.gb.html#Ch [accessed July 2003]).

47. George W. Bush, "President Discusses Iraq in National Press Conference," Washington, D.C., March 6, 2003 (www.whitehouse.gov/news/releases/2003/03/20030306-8.html [accessed July 2003]).

48. Colin Powell, "Interview with the *New York Times*," Washington, D.C., March 29, 2003 (www.state.gov/secretary/rm/2003/19171.htm [accessed July 2003]). See also Gerard Baker and others, "Blair's Mission Impossible: The Doomed Effort to Win a Second Resolution," *Financial Times*, May 29, 2003, p. 11.

CHAPTER TEN

1. George W. Bush, "Remarks at John Cornyn for Senate Reception," Houston, September 26, 2002 (www.whitehouse.gov/news/releases/2002/09/20020926-17.html [accessed July 2003]).

2. George W. Bush, "Interview with NBC's Tom Brokaw," Washington, D.C., April 24, 2003 (www.msnbc.com/news/905108.asp [accessed July 2003]).

3. Ari Fleischer, "Press Briefing," Washington, D.C., April 9, 2003 (www.whitehouse.gov/news/releases/2003/04/20030409-8.html [accessed July 2003]).

4. Thomas Friedman, "Postcard from Iraq," *New York Times*, May 21, 2003, p. A31.

5. George W. Bush, "Press Conference with British Prime Minister Tony Blair," Camp David, Md., March 27, 2003 (www.whitehouse.gov/news/releases/2003/03/20030327-3.html [accessed July 2003]).

6. Bill Keller, "Why Colin Powell Should Go," *New York Times*, March 22, 2003, p. A11.

7. Donald Rumsfeld, "Defense Department News Briefing," Pentagon, April 11, 2003 (www.defenselink.mil/transcripts/2003/tr20030411-secdef0090.html [accessed July 2003]).

8. Quoted in Romesh Ratnesar and Simon Robinson, "Life under Fire," *Time*, July 14, 2003, p. 28.

9. Paul Wolfowitz, "Testimony on Iraq Reconstruction," Prepared Statement

before the Senate Foreign Relations Committee, Washington, D.C., May 22, 2003 (www.defenselink.mil/speeches/2003/sp20030522-depsecdef0223.html [accessed July 2003]).

10. Quoted in John Hendren, "A Huge Postwar Force Seen," *Los Angeles Times*, February 26, 2003, p. A1.

11. Paul Wolfowitz, "Statement on Defense Priorities," *Department of Defense Budget Priorities for Fiscal Year 2004*, Hearing before the House Committee on the Budget, 108 Cong. 1 sess. (Government Printing Office, 2003), pp. 8–10 (http://frwebgate.access.gpo.gov/cgi-bin/getdoc.cgi?dbname=108_house_hearings&docid=f:85421.pdf [accessed July 2003]).

12. Michael Gordon and Eric Schmitt, "U.S. Plans to Reduce Forces in Iraq, with Help of Allies," *New York Times*, May 3, 2003, p. A1.

13. Quoted in Susan Sachs, "2 More Servicemen Killed in New Attacks in Baghdad," *New York Times*, May 9, 2003, p. A15.

14. George W. Bush, "Remarks Discussing Afghanistan and Iraq," Washington, D.C., July 1, 2003 (www.whitehouse.gov/news/releases/2003/07/20030701-9.html [accessed July 2003]).

15. Quoted in Thom Shanker, "Lesson for Iraq Seen in Balkan Aftermath," *New York Times*, May 22, 2003, p. A16.

16. Quoted in Jonathan Weisman and Mike Allen, "Officials Argue for Fast U.S. Exit from Iraq," *Washington Post*, April 21, 2003, p. A1.

17. Quoted in Eric Schmitt and David E. Sanger, "Looting Disrupts Detailed U.S. Plan to Restore Iraq," *New York Times*, May 19, 2003, p. A10.

18. George W. Bush, "Speech on Progress in Operation Iraqi Freedom," St. Louis, Mo., April 16, 2003 (www.whitehouse.gov/news/releases/2003/04/20030416-9.html [accessed July 2003]).

19. Quoted in Patrick E. Tyler, "Overseer Adjusts Strategy as Turmoil Grows in Iraq," *New York Times*, July 13, 2003, p. 8.

20. Richard Armitage, "Interview with Ralitsa Vasiliva of CNNI," Washington, D.C., April 7, 2003 (www.state.gov/s/d/rm/19385.htm [accessed July 2003]).

21. Quoted in Richard Wolffe and Trent Gegax, "The Best-Laid Plans," *Newsweek*, July 21, 2003, p. 32.

22. Dick Cheney, NBC's *Meet the Press*, Washington, D.C., March 16, 2003 (www.mtholyoke.edu/acad/intrel/bush/cheneymeetthepress.htm [accessed July 2003]).

23. Quoted in Schmitt and Sanger, "Looting Disrupts Detailed U.S. Plan to Restore Iraq."

24. Quoted in Vernon Loeb, "Occupation of Iraq Has No Time Limit," *Washington Post*, May 10, 2003, p. A1.

25. Quoted in Thomas E. Ricks, "U.S. Alters Tactics in Baghdad Occupation," *Washington Post*, May 25, 2003, p. A18.

26. Quoted in Scott Wilson, "Bremer Adopts Firmer Tone," *Washington Post*, May 26, 2003, p. A13.

27. George W. Bush, "Remarks in Announcement of the New Coordinator of U.S. Government Activities to Combat HIV/AIDS Globally," Washington, D.C., July 2, 2003 (www.whitehouse.gov/news/releases/2003/07/20030702-3.html [accessed July 2003]).

28. Quoted in Thom Shanker, "Rumsfeld Doubles Estimate for Cost of Troops in Iraq," *New York Times*, July 10, 2003, p. A1.

29. Paul Wolfowitz, "Interview with Sam Tanenhaus of *Vanity Fair*," Washington, D.C., May 9, 2003 (www.defenselink.mil/transcripts/2003/tr20030509-depsecdef0223.html [accessed July 2003]).

30. Tony Blair, "Press Conference prior to Departure for Camp David," London, March 25, 2003 (www.number-10.gov.uk/output/Page3347.asp [accessed July 2003]).

31. Dick Cheney, "Remarks to the Veterans of Foreign Wars 103rd National Convention," Nashville, Tenn., August 26, 2002 (www.whitehouse.gov/news/releases/2002/08/20020826.html [accessed July 2003]).

32. George W. Bush, "Remarks to the United Nations General Assembly," New York, September 12, 2002 (www.whitehouse.gov/news/releases/2002/09/20020912-1.html [accessed July 2003]).

33. George W. Bush, "Remarks on Iraq," Cincinnati, October 7, 2002 (www.whitehouse.gov/news/releases/2002/10/20021007-8.html [accessed July 2003]).

34. George W. Bush, "President Delivers State of the Union," Washington, D.C., January 28, 2003 (www.whitehouse.gov/news/releases/2003/01/20030128-19.html [accessed July 2003]).

35. Quoted in Bruce B. Auster, Mark Mazzetti, and Edward T. Pound, "Truth and Consequences," *U.S. News & World Report*, June 9, 2003, p. 14.

36. Mark Huband and Stephen Fidler, "No Smoking Gun," *Financial Times*, June 4, 2003, p. 11.

37. Colin Powell, "Remarks to the United Nations Security Council," New York, February 5, 2003 (www.state.gov/secretary/rm/2003/17300.htm [accessed July 2003]).

38. William Raspberry, "A Case for Powell, but Not War," *Washington Post*, February 10, 2003, p. A21.

39. ABC News/*Washington Post* Poll, February 5, 2003 (www.pollingreport.com/iraq4.htm [accessed July 2003]), emphasis in original.

40. Dominique de Villepin, "Remarks to the UN Security Council," New York, 4701st Meeting, S/PV.4701, February 5, 2003 (www.un.org/Depts/dhl/resguide/scact2003.htm [accessed July 2003]).

41. George Tenet, Testimony before the Senate Select Intelligence Committee, 108 Cong. 1 sess., February 11, 2003 (transcript available from Federal News Service at www.nexis.com [accessed July 2003]).

42. George W. Bush, "Remarks in Address to the Nation," Washington, D.C., March 17, 2003 (www.whitehouse.gov/news/releases/2003/03/20030317-7.html [accessed July 2003]).

43. Ari Fleischer, "Press Briefing," Washington, D.C., March 21, 2003 (www.whitehouse.gov/news/releases/2003/03/20030321-9.html [accessed July 2003]).

44. General Tommy R. Franks, "Briefing on Military Operations in Iraq," Doha, Qatar, March 22, 2003 (www.centcom.mil/CENTCOMNews/Transcripts/20030322.htm [accessed July 2003]).

45. Donald Rumsfeld, "Remarks on ABC '*This Week* with George Stephanopoulos,'" March 30, 2003 (www.defenselink.mil/news/Mar2003/t03302003_t0330sdabcsteph.html [accessed July 2003]).

46. Barton Gellman, "Covert Unit Hunted for Iraqi Arms," *Washington Post*, June 13, 2003, p. A1.

47. Quoted in Barton Gellman, "Frustrated, U.S. Arms Team to Leave Iraq," *Washington Post*, May 11, 2003, p. A1.

48. Lieutenant General James Conway, "Video Briefing from Iraq," Pentagon, May 30, 2003 (www.defenselink.mil/transcripts/2003/tr20030530-0229.html [accessed July 2003]).

49. Judith Miller and William Broad, "Some Analysts of Iraq Trailers Reject Germ Use," *New York Times*, June 7, 2003, p. A1; and Peter Beaumont, Antony Barnett, and Gaby Hinsliff, "Iraqi Mobile Labs Nothing to Do with Germ Warfare, Report Finds," *Observer*, June 15, 2003, p. 2.

50. *Iraqi Mobile Biological Warfare Agent Production Plants*, Central Intelligence Agency and Defense Intelligence Agency, May 28, 2003, p. 1 (www.cia.gov/cia/reports/iraqi_mobile_plants/index.html [accessed July 2003]).

51. Quoted in Dana Milbank, "Bush Remarks Confirm Shift in Justification for War," *Washington Post*, June 1, 2003, p. A18.

52. George W. Bush, "Remarks on Middle East, Iraq at Cabinet Meeting," Washington, D.C., June 9, 2003 (www.whitehouse.gov/news/releases/2003/06/20030609-4.html [accessed July 2003]).

53. Quoted in Bill Nichols, "Weapons Search Could Take Years," *USA Today*, May 16, 2003, p. 1.

54. Michael R. Gordon, "Agency Challenges Evidence against Iraq Cited by Bush," *New York Times*, January 10, 2003, p. A10; and Richard Leiby and Walter Pincus, "Ex-Envoy: Nuclear Report Ignored," *Washington Post*, July 6, 2003, p. A13.

55. Mohamed ElBaradei, "The Status of Nuclear Weapons Inspections in Iraq: An Update," Statement to the United Nations Security Council, New York, March 7, 2003 (www.iaea.org/worldatom/Press/Statements/2003/ebsp2003n006.shtml [accessed July 2003]).

56. Walter Pincus, "Basis for Arms Claims Affirmed," *Washington Post*, July 4, 2003, p. A20.

57. Donald Rumsfeld, "Testimony on Iraq," Hearing before the Senate Armed Services Committee, Washington, D.C., July 9, 2003 (www.defenselink.mil/speeches/2003/sp20030709-secdef0364.html [accessed July 2003]).

58. "Defense Agency Issues Excerpt on Iraqi Chemical Warfare Program," June 7, 2003 (http://usinfo.state.gov/topical/pol/arms/03060720.htm [accessed July 2003]), emphases added.

59. Hans Blix, *Fourth Consolidated Report of the Director General of the International Atomic Energy Agency*, S/1997/779, October 8, 1997 (www.iaea.org/worldatom/Programmes/ActionTeam/reports/s_1997_779.pdf [accessed July 2003]); and Hans Blix, *Thirteenth Quarterly Report of the Executive Chairman of the United Nations Monitoring, Verification, and Inspection Commission*, S/2003/580, May 30, 2003 (www.un.org/Depts/unmovic/index.htm [accessed July 2003]), appendix I.

60. George W. Bush, "Press Conference with South African President Mbeki," Pretoria, July 9, 2003 (www.whitehouse.gov/news/releases/2003/07/20030709.html [accessed July 2003]).

61. Wolfowitz, "Interview with Sam Tanenhaus of *Vanity Fair*."

62. Quoted in James Risen, David E. Sanger, and Thom Shanker, "In Sketchy Data, White House Sought Clues to Gauge Threat," *New York Times*, July 20, 2003, p. 1.

63. George F. Will, "The Bush Doctrine at Risk," *Washington Post*, June 22, 2003, p. B7, emphasis added.

64. George W. Bush, "Remarks on the Future of Iraq," Speech to the American Enterprise Institute, Washington, D.C., February 26, 2003 (www.whitehouse.gov/news/releases/2003/02/20030226-11.html [accessed July 2003]).

65. Quoted in Carl Cannon, "Memory and More in the Mideast," *National Journal*, June 7, 2003, p. 1780.

66. George W. Bush, "Remarks on the Need for New Palestinian Leadership," Washington, D.C., June 24, 2002 (www.whitehouse.gov/news/releases/2002/06/20020624-3.html [accessed July 2003]).

67. Quoted in Cannon, "Memory and More in the Mideast," p. 1780; emphasis in the original.

68. George W. Bush, "Remarks at Meeting with Arab Leaders," Sharm el-Sheikh, Egypt, June 3, 2003 (www.whitehouse.gov/news/releases/2003/06/20030603-2.html [accessed July 2003]).

69. Quoted in James Carney, "How Bush Got Religion," *Time*, June 16, 2003, p. 42.

70. George W. Bush, "Briefing on the Middle East," Aboard Air Force One, En Route to Doha, Qatar, June 4, 2003 (www.whitehouse.gov/news/releases/2003/06/20030604-3.html [accessed July 2003]).

71. Quoted in Cannon, "Memory and More in the Mideast," p. 1780.

CHAPTER ELEVEN

1. Colin Powell, "Interview by the *New York Times*," Washington, D.C., March 29, 2003 (www.state.gov/secretary/rm/2003/19171.htm [accessed July 2003]).

2. George W. Bush, "Remarks aboard the USS *Abraham Lincoln* Announcing End to Combat Operations in Iraq," San Diego, May 1, 2003 (www.whitehouse.gov/news/releases/2003/05/iraq/20030501-15.html [accessed July 2003]).

3. Quoted in Steven Weisman, "U.S. Threatens to Impose Penalties against Syrians," *New York Times*, April 15, 2003, p. B3.

4. Richard Perle, "Next Stop Iraq," Remarks at the Foreign Policy Research Institute's Annual Dinner, Philadelphia, November 14, 2001 (www.fpri.org/transcripts/annualdinner.20011114.perle.nextstopiraq.html [accessed July 2003]).

5. Donald Rumsfeld, "Department of Defense News Briefing," Pentagon, March 28, 2003 (www.defenselink.mil/news/Mar2003/t03282003_t0328sd.html [accessed July 2003]).

6. Quoted in David E. Sanger, "Viewing the War as a Lesson to the World," *New York Times*, April 6, 2003, p. B1.

7. Colin Powell, "Remarks at the American Israel Public Affairs Committee's Annual Policy Conference," Washington, D.C., March 30, 2003 (www.state.gov/secretary/rm/2003/19174.htm [accessed July 2003]).

8. Quoted in David E. Sanger, "What Victory in Iraq Means for U.S. Foreign Policy," *New York Times*, April 13, 2003, sec. IV, p. 5.

9. *Patterns of Global Terrorism 2002*, Office of the Coordinator for Counterterrorism, Department of State, Washington, D.C., April 30, 2003 (www.state.gov/s/ct/rls/pgtrpt/2002/html/19988.htm [accessed July 2003]).

10. George W. Bush, "Remarks at Army and Navy Medical Centers," Bethesda, Maryland, April 11, 2003 (www.whitehouse.gov/news/releases/2003/04/20030411-13.html [accessed July 2003]).

11. Julian Borger and others, "Bush Vetoes Syria War Plan," *Guardian*, April 15, 2003, p.1.

12. Quoted in Dana Milbank, "White House Escalates Diplomatic Pressure on Syria," *Washingtonpost.com*, April 14, 2003 (www.washingtonpost.com/ac2/wp-dyn/A22809-2003Apr14 [accessed July 2003]).

13. Ari Fleischer, "Press Briefing," Washington, D.C., April 14, 2003 (www.whitehouse.gov/news/releases/2003/04/20030414-5.html#6 [accessed July 2003]).

14. Quoted in Michael Hirsh, "No New Wars," *Newsweek.com*, April 22, 2003 (www.msnbc.com/news/903717.asp [accessed July 2003]).

15. Colin Powell, "Press Availability with Her Excellency Anna Lindh, Minister of Foreign Affairs of Sweden," Washington, D.C., March 6, 2001 (www.state.gov/secretary/rm/2001/1116.htm [accessed July 2003]).

16. Ibid.

17. George W. Bush, "Remarks by President Bush and President Kim Dae Jung of South Korea," Washington, D.C., March 7, 2001 (www.whitehouse.gov/news/releases/2001/03/20010307-6.html [accessed July 2003]).

18. Colin Powell, "Remarks to the Pool," Washington, D.C., March 7, 2001 (http://usinfo.state.gov/regional/ea/easec/kimpwll.htm [accessed July 2003]).

19. George W. Bush, "Statement by the President," Washington, D.C., June 13, 2001 (www.whitehouse.gov/news/releases/2001/06/20010611-4.html [accessed July 2003]).

20. Colin Powell, "Roundtable Interview with European Journalists," Washington, D.C., October 28, 2002 (www.state.gov/secretary/rm/2002/14773.htm [accessed July 2003]).

21. Richard Boucher, "Statement on the North Korean Nuclear Program," Washington, D.C., October 16, 2002 (www.state.gov/r/pa/prs/ps/2002/14432.htm [accessed July 2003]).

22. Quoted in Doug Struck and Glenn Kessler, "Hints on N. Korea Surfaced in 2000," *Washington Post*, October 19, 2002, p. A19.

23. Quoted in Philip Shenon, "North Korea Says Nuclear Program Can Be Negotiated," *New York Times*, November 3, 2002, p. 4.

24. Colin Powell, "Interview on NBC's *Meet the Press* with Tim Russert," Washington, D.C., December 29, 2002 (www.state.gov/secretary/rm/2002/16240.htm [accessed July 2003]).

25. Quoted in Judy Keen, "Bush Has Little Use for Diplomatic Niceties," *USA Today*, March 18, 2003, p. 4A.

26. Quoted in James Dao, "Powell Seeks Asian Response for New U.S.-Backed Resolution," *New York Times*, February 23, 2003, p. 13.

27. Ju-Yeon Kim, "North Korea Turns Bellicose and Inter-Korea Talks Collapse," Associated Press Worldstream, March 19, 1994.

28. Karen Elliott House, "The Lesson of North Korea," *Wall Street Journal*, January 3, 2003, p. A10. See also Charles Krauthammer, "A Place for Temporary Appeasement," *Washington Post*, March 7, 2003, p. A23; and William Kristol, "The End of the Beginning," *Weekly Standard*, May 12, 2003, p. 9.

29. George W. Bush "Presidential News Conference," Washington, D.C., March 6, 2003 (www.whitehouse.gov/news/releases/2003/03/20030306-8.html [accessed July 2003]).

30. Colin Powell, "Hearing of the Foreign Operations Subcommittee of the Senate Appropriations Committee," *Federal News Service*, April 30, 2003.

31. George W. Bush, "Interview with Tom Brokaw of NBC News," Washington, D.C., April 24, 2003 (www.msnbc.com/news/905108.asp [accessed July 2003]).

32. Quoted in David E. Sanger, "Bush Shifts Focus to Nuclear Sales by North Korea," *New York Times*, May 5, 2003, p. A1.

33. Colin Powell, "Interview on NBC's *Meet the Press* with Tim Russert," Washington, D.C., May 4, 2003 (www.state.gov/secretary/rm/2003/20163.htm [accessed July 2003]).

34. David E. Sanger, "Cracking Down on the Terror-Arms Trade," *New York Times*, June 15, 2003, sect. IV, p. 4.

35. Quoted in Douglas Jehl and Eric Schmitt, "U.S. Suggests a Qaeda Cell in Iran Directed Saudi Bombings," *New York Times*, May 21, 2003, p. A18.

36. Quoted in Richard Bernstein, "Rumsfeld Says Iran Is Developing Nuclear Arms under Guise of Civilian Program," *New York Times*, June 12, 2003, p. A16.

37. Mohamed ElBaradei, "Implementation of the NPT Safeguards Agreement in the Islamic Republic of Iran," Report to the IAEA Board of Governors, June 6, 2003 (www.iaea.org/worldatom/Documents/Board/2003/gov2003-40.pdf [accessed July 2003]), p. 7.

38. Ari Fleischer, "Press Briefing," Washington, D.C., April 23, 2003 (www.whitehouse.gov/news/releases/2003/04/20030423-2.html [accessed July 2003]).

39. Quoted in Steven Weisman, "U.S. Still Critical of Iran despite al Qaeda Arrests," *New York Times*, May 28, 2003, p. A14.

40. *Patterns of Global Terrorism 2002*, Office of the Coordinator for Counterterrorism, Department of State.

41. Quoted in Sonni Efron, "Looking Past Baghdad to the Next Challenge," *Los Angeles Times*, April 6, 2003, p. A10.

42. Kristol, "The End of the Beginning," p. 9.

43. George W. Bush, "Remarks in Meeting with Bipartisan Senators on Medicare Reform," Washington, D.C., June 18, 2003 (www.whitehouse.gov/news/releases/2003/06/20030618-6.html [accessed July 2003]).

44. Bush, "Interview with Tom Brokaw of NBC News."

45. George W. Bush, "Statement on Iran," Washington, D.C., July 12, 2002 (www.whitehouse.gov/news/releases/2002/07/20020712-9.html [accessed July 2003]).

46. Glenn Kessler, "U.S. Halts Overtures to Iran's Khatami," *Washington Post*, July 23, 2002, p. A1.

Chapter Twelve

1. Bill Keller, "Does Not Play Well with Others," *New York Times Book Review*, June 22, 2003, p. 9.

2. Quoted in Fareed Zakaria, "The Arrogant Empire," *Newsweek*, March 24, 2003, p. 29.

3. George W. Bush, "Remarks with President Mogae of Botswana in a Photo Opportunity," Gaberone, Botswana, July 10, 2003 (www.whitehouse.gov/news/releases/2003/07/20030710-3.html [accessed July 2003]).

4. George W. Bush, "State of the Union Address," Washington, D.C., January 28, 2003 (www.whitehouse.gov/news/releases/2003/01/20030128-19.html [accessed July 2003]).

5. Quoted in Peter Beinart, "South End," *New Republic*, January 27, 2003, p. 6.

6. Colin Powell, "Press Availability with NATO Secretary General Lord

Robertson," Washington, D.C., February 20, 2003 (www.state.gov/secretary/rm/2003/17818.htm [accessed July 2003]).

7. "Bungling Bully," *Financial Times,* July 3, 2003, p. 12.

8. Quoted in Michael R. Gordon, "Treaty Offers Pentagon New Flexibility for New Set of Nuclear Priorities," *New York Times,* May 14, 2002, p. A8.

9. "The Second 2000 Gore-Bush Presidential Debate: October 11, 2000," Wake Forest University, Winston-Salem, N.C. (www.debates.org/pages/trans2000b.html [accessed July 2003]).

10. "America's Image Further Erodes, Europeans Want Weaker Ties," Nine Country Survey by the Pew Research Center for the People and the Press, March 18, 2003 (people-press.org/reports/pdf/175.pdf [accessed July 2003]).

11. *Views of a Changing World: June 2003,* Report from the Global Attitudes Project (Washington, D.C.: Pew Research Center for the People and the Press, June 2003), p. 19 (http://people-press.org/reports/pdf/185.pdf [accessed July 2003]).

12. Quoted in Mike Allen and Susan Glasser, "Bush Urges an Alliance against Terror," *Washington Post,* June 1, 2003, p. A1.

13. George W. Bush, "President Holds Primetime News Conference," Washington, D.C., October 11, 2001 (www.whitehouse.gov/news/releases/2001/10/20011011-7.html [accessed July 2003]).

14. George W. Bush, "New SEC Chairman Sworn In," Washington, D.C., February 18, 2003 (www.whitehouse.gov/news/releases/2003/02/20030218-1.html [accessed July 2003]).

15. Mary McGrory, "Pit-Stop Presidency," *Washington Post,* October 27, 2002, p. B7.

16. Bill Emmott, "A Survey of America's World Role," *Economist,* June 29, 2002, p. 20.

17. We elaborate on this construct in our forthcoming book, *Power and Cooperation: An American Foreign Policy for the Age of Global Politics.* A shorter version of this argument appears in Henry Aaron, James Lindsay, and Pietro Nivola, eds., *Agenda for the Nation* (Brookings, 2003), pp. 287–328.

18. Condoleezza Rice, "Question & Answer Session," International Institute for Strategic Studies, London, June 26, 2003 (www.iiss.org/conferencepage.php?confID=60 [accessed July 2003]).

19. Al Kamen, "Road Map in the Back Seat?" *Washington Post,* June 27, 2003, p. A27.

20. Rice, "Question & Answer Session."

21. Quoted in Howard Fineman and Martha Brant, "This Is Our Life Now," *Newsweek,* December 3, 2001, p. 28.

22. George W. Bush, "Independence Day Speech," Dayton, July 4, 2003 (www.whitehouse.gov/news/releases/2003/07/20030704-1.html [accessed July 2003]).

ACKNOWLEDGMENTS

WRITING THIS BOOK was a great joy. Many people helped make it so. Strobe Talbott and James Steinberg gave us their unquestioned support from the moment we first suggested writing about how George W. Bush had remade American foreign policy. They, along with Bruce Jentleson, Tod Lindberg, Michael O'Hanlon, and Kenneth Pollack, read all or part of the manuscript. The book is all the better for their comments and suggestions.

Our thanks extend to others as well. Fred Greenstein gave us the opportunity to develop our initial argument in a paper for an April 2003 Princeton University conference assessing the Bush presidency. Karla Nieting Bilafer, Sarah Dorland, and Caroline Smith dug up old speeches, hunted down sources we could only faintly recall, and generally made researching and writing this book that much easier. Robert Faherty, Rebecca Clark, Lawrence Converse, Janet Walker, Susan Woollen, and all the others at the Brookings Institution Press worked diligently under a tight schedule to turn our manuscript into a finished product. The William and Flora Hewlett Foundation, the Carnegie Corporation of New York, and the Rockefeller Brothers Fund provided financial support.

We owe a special debt of gratitude to Stephen Smith. The world knows him as the vice president of communications at the Brookings Institution, but a select few know him as a dream editor. He deftly and diplomatically pushed us to tighten our prose, to sharpen our arguments, and to write with the reader in mind. We are deeply grateful for all his help.

Index